*The Regulation and Reform
of the American Banking System,
1900–1929*

EUGENE NELSON WHITE

The Regulation and Reform
of the American Banking System,
1900–1929

PRINCETON UNIVERSITY
PRESS

TO MY PARENTS,
MAXWELL AND HELEN NEWMAN WHITE

Contents

List of Tables

Preface

THIS IS a book about the regulation of banking in the United States in the first three decades of this century. It examines how federal and state banking reform affected the structure and performance of the banking system. There is a large literature on the history of money and banking in the United States generated by interest in the functioning of the banking system and the operation of monetary policy under previous institutional arrangements. Modern scholarship has not, however, fully explored the years between the turn of the century and the Great Depression. This is a striking omission as it was a time of significant change, witnessing an expansion of the financial system and the establishment of the Federal Reserve System.

I was first attracted to this subject in 1978 while taking a course in economic history at the University of Illinois at Champaign-Urbana. I was surprised by the absence of any modern studies on the banking system in this period, and I became curious about the subject. This book, which attempts to fill part of this gap, is based on my Ph.D. dissertation. I am indebted to the economic historians at the University of Illinois whose fine instruction, magnanimous assistance, and frequent seminars created an excellent climate for research. I owe my most important debt to my thesis adviser, Larry Neal, who was generous with his time and advice. His guidance and enthusiasm sustained me during the arduous task of writing my dissertation. His suggestions and careful reading of the manuscript are deeply appreciated. Jeremy Atack critiqued the econometric analysis and pointed out logical lacunae while I was writing. Tom Ulen's knowledge of the literature of industrial organization and regulation opened up new perspectives on my research. Paul Uselding's criticisms in seminars helped me to define the questions I posed with greater precision. My statistical inquiries were given special attention by Paul Newbold, George Judge, Kimio Morimune, and Carl Pasurka. I should not fail to mention the fine collection of books on banking and federal and state documents in the library of the University of Illinois, which provided me with most of the information on which this book is based.

Among the many others who have made valuable suggestions, I would like to single out my fellow economic historian at Rutgers, Hugh Rockoff, for his contributions. John James of the University of Virginia and Michael Bordo of the University of South Carolina provided me with many useful comments on a number of occasions. This book has also benefited from seminar presentations of various chapters. I received many useful suggestions at the 1980 Cliometrics meetings at the University of Chicago and at seminars at the University of Delaware, the University of Connecticut-Storrs, the University of Kansas, and the University of Georgia. Responsibility for all remaining errors rests, of course, with the author.

Some of the ideas in this book have benefited from the criticism of anonymous referees of various journals. Some of the material in Chapter 1 was originally published in "The Membership Problem of the National Banking System," *Explorations in Economic History*, 19 (April 1982), and the subject matter of Chapter 4 was previously presented in "State-Sponsored Insurance of Bank Deposits in the United States, 1907–1929," *Journal of Economic History*, 41 (September 1981). Permission from the editors of these journals to draw upon these articles is gratefully acknowledged.

E. N. W.
November 1981

The Regulation and Reform
of the American Banking System,
1900–1929

Introduction

BANKING has been one of the most regulated industries in the United States. Much of the legislation governing banking has been generated by the struggle between the federal and state governments for control of the banking system. In spite of many changes, the distinctive "dual banking system" that emerged from this competitive regulation is still an important feature of American banking today. This book focuses on the years 1900–1929 when both the state and the federal governments had begun to reform their banking laws.

The difficulties the reformers had in providing adequate answers to the problems of the banking system highlight both the political impediments to fundamental change and the relationships between what were often treated as the separate issues of membership, branch banking, deposit insurance, and correspondent banking. Contemporary critics of the banking system generally failed to recognize that many of its problems had arisen because of the constraints placed on banking by state and federal legislation in the nineteenth century. This regulation created an industry composed of thousands of small single-office or unit banks, thus impairing the integration of money markets and increasing the industry's vulnerability to financial crises and panics. In retrospect, it is difficult to account for the response of reformers to the weaknesses of the banking system. They did not seek to reverse the effects of past legislation, which had produced the defective system; rather they sought to establish new institutions to correct its malfunctioning while preserving its structure. It appears that reform was forced to take this direction because of the powerful opposition of the established banking interests to fundamental changes in the law. Eager to protect the profitable positions they had attained under the existing rules, country and city bankers alike were generally averse to revising the statutes regulating the structure of their industry. As a consequence, unit banking and other features of the existing system were generally accepted, and the banking reform movement tended to focus on peripheral instead of basic problems.

Contemporary observers' and reformers' avoidance of the issue of restructuring the banking industry is paralleled by the tendency of modern scholars to seek out macroeconomic causes for the periodic financial crises, while ignoring the important role the structure of the banking industry played in determining the susceptibility of the nation's financial system to crises. This book takes a different approach and examines how the major issues of the period were the product of the state and federal legislation that had shaped the banking system.

The most important pieces of legislation regulating banking in the first three decades of the twentieth century were the National Banking Act of 1864 and the Federal Reserve Act of 1913. A common objective of both acts was to bring all commercial banks under the control of the federal government. Neither one was successful, and banking reformers were always concerned with the maintenance and expansion of the federal system. The membership problem of the federal banking system serves as an appropriate starting point for analyzing the problems of banking because it was entirely the product of state and federal regulations.

The first chapter begins with the passage by Congress of the National Banking Act of 1864, which attempted to replace state with federal control of the banking industry. After an initial success, the National Banking System began to lose its grip on banking, as financial innovation and weaker state regulations diminished the attractiveness of national bank charters. In rural regions, lower state capital and reserve requirements and weaker portfolio restrictions made incorporation more profitable under state law than under federal law; while in the more urban areas of the country, lower state reserve requirements and fewer limitations on innovations in intermediation encouraged the spread of state-chartered trust companies which vigorously competed with national banks. The ability to increase membership in the federal system was, however, not simply a question of providing the appropriate economic incentives to induce banks to join. The alternatives open to the federal authorities were limited by the political influence of the unit bankers who opposed any legislation repealing the restrictions on branch banking. Furthermore, the effectiveness of any regulatory change was compromised by the ability of the states to offer offsetting inducements to join their banking systems.

One of the major problems of the American banking system in this period was its vulnerability to panics. The federal and state restrictions on branch banking had created thousands of relatively undiversified financial institutions sensitive to changes in the conditions of the local economy. In an effort to diversify their investments, facilitate check clearing, and meet certain reserve requirements, country banks placed substantial funds in the larger city banks. Although this flow of funds served to integrate money and capital markets, it led to a pyramiding of bank reserves in New York and a few other cities. These funds were subject to withdrawal on demand or short notice. Under normal financial conditions, the system performed well; however it could intensify the effects of a downturn in the economy. Problems arose when poor business conditions and the failure of some financial institutions caused the public to panic and rapidly withdraw its deposits. Country banks lost confidence in their city correspondents and quickly withdrew their funds, paralyzing the financial system.

The most serious of these crises was the panic of 1907, which gave the banking reform movement a new momentum. The second chapter covers the evolution of federal banking reform, culminating with the passage of the Federal Reserve Act. The reform movement is seen as having been decisively shaped by the interests of the banking community. Aware of country bankers' suspicions that a central bank would fall into the hands of the politicians in Washington or the great financiers of Wall Street, reformers cast the Federal Reserve System in the mold of a system of regional clearinghouses, institutions familiar to and respected by country bankers. The failure of the National Banking System to hold on to its initial, almost complete coverage of the banking system led reformers to include provisions in the Federal Reserve Act designed to reestablish federal control of commercial banks. The stability of the banking system was to be improved by reducing the power of the major city correspondent banks, which stood accused of unsoundly investing interior banks' reserves on deposit with them in the stock market. Instead, reserves would be carried safely with the Federal Reserve banks, which would provide facilities for clearing interbank payments. The banking system was to be strengthened by the opening of a discount window where member banks could rediscount eligible assets, thereby providing a means to maintain liquidity even in a panic.

Like its predecessor, the Federal Reserve System fell short of fulfilling the intentions of its founders. The correspondent banking system remained in place. The continued interbank intermediation by correspondent banks made it unnecessary for many smaller banks to join the Federal Reserve to benefit from the additional liquidity provided by discounting operations. The Federal Reserve banks' clearing operations were also a limited success. Ironically, the growth of branching was gradually accomplishing some of the Federal Reserve's goals. Branching created larger banks which were more frequent users of the Federal Reserve's services and were more likely to become members. An alternative program of reform could have replaced the existing banking structure with a system of nationwide branch banking in which there were no limitations on the size and scope of a bank's operations. This was a viable alternative as the case of Canada demonstrates. There free entry into the banking system and few regulations established a stronger, more stable, system.

The third chapter examines the membership problem of the Federal Reserve in the 1920s and the struggle over banking reform. The operations of the well-entrenched banking interests and the state regulators are found to have played an important role in keeping the Federal Reserve relatively weak. Analysis of the determinants of membership in the Federal Reserve in this period indicates that the same factors that kept banks out of the National Banking System were still discouraging state banks from joining the new federal system. The state institutions that did join were the larger state banks and trust companies which found themselves able, as state members of the Federal Reserve, to enjoy the benefits of both the state and the federal systems. Branching, as it promoted the growth of larger banks, became an important factor in determining membership; the expansion of branching was, however, severely limited by the successful opposition of unit banking lobbies in Washington and the state capitals.

After the panic of 1907, the states were also concerned with the weakness of the banking system. States in which small unit banks were particularly strong were attracted to the idea of deposit insurance to prevent future panics. The fourth chapter examines the eight states in the West and the South that set up deposit guarantee funds between 1907 and 1917. Aware that their limited resources made them especially vulnerable to panics, the small-town bankers sought a means to protect themselves without altering the banking structure. Deposit insurance appeared to provide the answer. For the populist politicians, as well as the country bankers, it promised to keep at bay the financial moguls of the East who favored more branching to decrease the banking system's vulnerability to panics. Initially, state deposit insurance enjoyed some success, but the agricultural depression of the 1920s brought in its wake a rising number of bank failures in the South and the West, eventually forcing all the state guarantee funds to fold.

The accomplishments of state and federal banking reform in this period were limited. The major achievement appears to have been the development of the Federal Reserve System from an association of clearinghouse–like institutions to something more truly resembling a central bank, but even this was compromised by a general misunderstanding of the coordination and effects of its monetary instruments. What stands out is the failure of banking reform to initiate any major changes in the structure of the banking system.

Basic changes in legislation regulating the banking industry had to await the disasters of the early 1930s, which left the unit bankers' powerful lobby in disarray. Yet, even at the height of the banking panics, Congress was hesitant to alter the nation's banking laws radically and chose, as before, to establish new institutions to rejuvenate the system. The banking reforms of the 1930s tried to restore the stability of the banking system without any major structural changes. This permitted both unit banking and the dual banking system to survive into the second half of the twentieth century.

While financial markets have changed considerably and many reforms have been instituted since 1929, the debates of the period are of current interest. The Depository Institutions Deregulation and Monetary Control Act of 1980 has attempted to solve the Federal Reserve System's continuing membership problem and to improve control of the money supply by granting to the Federal Reserve Board increased control over state-chartered banks. Although this act has made some important changes, it is similar to previous legislation that augmented federal control of banking institutions without a general reform of the laws regulating the banking industry. This is significant from a historical perspective because the increased influence of the federal banking authorities was gradually undermined by financial innovation and the responses of state legislatures.

1

The Dual Banking System before 1914

THE MOST salient and enduring feature of the American banking system since the Civil War has been the rivalry between the federal and state regulatory authorities over the establishment and control of banks. The origins of the Federal Reserve System's membership problem may be traced to the difficulties its predecessor, the National Banking System, experienced in maintaining its membership vis-à-vis the state banking systems. The National Banking System was created by Congress with the purpose of establishing a uniform currency issued by banks chartered and regulated by the Comptroller of the Currency. Although the nation was provided with a uniform currency, the federal government failed to gain control of the creation of new banks, as state banking authorities vied with the Comptroller to charter banks. Competition between state and federal regulators tended to weaken the regulation of banks to the point where entry into the industry was virtually unrestricted.[1] Federal control of the banking system deteriorated sharply in the early years of the twentieth century when the expansion of the economy led to a rapid growth of the banking industry. An almost complete prohibition on branch banking and low minimum capital re-

[1] Ross Robertson, *The Comptroller and Bank Supervision, An Historical Appraisal*, pp. 57–62 and Richard E. Sylla, *The American Capital Market, 1846–1914: A Study of the Effects of Public Policy on Economic Development*, pp. 47–78.

quirements produced a rise in the number of banks from 8,390 in 1900 to 23,594 in 1914. Only 3,487 of the new institutions were national banks. The failure of this atomistic banking industry, in the absence of a central bank, to prevent the panic of 1907 led Congress to reconstruct the federal system with the Federal Reserve absorbing the National Banking System. The history of the National Banking System speaks to the difficulty of solving the persistent problems of American banking and the political and economic constraints that narrowed the options open to policy makers.

The National Banking Act of 1864 and the Emergence of the Dual Banking System

The struggle between state and federal banking authorities began when the federal government entered the business of bank regulation with the passage of the National Currency Act in 1863 and the National Banking Act which superseded it in 1864. The adoption of the National Banking Act in the midst of the Civil War was largely prompted by the fiscal needs of the Union. The act determined the minimum capital and reserve requirements, limited branching, and placed restrictions on the portfolio composition of banks chartered under its auspices; but its proximate objective was to encourage banks to buy government bonds by allowing them to use these as backing for the issuance of bank notes. There was, however, no rush by the banks to join the new system, which required them to abandon their state charters, adhere to stiffer regulations, and submit to federal supervision. In the first year, only a few banks took out national charters. Frustrated, the government imposed a 10 percent tax on state bank notes in 1865. As bank notes were the primary form of liability issued by banks, this quickly forced most banks to join the National Banking System. This crossover and the subsequent growth of the two systems can be seen in Table 1.1.

Table 1.1
National and State Banks, 1860–1914

Year	Number of National Banks	Number of State Banks		Assets (in millions of dollars)	
		Comptroller's Series	Barnett's Series	National Banks	State Banks
1860	0	1,562		0	
1861	0	1,601		0	
1862	0	1,492		0	
1863	66	1,466		17	
1864	467	1,089		252	
1865	1,294	349		1,127	
1866	1,634	297		1,476	
1867	1,636	272		1,494	
1868	1,640	247		1,572	
1869	1,619	259		1,564	
1870	1,612	325		1,566	
1871	1,723	452		1,703	
1872	1,853	566		1,771	
1873	1,968	277		1,851	178
1874	1,983	368		1,852	237
1875	2,076	551		1,913	272
1876	2,091	663		1,826	278
1877	2,078	592	794	1,774	383
1878	2,056	475	807	1,751	278
1879	2,048	616	813	2,020	315
1880	2,076	620	811	2,036	354
1881	2,115	652	816	2,326	419
1882	2,239	672	832	2,344	438
1883	2,417	754	926	2,365	512
1884	2,625	817	1,017	2,283	521
1885	2,689	975	1,124	2,422	553
1886	2,809	849	1,207	2,475	528
1887	3,014	1,413	1,531	2,637	684
1888	3,120	1,403	1,746	2,731	671
1889	3,239	1,671	2,097	2,988	796
1890	3,484	2,101	2,534	3,484	871
1891	3,652	2,572	3,102	3,113	906
1892	3,759	3,191	3,484	3,494	1,040
1893	3,807	3,579	3,700	3,213	1,130
1894	3,770	3,586	3,705	3,422	1,077
1895	3,715	3,774	3,818	3,471	1,147
1896	3,689	3,708	3,917	3,354	1,107
1897	3,610	3,857	3,978	3,563	1,138

Table 1.1 (*cont.*)

Year	Number of National Banks	Number of State Banks		Assets (in millions of dollars)	
		Comptroller's Series	Barnett's Series	National Banks	State Banks
1898	3,581	3,965	4,062	3,978	1,356
1899	3,582	4,191	4,253	4,709	1,636
1900	3,731	4,369	4,405	4,944	1,756
1901	4,163	4,983	4,906	5,674	2,130
1902	4,532	5,375	5,433	6,007	2,271
1903	4,935	5,962	6,111	6,285	2,491
1904	5,327	6,923	6,984	6,653	2,863
1905	5,664	7,794	7,920	7,325	3,190
1906	6,046	8,862	9,334	7,781	3,677
1907	6,422	9,967	10,352	8,472	4,119
1908	6,817	11,220	11,295	8,710	3,993
1909	6,886	11,319		9,365	3,338
1910	7,138	12,166		9,892	3,694
1911	7,270	12,864		10,378	3,747
1912	7,366	13,381		10,857	3,897
1913	7,467	14,011		11,032	4,143
1914	7,518	14,512		11,477	4,353

SOURCES: The number of national banks and their assets were obtained from U.S. Department of Commerce, *Historical Statistics of the United States*, pp. 1024–1031. The Comptroller's series of state banks and state bank assets were gleaned from U.S. Comptroller of the Currency, *Annual Reports*, various years. The other series of state banks comes from George Barnett, *State Banks and Trust Companies since the Passage of the National-Bank Act*. This series includes additional state banks that did not submit reports to the Comptroller but did send information to *Homan's Bankers Almanac and Register*.

Yet the state banks were not to be eliminated with a stroke of the executive pen. Taxing them out of the business of note issue only pushed them into a faster development of deposit banking. State banks rebounded, and by 1874 their total deposits exceeded the total note issue of the national banks.[2] The development of a substitute liability to issue allowed banks to select a state or a national charter on the basis of their

[2] U.S. Department of Commerce, *Historical Statistics of the United States*, pp. 1025–1032.

relative advantages as determined by each system's regulations.

Branch Banking and Capital Requirements

Two regulations, common to both systems—branching restrictions and minimum capital requirements—affected a bank's choice of charter and limited the potential scale of its operations by setting a lower and an upper bound respectively on bank size.

Branch banking was not given an opportunity to establish itself in the post–Civil War United States. There had been some limited branching in the antebellum period, particularly in the West and the South, but this was virtually eliminated in the 1860s.[3] No specific prohibition of branch banking was written into the law, but Section 8 of the National Banking Act required that a national bank's "usual business shall be transacted at an office or banking house located in the place specified in its organization certificate."[4] The second Comptroller of the Currency, Freeman Clarke (1865–1866), interpreted this as a prohibition on branch banking. He set a precedent when he ruled that the Washington County Bank of Williamsport, Maryland, had to divest itself of its branch or forfeit its national charter.[5] Regardless of Congress' original intention this ruling set the standards by which national banks would be organized until the 1920s.

Although nationwide branch banking was ruled out, statewide branching would still have been possible if state legislatures had been more favorably disposed, but the states were generally hostile to the establishment of branch banking within their jurisdiction. A study commissioned by the National Monetary Commission in 1910 concluded that "under none of the state banking laws has there been built up an important system

---

[3] Robertson, *The Comptroller*, pp. 27–29.
[4] Ibid., p. 197.
[5] Ibid., pp. 81–85.

of branch banks. This has been partly due to the very general wish of each American community, no matter how small, to have its banks managed by its own citizens and partly to the fact that in most of the states, the establishment of branch banks is either explicitly forbidden or in no way provided for by law."[6]

Apparently these restrictions on branching were not a serious impediment to banking in the first thirty years after the passage of the National Banking Act. There was little discussion of the subject by the public, bankers, academics, or Congress before the 1890s.[7] Only at the turn of century did branch banking reappear. According to the National Monetary Commission's study of state banking regulations in force in 1909, ten states—Arizona, Delaware, Florida, Georgia, Louisiana, Massachusetts, New York, Oregon, Rhode Island, and Tennessee—allowed some limited forms of branching. Branches were usually restricted to a specific number of offices or were forced to confine their operations to their home-office city. Only California, after the passage of a new banking act in 1909, allowed state-wide branch banking.[8] Whether because of these legal prohibitions or the limited advantages obtained by opening branch offices, branch banking was still in its infancy in the first decade of the twentieth century. In 1900, the first year for which reliable statistics are available, 87 banks operated branches accounting for 1.6 percent of all bank offices and 1.8 percent of all commercial-bank loans and investments. By 1910 branching had spread a little further. There were 292 banks operating branches in this year, representing 3.4 percent of all bank offices and 8.9 percent of loans and investments.[9]

[6] George Barnett, *State Banks and Trust Companies since the Passage of the National-Bank Act*, p. 135.

[7] Gerald C. Fisher, *American Banking Structure*, p. 26.

[8] Samuel A. Welldon, *Digest of State Banking Statutes*.

[9] Board of Governors of the Federal Reserve System, *Banking and Monetary Statistics, 1914–1941*, p. 297.

The growth in demand for banking services prior to 1914 was thus met by new banks opening their doors rather than by existing banks opening new offices. The number and size of these banks depended primarily on the population density of the area and the minimum capital requirements specified by the chartering authority. In a large city where population density was high, fewer banks were needed, and additional demand could be handled partially by existing banks expanding the size of their operations. In rural areas of the country, low population density required numerous, widely dispersed banking offices. Many banks were needed to serve the growing demand for bank services in the presence of the strict limits placed on branching, and the number of these banks was constrained by the legal minimum capital requirements.

A bank's capital served as a buffer for the depositors against losses incurred in normal business operations, and the federal and state authorities sought to provide a minimum level of security for the holders of a bank's liabilities by setting capital requirements. In consideration of the need to provide banking services to small communities, these were often graded according to the population of the community. The National Banking Act fixed three capital requirements. For towns with a population under 6,000 a bank had to have a minimum capital of $50,000; where the population was between 6,000 and 50,000, $100,000 was required; and in larger cities a $200,000 minimum was specified. Banks could begin operations with 50 percent of their required capital, but the remainder had to be paid in within five months at a rate of 10 percent a month. Each new bank was also required to place one-tenth of its net semiannual profits in a surplus fund until this equaled 20 percent of its required capital. This surplus was to be used in case of unexpected losses, and if at any time the fund fell below 20 percent of capital, no dividends could be paid until it was restored. Banks were to suspend operations if their losses exceeded retained earnings and surplus. The only significant change in these requirements was made by the Gold Standard Act of 1900 which lowered the minimum capital required for towns under 3,000 to $25,000.[10]

Unfortunately, knowledge of how state capital requirements changed over time is sketchy, as there are only two surveys of state legislation. These are found in the Comptroller of the Currency's *Annual Report* of 1895 and Samuel Welldon's 1909 compilation of state and territorial laws for the National Monetary Commission.[11] The 1895 and 1909 regulations graded by population are presented in Table 1.2 and Table 1.3 respectively. Although there is considerable variation in the state laws and there were several exceptions, it was usually the case that state charters required the same or less capital than a national charter for a town of a given size. State banks thus had a decided edge, all other things being equal, in establishing themselves in marginal markets. In 1895 only Louisiana and Massachusetts and in 1909 only Massachusetts had statutory minimums greater than the national requirement for the smallest towns. State legislation also tended to be a little more lax in setting surplus requirements. In 1909 seven states stipulated a higher ration of surplus to initial capital, and nineteen followed the 20 percent rule of the National Banking System, with the remainder setting lower requirements or none at all.[12]

The first and only systematic study of the regulatory rivalry between the state and federal authorities was carried out by George Barnett in his *State Banks and Trust Companies since the Passage of the National-Bank Act*, written for the National Monetary Commission, which was investigating the weaknesses of the National Banking System. Using Welldon's compilation of state regulations, Barnett concluded that the states and

---

[10] Robertson, *The Comptroller*, appendix.
[11] Welldon, *Digest of State Banking Statutes*.
[12] Barnett, *State Banks and Trust Companies*, pp. 59–60.

Table 1.2
Minimum Capital Required to Establish a Bank by Federal and
State Laws, 1895
(in thousands of dollars)

	Less than 3,000	*3,000 and over*	*6,000 and over*	*25,000 and over*	*Over 50,000*
			Town Size		
National banks	50	50	100	100	200
State banks					
Alabama	50	50	50	50	50
Arizona	Specified in each bank's charter of incorporation				
Arkansas	No banking legislation—effectively zero				
California	25	25	50	100	200
Colorado	30	30	30	30	30
Connecticut	Specified in each bank's charter of incorporation				
Delaware	Specified in each bank's charter of incorporation				
Florida	15	25	50	50	50
Georgia	25	25	25	25	25
Idaho	Specified in each bank's charter of incorporation				
Illinois	25	25	50	100	200
Indiana	25	25	25	25	25
Iowa	25	50	50	50	50
Kansas	5	5	5	5	5
Kentucky	Specified in each bank's charter of incorporation				
Louisiana	100	100	100	100	100
Maine[a]	Specified in each bank's charter of incorporation				
Maryland	50	50	50	50	300
Massachusetts[a]	100	100	100	100	100
Michigan	15	15	15	50	50
Minnesota	10	25	25	25	25
Mississippi	No banking legislation—effectively zero				
Missouri	10	10	10	10	100
Montana	20	20	20	20	20
Nebraska[b]	5	25	30	50	50
Nevada	Specified in each bank's charter of incorporation				
New Hampshire	Specified in each bank's charter of incorporation				
New Jersey	50	50	50	50	50
New Mexico	30	30	30	30	30
New York	25	50	50	50	100
North Carolina	Specified in each bank's charter of incorporation				
North Dakota	5	5	5	5	5
Ohio	25	25	25	25	25
Oklahoma	No banking legislation—effectively zero				

Table 1.2 (*cont.*)

	Town Size				
	Less than 3,000	3,000 and over	6,000 and over	25,000 and over	Over 50,000
Oregon	Specified in each bank's charter of incorporation				
Pennsylvania	50	50	50	50	50
Rhode Island	Specified in each bank's charter of incorporation				
South Carolina	No banking legislation—effectively zero				
South Dakota^c	5	25	25	25	25
Tennessee	Specified in each bank's charter of incorporation				
Texas	The state chartered no banks				
Utah	25	25	25	25	25
Vermont^a	Specified in each bank's charter of incorporation				
Virginia	Specified in each bank's charter of incorporation				
Washington	25	25	25	25	25
West Virginia	25	25	25	25	25
Wisconsin	25	25	25	25	25
Wyoming	Specified in each bank's charter of incorporation				

SOURCE: U.S. Comptroller of the Currency, *Annual Report*, 1895.

[a] No state banks were chartered, only trust companies with banking departments.

[b] The minimum capital requirement for a bank in towns of population less than 1,000 was $5,000, in towns of 1,000–1,500, $10,000, and in towns of 1,500–2,000, $15,000.

[c] The minimum capital requirement for a bank in towns with a population less than 500 was $5,000, in towns with a population of 500–1,000 it was $10,000, and where the population was over 1,000 it was $25,000.

territories could be roughly divided into two groups according to the amount of the smallest permissible capital. The first category included the eastern states and most of those in the Midwest, which had minimum requirements of $25,000. The second group contained the remaining midwestern states, and those in the South and the West which generally allowed banks to incorporate with as little as $10,000. This tendency reflected, in part, the difficulty of accumulating a large initial capital in small towns and rural areas.

Many state bank supervisors complained that these minimum capital requirements were too low to ensure the safety

Table 1.3
Minimum Capital Required to Establish a Bank, by Federal and State Laws, 1909
(in thousands of dollars)

	Town Size				
	Less than 3,000	3,000 and over	6,000 and over	25,000 and over	Over 50,000
National banks	25	50	100	100	200
State banks					
Alabama	15	25	25	25	25
Arizona	Specified in each bank's charter of incorporation				
Arkansas	No banking legislation—effectively zero				
California	25	25	50	100	200
Colorado	10	15	25	30	30
Connecticut	Specified in each bank's charter of incorporation				
Delaware	Specified in each bank's charter of incorporation				
Florida	15	25	50	50	50
Georgia	15	15	15	15	15
Idaho	10	25	100	100	100
Illinois	25	25	50	100	200
Indiana	25	25	25	25	25
Iowa	25	50	50	50	50
Kansas	10	25	25	50	50
Kentucky	15	15	15	15	15
Louisiana	10	30	30	100	100
Maine[a]	Specified in each bank's charter of incorporation				
Maryland	10	20	30	50	100
Massachusetts[a]	100	100	100	100	100
Michigan	20	25	50	100	100
Minnesota	10	25	25	25	25
Mississippi	10	15	15	15	15
Missouri	10	10	10	10	100
Montana	20	20	20	20	20
Nebraska[b]	10	35	50	100	100
Nevada	10	35	50	50	50
New Hampshire	Specified in each bank's charter of incorporation				
New Jersey	50	50	50	50	50
New Mexico	30	30	30	30	30
New York	25	50	50	50	100
North Carolina	5	10	25	25	25
North Dakota	10	35	50	50	50
Ohio	25	25	25	25	25
Oklahoma	10	25	50	100	100

Table 1.3 (*cont.*)

	Town Size				
	Less than 3,000	3,000 and over	6,000 and over	25,000 and over	Over 50,000
Oregon	10	30	50	50	50
Pennsylvania	25	25	50	50	50
Rhode Island	Specified in each bank's charter of incorporation				
South Carolina	No banking legislation—effectively zero				
South Dakota	10	25	50	50	50
Tennessee	Specified in each bank's charter of incorporation				
Texas	10	25	25	100	100
Utah	10	10	10	50	100
Vermont[a]	Specified in each bank's charter of incorporation				
Virginia	10	10	10	10	10
Washington	10	25	30	75	100
West Virginia	25	25	25	25	25
Wisconsin	10	20	30	50	50
Wyoming	10	25	100	100	100

SOURCE: Samuel A. Welldon, *Digest of State Banking Statutes*, and various state bank examiner's reports.

[a] No state banks were chartered, only trust companies with banking departments.

[b] The minimum capital requirement for a bank in towns of 100 to 500 people was $10,000, in towns of 500–1,000 it was $20,000, and in towns of 1,000–2,000 it was set at $25,000. In towns with a population greater than 2,000 a minimum of $35,000 was needed.

of a bank's operations, and they frequently pressed the state legislatures to raise them. Barnett believed that they had generally been successful in securing an upward revision in the minimum level, but he seems to have been mistaken. A comparison of the surveys of 1895 and 1909 reveals instead an inclination by the state legislatures to keep their capital requirements lower than those of the National Banking System when confronted with the 1900 downward revision of national bank requirements. Nine states—Alabama, Colorado, Georgia, Louisiana, Maryland, Pennsylvania, Utah, Washington, and Wisconsin—who in 1895 had minimum capital requirements at or below the national levels had lowered them by

1909 to maintain their position of relative advantage. Ten other states—Idaho, Kentucky, Mississippi, Nevada, North Carolina, Oklahoma, Oregon, Texas, Virginia, and Wyoming—passed "free banking" acts enabling banks to incorporate under fixed rules rather than apply directly to the state legislature or use the general laws of incorporation. All of these states set their smallest capital requirements at $5,000 to $15,000, well below the national minimum of $25,000. Five states did raise their capital requirements. Kansas, Nebraska, North Dakota, and South Dakota all had very low requirements of $5,000 and raised them to $10,000, still well below the national level. This move probably reflects the successful efforts of bank supervisors and others to persuade the legislature to raise the limit to prevent too many very small banks from incorporating. The last of these five states, Michigan, increased its capital requirement to $20,000, again keeping it below the national minimum.

The provision of the Gold Standard Act of 1900, which reduced the lowest minimum capital requirement for national banks and prompted many states to lower their requirements in turn, has a history that sheds light on the struggle over branch banking. In the early 1890s the Comptrollers of the Currency were favorably disposed toward legislation permitting some form of branching to accommodate the increased demand for banking facilities in rural areas. In 1895 Secretary of the Treasury Carlisle and President Cleveland both recommended that national banks be permitted some form of branching. In the following year Comptroller John Eckles proposed in his *Annual Report* that branches be allowed in places with a population less than 1,000.[13] Initially, there was little opposition to branching, but small unit banks quickly realized the potential threat and rallied to resist any legislation encouraging branching. Their cause was taken up by Charles

---

[13] U.S. Comptroller of the Currency, *Annual Report*, 1896, pp. 103–104.

Dawes who became Comptroller in 1898. From his influential position, Dawes helped to kill a bill in Congress providing for some branching. In its place, he promoted the idea of lowering capital requirements to increase the number of rural bank offices and obtained the provision in the Gold Standard Act.[14] This law increased the number of small national banks and, as already observed, caused a number of states to reduce their capital requirements as well, thereby allowing many more small state banks to be established. This development helped to create a more vigorous antibranching lobby which was successful in preventing any major alterations in federal law until the 1920s.

Portfolio Restrictions

Lower minimum capital requirements were not the only factor responsible for promoting the growth of state banks in rural areas. The National Banking Act had severely encumbered national banks' operations by restricting their capacity to lend on security of real estate. National banks in New York, Chicago, and Saint Louis, the central reserve cities, were forbidden to make real estate loans. Other nationally chartered banks were allowed to grant loans up to five years' maturity on real estate provided each individual loan amounted to less than 50 percent of the appraised value of the land. More important, total real estate loans could not exceed 25 percent of the bank's capital.[15] Consequently, real estate accounted for a small portion of national-bank assets, and state banks had a virtually open field to make loans on security of real estate. Welldon's survey of state legislation found only twelve states that imposed any restrictions on commercial banks' real estate loans. Many of these legal limitations probably imposed little if any constraint on a bank's portfolio choice. States in

[14] Fisher, *American Banking Structure*, pp. 27–28.
[15] Robertson, *The Comptroller*, appendix.

this category include California and North Dakota, which limited loans to first liens. In Minnesota the value of the land used as collateral had to be at least two times greater than the sum of the loan. The Ohio and Texas state legislatures limited the total loans constraining real estate to 50 percent of total assets, a fraction not reached by banks in any state. Other weak constraints were found in South Carolina and Wisconsin, where total real estate loans could not exceed 50 percent of capital and deposits. Even in states in which the legal limitations were stronger, they were still substantially weaker than those placed on national banks. Michigan restricted real estate loans to 50 percent of bank capital; and New York allowed these to amount to 15 percent of assets in towns of less than 1,500, rising up to 40 percent in the largest cities. North Dakota limited loans "wholly dependent" on real estate to 15 percent of capital and surplus. Oklahoma permitted real estate loans to be given up to a maximum of 20 percent of all loans, and state banks in Pennsylvania were only permitted to contract these loans up to one-half of time deposits or 25 percent of capital, surplus, and profits, whichever was smaller.

In light of these weaker portfolio restrictions, it is not surprising to find that state banks were able to capture this part of the market. This is apparent in the special report on state-bank assets and liabilities compiled in 1909 by the National Monetary Commission and published in the *Annual Report* of the Comptroller of the Currency in that same year. The average percentage of loans and discounts secured by mortgages or liens on realty and mortgages owned by state banks amounted to 11.8 percent of total assets while these constituted only 0.6 percent of national banks' total assets.[16] These assets formed an even larger portion of state-bank assets in agricultural areas. The National Monetary Commission's study revealed that banks in cities had few loans on real estate in their portfolios, most

[16] U.S. Comptroller of the Currency, *Annual Report*, 1909, pp. 720–733.

of their business being concentrated in the financing of trade and industry. State banks in New York City held only 2 percent of their assets in mortgages or loans and discounts secured by real estate, while banks in the rest of the state had 8.4 percent in these assets. State banks in typically rural, agricultural states like Colorado, Kansas, Minnesota, and Mississippi had 31.3, 11.2, 21.1, and 23.4 percent, respectively, of their assets in real estate. This contrasted with the state banks of the more urban, industrial states. For example, banks in Connecticut, New Jersey, and Rhode Island had 1.1, 4.8, and 2.1 percent of their assets in real estate.[17] State charters with these weak limitations on real estate loans coupled with lower minimum capital requirements offered a bank a substantial advantage over a national charter in agricultural areas where there was low population density.

The Regulation of Liabilities

Regulations restricting the creation of liabilities were another major factor affecting a bank's choice of charter. During the era of the National Banking System, these took the form of reserve requirements on deposits and limitations on banknote issue. In designing the National Banking Act, Salmon P. Chase, the Secretary of the Treasury, had intended the privilege of bank-note issue to attract banks into the new system.[18] The new national bank-note currency was, however, limited by several requirements that affected the profitability of issue. The Act of March 3, 1865, limited note issue to 90 percent of the value of a national bank's paid-in capital. In order to issue notes, banks had to acquire government bonds. With these as backing, bank notes equal to 90 percent of the par value of the bonds could be issued. This act also limited the

[17] Ibid.
[18] Phillip Cagan, "The First Fifty Years of the National Banking System," pp. 15–19.

aggregate note issue to $300 million. This had to be raised in 1870 when the ceiling was reached. The new limit was quickly attained, but the problem was resolved by the Resumption Act of 1875 which eliminated the note ceiling. The last change in the rules for note issue was made in the Gold Standard Act of 1900 when Congress allowed banks to issue bank notes equal to 100 percent of the par or market value of the eligible bonds (whichever was lower) up to a limit of 100 percent of their paid-in capital.

Contemporaries were puzzled by the fact that after 1875 the number of national bank notes outstanding declined. Economic historians have attributed this to the falling profitability of note issue. The cost of bond-backed note issue rose sharply in the 1880s as long-term interest rates fell, leading to a rise in the prices of U.S. bonds. Bank-note issue became profitable again in the mid-1890s, and it expanded rapidly; however banks' circulation remained well below the legal limit in spite of the apparently high profit on bank notes.[19] Some historians have tried to explain low note issue as a consequence of the correspondent banking system or the fear after 1907 that banking reform would eliminate bonds as backing for currency, thereby reducing the value of the millions of dollars worth of bonds that banks held.[20] The most satisfactory explanation has been offered by John James who used a model of portfolio selection. He argued that bonds to back notes yielded banks a low interest rate which offset, to some degree, the cost of issuing notes. When and where market interest rates are low, it was profitable to invest in bank notes for loans, but higher rates made it preferable to create deposits instead. James found that this explained fairly well the variation in note issue from one region to another and over time as interest

[19] Phillip Cagan, *Determinants and Effects of Changes in the Money Stock, 1875–1960*, pp. 87–95.

[20] Charles A. E. Goodhart, "Profit on National Bank Notes, 1900–1913."

rates changed.[21] Backing currency with bonds apparently altered the composition of liabilities more than it changed their volume.

The National Banking Act also limited the issuance of liabilities by imposing reserve requirements on bank notes and all deposits. The intent of these requirements was to force banks to hold more reserves than they would otherwise have held, thus restricting the expansion of deposits and loans as additional reserves became available. Banks' profits and the money supply were consequently limited. The law scaled these reserve requirements according to a bank's location. Country banks were to hold a reserve equal to 15 percent of their aggregate notes and deposits. Two-fifths of this was to be held in lawful money in their vaults, and up to three-fifths could be held in the form of deposits in any national bank in one of the nine designated reserve cities. This was a very attractive way of holding reserves, as interest was paid on these holdings. Reserve-city banks were required to keep reserves of 25 percent.

These provisions were modified by the Act of June 20, 1874, which abolished the reserve requirements against note circulation. In its place banks were required to subscribe to a redemption fund at the Treasury equal to 5 percent of each bank's outstanding circulation to be used to redeem notes.[22] Also established by this act were eighteen new reserve cities. Banks in these places were allowed to hold half of their required reserves of 25 percent on deposit in the central reserve city, New York. The three-tier system was again expanded in 1887 when the law was changed, permitting the Comptroller of the Currency to designate any city with a population of 50,000 or more a reserve city and any city over 200,000 a central reserve city if three-fourths of the resident national

[21] John A. James, "The Conundrum of the Low Issue of National Bank Notes."

[22] John A. James, *Money and Capital Markets in Postbellum America*, p. 78.

banks requested it. Chicago and Saint Louis became central-reserve-cities in that year, and by 1913 there were forty-seven reserve cities.[23]

The imposition of reserve requirements did not, however, necessarily affect the composition of a bank's portfolio or reduce its profitability. While this certainly would have happened if a bank was forced to keep more vault cash than it would have done otherwise, most of the reserves required were allowed to be held in the form of deposits at other banks, that is, as bankers' balances. These balances served several important functions. In a system of thousands of unit banks, some mechanism was needed whereby banks could clear the claims they held against one another. In the cities, banks formed clearinghouses where, on a permanent and regular basis, they could clear payments. To serve banks that needed to clear claims against banks in other locations, a system of correspondent banking developed, whereby banks in other cities or in the economic hinterland could clear payments through city banks on a regular basis by keeping on deposit with their city agent an agreed minimum balance. These bankers' balances established a customer relationship between country banks and their city correspondents. When country banks had excess funds these could be sent to the city and deposited with the correspondent to earn interest or be invested in the money market with the correspondent's expert assistance.[24]

This easy avenue through which funds could be moved in response to investment opportunities was a key to establishing a national short-term money market. It is thus not surprising that the largest portion of bankers' balances were held in New York, the center of the money market, followed by Chicago and Saint Louis. In 1913 central-reserve-city banks held about 75 percent of these net balances (with New York banks alone holding over 60 percent), reserve-city banks 16 percent, and

[23] Ibid., pp. 97–98.
[24] Ibid., pp. 95–104.

country banks 5 percent, with the remainder being held at state banks.[25] The designation of New York, Chicago, and Saint Louis as central-reserve-cities and other important cities as reserve cities allowed banks to count as part of their reserves funds that they might have kept there anyway and as such constituted no real burden on the banks.

In contrast to the National Banking System, the regenerated state banking systems were not immediately subjected to reserve requirements. As late as 1887 reserve requirements were only written into the laws of three states, Connecticut, Ohio, and Minnesota.[26] This situation had changed slightly when the Comptroller of the Currency surveyed state banking legislation in 1895. The data obtained from this survey and the National Monetary Commission's study are presented in Table 1.4. In 1895 there were still thirty-one states and territories that did not require their chartered banks to hold any reserves. Of the remaining seventeen states, seven imposed the same total reserve requirements on demand deposits as did the National Banking Act, eight required higher, and only two lower. By 1909 only thirteen states still did not set a minimum for reserves, while twenty-four conformed to the total reserve requirements for national banks on demand deposits and eleven ordered their banks to hold still higher reserve ratios of 20 to 25 percent. What led states to raise their reserve requirements is not certain, although the panics of 1893 and 1907, which motivated many other banking reforms, may have been responsible. Public concern over the strength of the banking system may have dominated the desire of banks and state legislatures to preserve this advantage for state banks.

From these statistics it would appear that the differential in reserve requirements favored national over state charters in many states, but this favorable differential disappears if

---

[25] Leonard L. Watkins, *Bankers' Balances*, p. 55.
[26] Barnett, *State Banks and Trust Companies*, p. 110.

Table 1.4
National and State Bank Reserve Requirements on Demand Deposits, 1895 and 1909

	Country	Reserve City	Central Reserve City	
National Banks	15 (3/5)	25 (1/2)	25 (0)	

| | 1895 | | 1909 | |
State Banks	Country Banks	Reserve Agent	Country Banks	Reserve Agent
Alabama	0	0	15 (3/5)	designated
Arizona	0	0	15 (3/5)	designated
Arkansas	0	0	0	0
California	0	0	15 (3/5)	20 (3/5)
Colorado	0	0	0	0
Connecticut	10 (any)	designated	15 (11/15)	designated
Delaware	0	0	0	0
Florida	20 (3/5)	designated	20 (3/5)	designated
Georgia	25 (any)	designated	25 (any)	designated
Idaho	0	0	15 (1/2)	designated
Illinois[a]	0	0	0	0
Indiana	0	0	0	0
Iowa[a]	0	0	0	0
Kansas	20 (1/2)	designated	20 (3/4)	25 (3/5)
Kentucky	0	0	15 (1/3)	25 (1/3)
Louisiana	33 (1/3)	designated	25 (8/25)	designated
Maine	15 (2/3)	designated	15 (2/3)	designated
Maryland	0	0	0	0
Massachusetts	15 (3/5)	15 (1/2)	15 (3/5)	15 (1/2)
Michigan	15 (2/3)	20 (2/3)	20 (3/4)	designated
Minnesota	20 (any)	designated	20 (1/2)	designated
Mississippi	0	0	0	0
Missouri	15 (any)	designated	15 (any)	designated
Montana	20 (1/2)	designated	15 (any)	designated
Nebraska	15 (1/3)	designated	15 (3/5)	20 (3/5)
Nevada	0	0	15 (2/3)	designated
New Hampshire	0	0	0	0
New Jersey	0	0	15 (3/5)	designated
New Mexico	0	0	15 (3/5)	designated
New York[b]	10 (1/2)	15 (1/2)	15 (3/5)	25 (2/5)
North Carolina	0	0	15 (3/5)	designated
North Dakota	20 (1/2)	designated	20 (3/5)	designated
Ohio	15 (any)	designated	15 (3/5)	designated
Oklahoma	0	0	20 (2/3)	25 (2/3)
Oregon	0	0	15 (2/3)	25 (2/3)

Table 1.4 (cont.)

	Country	Reserve City	Central Reserve City	
Pennsylvania	0	0	15 (2/3)	designated
Rhode Island	0	0	15 (3/5)	25 (3/5)
South Carolina	0	0	0	0
South Dakota	20 (1/2)	designated	20 (1/2)	25 (1/2)
Tennessee	0	0	0	0
Texas	0	0	25 (1/3)	designated
Utah	0	0	15 (any)	20 (any)
Vermont	0	0	0	0
Virginia	15 (3/5)	designated	15 (3/5)	designated
Washington	0	0	20 (any)	designated
West Virginia	0	0	15 (3/5)	designated
Wisconsin	0	0	15 (any)	25 (any)
Wyoming[a]	0	0	0	0

SOURCES: U.S. Comptroller of the Currency, *Annual Report*, 1895 and Samuel A. Welldon, *Digest of State Banking Statutes*.

NOTE: In most states, the bank examiner designated specific banks to serve as reserve agents. Usually any state or national bank that met the country bank reserve requirements and the bank examiner's approval could serve as a reserve agent. Reserve requirements are in percentages. The number in parentheses is the portion of reserves that could be held on deposit with reserve agents.

[a] No legal reserve requirement; however, in Illinois and Iowa the bank examiner imposed a requirement of 15% where 3/5 could be held on deposit, and in Wyoming the state examiner required a reserve of 25% in 1895.

[b] New York had a hierarchy of reserve requirements in 1909. In cities where the population was less than 1 million, a reserve of 15% (3/5) was required, where the population was between 1 and 1.8 million it was 20% (1/2), and where the population exceeded 1.8 million it was 25% (2/5).

only the vault cash requirement, which may have been the only binding constraint, is counted. Among those states that imposed a 15 percent reserve requirement on country banks, nine set lower, thirteen the same, and only two higher vault cash reserve requirements on demand deposits. Of those eleven states that levied higher total reserve requirements, seven had lower vault cash requirements. Thus only six states imposed higher vault cash reserve requirements on their state banks, and in all but two states these were no greater than 1 percent.

While many states imposed reserve requirements on demand deposits similar to those required of national banks, state banks enjoyed a considerable advantage in the issuance of time deposits. The National Banking Act did not distinguish between demand and time deposits and subjected both to the same requirements. Most states, on the other hand, allowed their banks easier terms for the issuance of time deposits. In terms of total reserve requirements on time deposits, twenty-seven states set these lower than the national-bank level in 1909. Sixteen states kept to the national-bank rule, and five had higher requirements. As regards the vault cash requirements, thirty-seven had lower, nine the same, and only four higher reserve requirements on time deposits.

The National Banking Act clearly defined which banks could act as depositories for country bankers' reserves, but only nine states in 1909 had created any type of hierarchical reserve arrangement to parallel the national scheme. These states and their reserve requirements for reserve agents were as follows (the fraction of reserves that could be held on deposit are in parentheses, the balance being held in the banks' vaults): California, 20 percent ($\frac{3}{5}$); Kansas, 25 percent ($\frac{3}{5}$); Kentucky, 25 percent ($\frac{1}{3}$); Massachusetts, 15 percent ($\frac{1}{2}$); Rhode Island, 25 percent ($\frac{3}{5}$); South Dakota, 25 percent ($\frac{1}{2}$); Utah, 20 percent (any); and Wisconsin, 25 percent (any). New York alone established a pyramid of reserve requirements similar to the national system's. In towns with a population less than 1 million, banks were to hold reserves of 15 percent ($\frac{3}{5}$); where the population was more than 1 million but less than 1.8 million, banks were required to maintain reserves equal to 20 percent ($\frac{1}{2}$) of their deposits, and where the population was greater than 1.8 million, the reserve requirement was 25 percent ($\frac{2}{5}$). Almost all other states allowed any bank that met with the state bank examiner's approval to act as a reserve agent. This included, for most states, all national banks, helping to make them city correspondents for many state banks, as well as national banks, in the interior. It appears, then, that to the extent that reserve requirements constrained bank profitability, the state charters were more attractive since states generally imposed lower requirements.

One feature of regulation that was clearly an outcome of the panic of 1907 was the state legislation providing for the guarantee of deposits, which attempted to prevent future panics. In the years between 1907 and the passage of the Federal Reserve Act, Kansas, Nebraska, Oklahoma, South Dakota, and Texas passed laws to insure bank deposits. Under these laws, assessments on state banks were placed in a guarantee fund which would make payments to depositors of failed banks. Although the intention behind this legislation was to prevent a run on the banks, in effect it created another advantage for state charters, since many depositors would switch their deposits from national to state banks in order to insure them. States that adopted deposit insurance schemes saw their banking systems grow at a rapid rate while the national banks in their domain tended to stagnate.[27]

The Supervision and Examination of Banks

If this extensive regulation of banking by state and federal authorities was to be effective, a well-developed system of bank supervision was necessary. The responsibility for supervising national banks' adherence to regulations was delegated to the Office of the Comptroller of the Currency. While the Comptrollers experienced considerable difficulty in performing this task, enforcement of federal laws was stricter than that of state laws where supervision in most cases was noticeably lax.

National banks were required to make five call reports a year to provide the Comptroller with information on their

[27] For a more detailed discussion of deposit insurance, see Chapter 4.

balance sheets. Three of these were made on randomly chosen dates, and a high penalty ($100 for each day's delay) was set for failing to turn in the call day's balance sheet immediately. Many early Comptrollers set high standards for examination, ordering the bank examiners to look beyond a bank's ledger to the actions of the bank's management and the quality of a bank's loans and investment portfolio. Unfortunately, these good intentions were undermined by the National Banking Act's stipulation that examiners be compensated by fees levied on examined banks, out of which examiners were to pay their own expenses. This arrangement created perverse incentives. Examiners often performed a hurried job and followed easy and predictable routes, thereby alerting banks to an impending visit. The difficulties of supervision in the pre–Federal Reserve era come sharply into focus when one looks at the reforms instituted. The most important reform of the period was carried out by Comptroller Lawrence O. Murray (1908–1913), who ensured that charter applications would be made in person rather than by correspondence.[28]

The states were slow to back their legislation with effective supervision. As late as 1863 a large number of states made no provision for bank supervision, and only in the 1880s did they begin to remedy this. In 1885 ten states authorized regular examinations of banks, and nine had either a bank supervisor or a board of supervision. Between 1886 and 1900, twenty-one more states provided for examinations and ten established supervisory authorities. By 1914 all states required some type of annual examination, but it was not until 1931 that every state had a bank supervisor or regulatory board.[29] State supervision was superior to federal in that most states paid examiners a fixed salary. However, the quality of examiners was notoriously low, and many officials were political appointees. Supervisors and boards had very little discretion-

[28] Robertson, *The Comptroller*, pp. 71–79.
[29] Ibid., p. 69.

ary power to grant charters or appoint receivers, and they frequently complained in their reports about their inability to enforce the law strictly.[30] In the preceding discussion of banking regulation it was apparent how weaker state requirements encouraged banks to select a state rather than a national charter; the effects of less rigorous supervision on a bank's choice of charter are, however, less certain. While lax standards may have encouraged banks to join the state systems to avoid compliance with the law, the knowledge that national banks were subject to superior supervision could have attracted more depositors and made a national charter more attractive.

Private Banks and Trust Companies

State banks were not the national banks' only rivals. Private banks and trust companies were in close competition in their commercial banking activities with state and national banks. In the pre-1914 era, private banks served two distinct functions: as adjuncts to brokerage firms in large cities and as suppliers of credit to small agricultural communities.[31] Banks fulfilling the second function were the most important competitors of state and national banks. Their greatest period of growth occurred in the first two decades after the passage of the National Banking Act when the state systems had not yet recovered, and only private banks could serve those communities that could not sustain even the smallest national bank. The last twenty years before the passage of the Federal Reserve Act was a period of stagnation and decline for the private banks. Although data on private banks are poor, the Comptroller's reports offer a fairly accurate picture of the trend after 1896 when data were regularly received from private banks in all states. According to the series collected by the Comptroller of the Currency, the number of private banks

---

[30] Barnett, *State Banks and Trust Companies*, pp. 156–181.
[31] Ibid., p. 206.

rose from around 2,600 in the late 1890s to a peak of 3,017 in 1903. After this their number fell rapidly and stood at 2,201 in 1914. This decline continued through the 1920s. Barnett collected an alternative series which included many more private banks he found listed in *Homan's Bankers Almanac and Register*. This series and the comptroller's, presented in Table 1.5, record the same trends in the population of private banks.[32] According to Barnett, the main reason for this decrease was an absorption of private banks into the state systems as minimum capital requirements were lowered after the turn of the century.[33] He argued that many private banks preferred the corporate form of organization, but could not meet the federal or state minimum capital requirements. The lowering of these requirements after 1900 induced many private banks to take out state charters. Texas, which did not permit the incorporation of state banks, was the last stronghold of private banks. The legislature relented in 1905 and passed an act to allow for the incorporation of state banks. The new law led many private banks to take out state charters, as the minimum capital requirement in small towns was $10,000. The new state system grew rapidly as these new banks entered its rolls, rising from 29 members in 1905 to 515 in 1909.[34] Furthermore, many states began to put pressure on private banks to take out state charters. According to Barnett's 1910 study, eighteen states and territories had effectively co-opted private banks by requiring them to adhere to the same rules as state banks.[35] Other states hampered the operation of private banks by pre-

---

[32] The two series are fairly well correlated. From 1896, when the Comptroller's reporting of private banks improved, to 1909 the coefficient of correlation for the two series is 0.699.

[33] Barnett, *State Banks and Trust Companies*, p. 209.

[34] Joseph M. Grant and Lawrence L. Crum, *The Development of State-Chartered Banking in Texas*, p. 246.

[35] These states were Alabama, Arizona, California, Colorado, Florida, Idaho, Indiana, Kansas, Mississippi, Missouri, New Jersey, New Mexico, North Carolina, Oregon, South Carolina, South Dakota, Utah, and Wyoming.

Table 1.5
Private Banks, 1886–1914

| Year | Number of Private Banks | | Private Bank Assets (in millions of dollars) |
	Comptroller's Series	Barnett's Series	
1886	1,001	3,689	145
1887	1,203	3,966	174
1888	1,324	4,064	163
1889	1,344	4,215	142
1890	1,235	4,305	164
1891	1,161	4,230	151
1892	848	4,004	146
1893	904	4,031	107
1894	1,070	3,844	105
1895	824	3,924	130
1896	2,597	3,810	94
1897	2,637	3,806	78
1898	2,698	3,853	91
1899	2,761	4,168	87
1900	2,825	5,287	126
1901	2,855	5,060	149
1902	2,896	4,976	169
1903	3,017	5,417	169
1904	2,914	5,484	123
1905	2,777	5,291	165
1906	2,726	4,823	144
1907	2,784	4,947	195
1908	2,525	4,576	161
1909	2,467	4,407	246
1910	2,442		160
1911	2,374		183
1912	2,319		196
1913	2,305		182
1914	2,201		196

SOURCES: The Comptroller's series and the private bank assets were obtained from U.S. Comptroller of the Currency, *Annual Report*, various years. There is a break in the series in 1895–1896 when more states began to report the number of private banks. The second series of private banks was compiled by George Barnett and presented in his study for the National Monetary Commission, *State Banks and Trust Companies, since the Passage of the National-Bank Act*. This series includes additional private banks that did not report to the Comptroller but did submit information to *Homan's Bankers Almanac and Register*.

venting them from using any name that would indicate they performed banking services or by requiring them to put up a bond.[36]

The effect of these restrictions is recorded in the declining number of private banks in a period during which state and national banks experienced rapid growth. For the purposes of analyzing the problems of the National Banking System, it will be assumed, then, that private banks did not constitute a threat to the national system's ability to sustain and enlarge its membership.

In contrast to private banks, trust companies entered into a period of very rapid growth in the last twenty years of the National Banking System. Originally, trust companies were designed as corporations that would serve the relatively wealthy while savings banks served the laboring classes. To meet the demands of this clientele, trust companies obtained the power to receive deposits of money in trust and to purchase securities of business firms. However trust companies were not limited to these activities and soon moved into the business of banking as well, competing for deposits, lending on collateral securities, and buying paper in the market.[37] The potential threat to the federal system was clearly recognized in the Federal Reserve Act, which permitted trust companies to join under the same conditions as state banks. The growth of trust companies was even greater than that of the state banks. Three alternative series for trust companies are presented in Table 1.6. The Comptroller of the Currency's series, although lacking data on all trust companies, is continuous, in contrast to Barnett's series, which adds to the Comptroller's additional trust companies found in *Homan's Bankers Almanac and Register*, but does not cover the whole period. Perhaps the most complete is Bell's series, which uses the United States Mortgage and Trust Company of New York's annual publication,

[36] Barnett, *State Banks and Trust Companies*, pp. 214–219.
[37] Larry Neal, "Trust Companies and Financial Innovation," pp. 36–38.

Table 1.6
Trust Companies, 1886–1914

Year	Number of Trust Companies			Trust Company Assets (in millions of dollars)	
	Comptroller's Series	Barnett's Series	Bell's Series	Comptroller's Series	Bell's Series
1886	42	52	115	278	
1887	58	52	150	319	
1888	120	63	165	383	
1889	120	63	200	441	
1890	149	102	255	503	
1891	171	125	292	537	
1892	168	124	315	600	
1893	228	214	335	726	
1894	224	228	345	705	
1895	242	241	364	807	
1896	260	257	380	855	
1897	251	264	390	843	
1898	246	268	415	942	
1899	260	276	450	1,071	
1900	290	492	518	1,330	
1901	334	561	635	1,614	
1902	417	636	785	1,983	
1903	531	827	912	2,298	2,910
1904	585	924	994	2,380	3,138
1905	683	1,041	1,115	2,865	3,801
1906	742	1,337	1,304	2,959	3,943
1907	794	1,485	1,480	3,071	4,220
1908	842	1,496	1,470	2,865	3,917
1909	1,079		1,504	4,068	4,610
1910	1,091		1,527	4,217	4,610
1911	1,251		1,616	4,665	5,168
1912	1,410		1,579	5,107	5,490
1913	1,515		1,732	5,124	5,475
1914	1,564		1,812	5,489	5,924

SOURCES: The Comptroller's series and the trust company assets were obtained from the U.S. Comptroller of the Currency, *Annual Report*, various years. The second series was compiled by George Barnett and presented in his study for the National Monetary Commission, *State Banks and Trust Companies since the Passage of the National-Bank Act*. Barnett obtained his series from *Homan's Bankers Almanac and Register*, which, except for the earlier years, received more bank reports than the Comptroller. John Fred Bell compiled series on the number and assets of trust companies for his Ph.D. dissertation, "The Growth and Development of Banking Activities of Trust Companies." For this most complete series, Bell used the annual publication, *Trust Companies of the United States*.

Trust Companies of the United States. Although there are differences in the two series, they are closely correlated as they reflect the same trends.[38] According to Barnett, as late as 1890, there were only 102 trust companies in the United States, with 48 located in New England and 45 in the mid-Atlantic states. By 1900 they numbered 492, still heavily concentrated on the East Coast. New England had 90, the Mid-Atlantic 211, the South 97, and the Midwest 47 in that year. Almost a decade later, in 1909, 1,079 trust companies were in business, with 278 located in Pennsylvania alone. Indiana, New York, and New Jersey followed with 93, 85, and 78 trust companies each. Other states with over 40 were Maine, Massachusetts, Texas, Kentucky, Illinois, and Missouri. Connecticut and Vermont had over 20, and the rest of the states had fewer.[39]

As relatively new institutions, trust companies were responsible for innovation in the financial sector.[40] Trust companies had many of the attributes of state banks and shared the same general advantage of weaker regulations vis-à-vis national banks. Before the 1890s, trust companies had been subject to little regulation; but the states, recognizing the development of a new type of commercial bank to rival their state-chartered banks, began to bring them under state supervision. The state legislatures and banking authorities tried to equalize the differences in regulation between state banks and trust companies either by imposing new restrictions on trust companies or by allowing state banks to engage in operations previously limited to trust companies. By the early twentieth century many trust companies were almost indistinguishable from state banks; however, in some states, differences persisted with trust companies having the advantages

---

[38] The coefficients of correlation for the number of companies were: Comptroller-Bell, 0.911; Bell-Barnett, 0.996; and Comptroller-Barnett, 0.998. For Comptroller-Bell assets, the coefficient was 0.979.

[39] Barnett, *State Banks and Trust Companies*, p. 248.

[40] Neal, "Trust Companies and Financial Innovation," pp. 35–45.

of lower reserve requirements, lower taxation, and trust operations.[41]

In many states, trust companies had successfully invaded or supplanted state banks in the field of commercial banking. In Massachusetts, Maine, and Vermont, no state banks were chartered in the last decade before the Federal Reserve System was established. All commercial banking was performed by trust companies with banking departments. In Pennsylvania, where trust companies were also well developed, they were regulated by the same authority as state banks and subject to very similar regulations, blurring the distinction between commercial bank and trust company. Connecticut chartered trust companies under the same legislation as state banks. Missouri, Indiana, and Kentucky imposed the same capital and reserve requirements on trust companies as they did on state banks. Illinois had no formal reserve requirements for either; but while it set minimum capital requirements for state banks, it did not do so for trust companies. Texas had no reserve requirements for trust companies, but it placed higher capital requirements on them than on state banks. The relatively higher minimum capital requirements for trust companies vis-à-vis state banks in New York and New Jersey probably did not constrain trust companies, since capital was easier to obtain in the metropolitan area and reserve requirements were lower.[42] In New York, trust companies were particularly prominent and experienced more rapid growth than the more closely regulated state banks. Between 1897 and 1907, total New York state- and national-bank assets increased by 82.1 percent and 96.7 percent while trust companies' assets rose 244.1 percent.[43]

Where trust companies entered commercial banking, they

[41] John Fred Bell, "The Growth and Development of Banking Activities of Trust Companies," pp. 66–102.

[42] Welldon, *Digest of State Banking Statutes*, Table 3 and accompanying text.

[43] Barnett, *State Banks and Trust Companies*, p. 235.

clearly consisted a major, additional threat to the National Banking System. For the purposes of this study, where trust companies supplanted state banks entirely, they are simply treated as state banks. In states in which there were state banks and trust companies with commercial banking operations, the latter are treated as state banks with appropriate adjustments for differences in regulations. Trust companies in many ways were rivals of both state and national banks, but as state-chartered creations they may, together with state banks, be considered as part of the state systems that gradually eroded the National Banking System's prominence.

The Determinants of Membership in the National Banking System

The weaker regulations imposed on state-chartered institutions in comparison to national banks have been recognized as important factors affecting the membership of the National Banking System. However, there has been no attempt to measure empirically the relative impact of the various regulations on a bank's decision to join one system or the other. Barnett's 1910 study is the only previous work. His evaluation of the effects of the differences in regulation, although insightful, is impressionistic. Barnett believed that the most important factors inducing a bank to take out a state charter were lower capital and reserve requirements and looser portfolio restrictions. A bank selecting a national charter, on the other hand, would find it easier to attract stockholders and depositors since the superior, nationally uniform supervision promised greater security. Furthermore, national banks had the privilege of note issue, which Barnett considered an additional source of profit.[44] Given these hypotheses and the other possible factors

[44] Ibid., pp. 220–234.

affecting a bank's choice of charter, an empirical evaluation is necessary to sort out which regulations did constrain a bank's activities and influence its membership decision.

No econometric analysis of the determinants of why banks joined the national or the state banking system has been attempted, but there are many studies that look at the question of membership in the Federal Reserve System. Most of these studies treat Federal Reserve membership in terms of its costs and benefits. Reserves required to be held at the Federal Reserve without interest are the most important cost imposed on member banks. The benefits that offset part of this burden include free services such as check collection, coin and currency handling, wire transfers, safekeeping of securities, and borrowing at the discount window. One approach attempts to explain why banks leave the Federal Reserve by determining whether or not the implicit rate of return on required reserves is low. R. Alton Gilbert carried out this exercise and found the return in the 1970s to be very low, 1.69 percent for large banks, and 0.59 percent for small banks, suggesting that there was good reason for banks to leave the Federal Reserve.[45] Looking at the relative burdens on members and nonmembers, Robert Knight applied a cost-benefit analysis and discovered that the burden of required reserves for Federal Reserve members was greater than that for state bank nonmembers.[46]

An alternative method has been to regress the ratio of the number of member to total commercial banks or the ratio of member deposits to total deposits of commercial banks on variables that reflect the possible costs or benefits of membership. C. J. Prestopino carried out a cross-section analysis

[45] R. Alton Gilbert, "Utilization of Federal Reserve Bank Services by Member Banks: Implications for the Costs and Benefits of Membership," p. 9.

[46] Robert E. Knight, "Comparative Burdens of Federal Reserve Member and Nonmember Banks."

for 1968 and found that the higher reserve requirements of the Federal Reserve were a significant factor.[47] Carl Gambs and Robert Rasche's time series regressions for the period 1962–1973 showed that reserve requirements and interest rates, reflecting the opportunity cost of holding reserves, were important.[48] In a more long-term study covering the period from 1923 to 1976, Joanna Frodin examined member-bank to total commercial-bank deposits as a function of the net aggregate cost or benefit per dollar of member-bank deposits and per dollar of member-bank capital accounts. She found net cost to be an important factor.[49] In an effort to analyze the separate effects of each element of cost and benefit, Benjamin Klein estimated ordinary least squares and autoregressive integrated moving average regressions of the percentage of member banks and member-bank deposits to total commercial banks and total commercial-bank assets as a function of the cost of reserves per dollar of member deposits, the subsidy per dollar from borrowing, the insurance from failure provided by the discount window, and the lagged dependent variable. He found these all to be significant factors in the current decline in Federal Reserve membership.[50]

Although these studies all support the hypothesis that the higher cost of membership has reduced Federal Reserve membership, the difficulty encountered in all of them has been to evaluate correctly the benefits and costs of membership, assigning exact dollar values to each. This is a difficult task, and deficiencies in the pre-1914 banking data make it even harder. Even for the last few years prior to the passage

[47] C. J. Prestopino, "Do Higher Reserve Requirements Discourage Federal Reserve Membership?"

[48] Carl Gambs and Robert Rasche, "Costs of Reserves and the Relative Size of Member and Nonmember Bank Demand Deposits."

[49] Joanna Haywood Frodin, "The Tax/Subsidy Relation between Member Banks and the Federal Reserve System."

[50] Klein's results are quoted in George J. Benston, *Federal Reserve Membership: Consequences, Costs, Benefits and Alternatives*, pp. 41–42.

of the Federal Reserve Act, the exact number of state banks is uncertain. While statistics are available for national banks, state bank records often fail to indicate whether the change in the number of banks is due to new members, conversions to national charters, failures, or voluntary liquidations. To construct a dependent variable along the lines of current studies with a ratio of the number or assets of national banks to all commercial banks or commercial-bank assets would be fraught with error.

As an alternative and, perhaps, superior formulation, the approach used here analyzes the problem of national-bank membership as the decision of a profit-maximizing firm entering the market.[51] Any prospective financial institution intending to go into the business of commercial banking in this period had a choice of incorporating under either state or federal law and would have chosen the type of charter whose regulation allowed the institution to earn higher profits. The firm was thus faced with a simple dichotomous choice. The appropriate statistical model is a qualitative-response model where the dependent variable reflecting a firm's choice of charter can take on either of two values, zero or one, representing respectively the selection of a national or a state charter. Probit analysis was used here. This approach establishes a

[51] To explain how the complex laws regulating banks affected membership it would be preferable to specify a microeconomic model of bank behavior in which the membership decision is taken in conjunction with other decisions about the size and composition of a bank's portfolio. This would lead to the estimation of a system of structural equations, one for each decision variable, where the interdependent nature of the decisions regarding profitability, liquidity, solvency, and membership could be taken into account. Unfortunately, this approach is not a practical one. There is no general model of bank behavior that could be adapted to analyze the membership question, and thus, how federal and state regulations affected a bank's membership decision must be accounted for by appropriate exogenous variables in a single reduced-form equation. For a survey of models of bank behavior and an analysis of the limitations see Ernst Baltensperger, "Alternative Approaches to the Theory of the Banking Firm."

readily interpretable probabilistic framework in which counterfactual questions can be easily handled.[52]

The sample chosen for examination includes all national banks and state-chartered commercial banking institutions (state banks and trust companies that engaged in commercial banking) that opened between October 31, 1908, and October 30, 1910. This represents two reporting periods for the Comptroller of the Currency, who was responsible for chartering national banks. This period was chosen because of the information available about state regulations in 1909 and the better quality of information about the number of new state banks. Before the panic of 1907 many states still did not regularly report the number and condition of the banks chartered under their auspices. After the panic almost every state provided annual or biennial reports by a state bank examiner or auditor. An extensive search of the bank examiners' reports found 2,242 state banks and trust companies were chartered in this period compared to 620 national banks.[53]

The selected determinants of a bank's choice of charter were minimum capital requirements, branching restrictions, the ratio of rural to total population, the total and vault cash reserve requirements for demand and time deposits, and state deposit insurance. Some independent variables were measured as the difference between the national and state regulations for 1909 for each bank. For example, in Colorado the minimum capital requirement for banks in towns with a population under 3,000 was $10,000 compared to the national requirement of $25,000. The difference of $15,000 was the independent variable used. It was hypothesized that the greater the difference in favor of the state, the greater the probability a bank would take out a state charter. If the capital constraint was a binding one, that is, if it effectively altered bank be-

---

[52] Probit assumes that the probability of a bank selecting a national charter is normally distributed. This technique and its application are explained in Appendix B.

[53] For a more detailed description of the data, see Appendix A.

havior, the estimated coefficient should be positive and significant. Similarly for reserve requirements, the larger the difference between national and state reserve requirements, the greater the probability a bank would incorporate under state law. If this was a significant factor, this variable should have a positive coefficient.

As already noted, state banks in rural areas tended to hold a much larger portion of their assets in mortgages and real estate–based loans than urban state banks or national banks. State banks were able to offer more loans and discounts on real estate owing to the weaker state restrictions on their portfolios. Thus, state banks had more profitable loans open to them in agricultural areas than national banks had. In order to capture the advantage that state institutions enjoyed by their ability to lend on real estate in rural areas, a variable representing the opportunity to offer such loans was necessary. For this purpose, a proxy, the ratio of rural to total state population for 1910, was chosen where rural population was defined by the Census of 1910 to be those people living in communities of 2,500 or less. It was hypothesized, that the higher this ratio was, that is, the more rural the state, the more likely a bank would be to take out a state charter to gain the advantage of looser portfolio restrictions. A positive coefficient was expected.

If a state allowed any type of branch banking, a dummy variable was set equal to one to capture the possible effects. Care was taken to ensure that only those banks actually allowed to branch were assigned a one instead of a zero. In New York, for example, the dummy variable was set equal to one only in New York City, where banks had this option. It was not thought possible to determine a priori whether branching would increase or decrease the probability of a bank taking out a state charter. Banks might be lured away from the national system increasing the number of banks incorporating under state law, or expand by opening new branches, thereby decreasing the number of state charters.

The sign of the coefficient could be either positive or negative accordingly.

There were two types of state deposit guarantee systems, compulsory and voluntary. A dummy variable was used for each, with the expectation that either type would induce more banks to join the state banking systems and yield positive coefficients. No separate variable was included to measure the advantages bestowed on national banks by the privilege of note issue.[54] A dummy variable might have been used, but since this corresponds exactly to the dichotomous division of charters it was not included. Instead these advantages and any other additional benefits should be captured in the intercept term. A significant, negative coefficient provides partial evidence that note issue conferred an advantage to a national charter and decreased the probability that a new bank would incorporate under state law.

The choice of charter model used here is:

$$Y_i = b_0 + b_1 x_{1i} + b_2 x_{2i} + b_3 x_{3i} + b_4 x_{4i} + b_5 x_{5i} + b_6 x_{6i} + b_7 x_{7i} + b_8 x_{8i} + b_9 x_{9i} \qquad (1)$$

where $Y_i = 0$ when the ith bank selected a national charter and $Y_i = 1$ when the ith bank chose a state charter. For the ith bank, the independent variables are x_{1i}, the difference between the state and national minimum capital requirement; x_{2i}, a dummy variable for branch banking; x_{3i}, the difference between the state and national total reserve requirements on demand deposits; x_{4i}, the difference between the state and

---

[54] The benefits of national bank-note issue depended on the profitability of issue. As previously mentioned, why banks failed to respond to a high rate of return on bank notes is imperfectly understood. Some proxy for regional or state profitability of bank-note issue might have been constructed using the inverse relationship between local interest rates and note issue observed by James. See James, "The Conundrum of the Low Issue of National Bank Notes." However, note issue might have also benefited the state banks and trust companies which, unlike national banks, could use national bank notes as lawful money when calculating their reserves. Thus, no individual variable for note issue was included, as the benefits from note issue are far from clear.

national vault cash reserve requirements on demand deposits; x_{5i}, the ratio of the rural to total population in a given state; x_{6i}, the difference between the state and national total reserve requirements on time deposits; x_{7i}, the difference between the state and national vault cash reserve requirements on time deposits; x_{8i}, a dummy variable for voluntary deposit insurance; and x_{9i}, a dummy variable for compulsory deposit insurance. The probit procedure transforms equation (1) with a cumulative normal density function to:

$$P(E_i) = F(b_0 + b_1 x_{1i} + b_2 x_{2i} + b_3 x_{3i} + b_4 x_{4i}$$
$$+ b_5 x_{5i} + b_6 x_{6i} + b_7 x_{7i} + b_8 x_{8i} + b_9 x_{9i}) \qquad (2)$$

or

$$P(E_i) = F(I_i). \qquad (3)$$

where $P(E_i)$ is both the probability of a single bank selecting a state charter and the percentage of banks in a given class choosing a state charter given the values of the independent variables. I_i is the critical value that yields that probability from the normal distribution.

The estimates and the approximate t-statistics for the coefficients of the model, using three different specifications, are presented in Table 1.7.[55] The large sample containing 2,862 observations should provide a clear indication of a variable's significance as efficiency is not a problem. Two measures of goodness of fit, the log likelihood ratio test statistic and the pseudo-R^2, are also given.[56] The log likelihood ratio test indicates that all estimated equations are highly significant.[57]

[55] The maximum likelihood estimation technique used ensured that the estimated coefficients and standard errors would be asymptotically consistent. The approximate t-statistics, the test of significance for the coefficients, has an asymptotic t distribution.

[56] These measures are discussed in Appendix B. For further information see George G. Judge, William E. Griffiths, R. Carter Hill, and Tsoung-Chao Lee, *The Theory and Practice of Econometrics*, pp. 600–601.

[57] The log likelihood ratio test statistic has a chi-square distribution where the degrees of freedom are equal to the number of independent variables.

Table 1.7
Choice of Charter Probit Estimates, 1908–1910

	Model I	Model II	Model III
Independent Variables			
Intercept	−0.1235	−0.0969	−0.0277
	(−1.3160)	(−1.0533)	(−0.3144)
Minimum capital	0.0074	0.0066	0.0069
requirement	(6.1667*)	(5.5000*)	(5.7500*)
Branch banking	−0.0276	−0.2474	−0.2239
	(−3.6481*)	(−3.3633*)	(−3.0094*)
Ratio of rural	1.1871	1.1079	0.9375
to total state	(9.1315*)	(8.6218*)	(7.7608*)
population			
Total reserve	−0.0273		−0.0110
requirements on	(−5.3529*)		(−2.5000*)
demand deposits			
Vault cash reserve	0.0700	0.0341	
requirements on	(6.0345*)	(3.6277*)	
demand deposits			
Total reserve	0.0285		0.0107
requirements on	(4.7500*)		(2.8919*)
time deposits			
Vault cash reserve	−0.0825	−0.0131	
requirements on	(−4.8529*)	(−1.1909)	
time deposits			
Voluntary deposit	0.5233	0.4525	0.5775
insurance	(3.8449*)	(3.7614*)	(4.5012*)
Compulsory deposit	0.2215	0.4870	0.4817
insurance	(2.2906*)	(5.9681*)	(5.5432*)
Goodness of Fit			
Log likelihood			
ratio test statistic	293.6*	257.6*	254.0*
Pseudo-R^2	0.118	0.106	0.105

NOTE: The numbers in parentheses are approximate *t*-statistics obtained by dividing the estimated coefficients by their estimated standard errors.
* Significant at the 0.05 level.

The pseudo-R^2 reported shows the percentage of variation explained by the equation. It appears to be on the low side;

At the 5 percent level, the critical value with seven degrees of freedom is 14.1; with nine degrees of freedom it is 16.9.

however this could have occurred if some of the regulations were not binding. If federal or state regulations were sometimes not effective in altering bank behavior (for example, if the minimum capital requirement was less than the amount of capital the bank would have freely chosen), then the choice of charter decisions would not be influenced by these requirements. Some of the variation may, thus, be unexplained even though the explanatory power as indicated by the log likelihood ratio test statistic is high.

In all estimations, the coefficients on the minimum capital requirement, vault cash reserve requirement on demand deposits, ratio of rural to total population, total reserve requirement on time deposits, compulsory deposit insurance, and voluntary deposit insurance variables are positive as hypothesized and significant at the 5 percent level. The significant coefficient on the branch banking variable to which no a priori sign could be attributed was negative in all cases. This points out that branching, in the state systems that permitted it, encouraged expansion through the opening of new offices rather than new banks. The intercept term in all three estimations is negative and not significant. If it had been significant, an argument could have been constructed that the residual regulations favored the establishment of new national banks. This is particularly important with regard to the question of the advantages conferred on national banks by the privilege of note issue. As there is no way to capture this in a variable, the intercept must be examined. Barnett argued that note issue was a potent attraction. The variable's lack of significance, however, appears to offer additional support to James's argument that it did not confer any particular advantage and that the failure of banks to issue notes up to the value of their capital, the legal maximum, was due to the relative attractiveness of deposit creation. A strong argument for this conclusion cannot be made as other, unknown, factors may be affecting the intercept term.

Analysis of the reserve requirements presented some problems, and these are what originally prompted the three specifications. The difficult-to-explain results were the signs on the total reserve requirement on demand deposits for Models I and III and the vault cash reserve requirements on time deposits in Model I. While the significant negative sign on the coefficient for total reserve requirements on demand deposits contradicts the initial hypothesis, there are some convincing economic reasons why this should be negative. The one important aspect of the pre-1914 dual banking system that the models ignore is the hierarchical reserve requirements, which contributed to a concentration of reserves held as bankers' balances in major financial centers. By requiring banks to hold a portion of their reserves on deposit with banks in reserve cities, federal and state authorities increased the deposits available to reserve-city banks and, thus, may have increased the profitability of these city banks. As previously explained, federal legislation designated certain cities as reserve cities where country banks could hold part of their legal reserves. In most states, many national banks were designated as reserve agents, and their well-established presence in the major towns and cities made them the major recipients of these funds. In both instances, national banks benefited from these arrangements. The desirability of acting as reserve agents can also be observed in the rise in the number of reserve cities from eighteen in 1887 to forty-three in 1913. Cities were only so designated by the Comptroller upon request of three-fourths of the national banks in their area. They would not have done so if it adversely affected their profitability. The burden of higher total and vault cash reserve requirements on demand deposits was offset for many national banks who benefited from serving as depositories for state and national country banks.

This explanation still leaves two puzzles unresolved: why the total reserve requirement on time deposits is positive in Model I and Model III and why when the total requirement is added in Model I the vault cash reserve requirement on time deposits' coefficient turns significant. The second problem may be one of multicollinearity:[58] all the reserve requirement variables were strongly correlated, and this may account for the switch in significance.[59] One attempt was made to track down multicollinearity by performing log likelihood ratio tests on groups of variables.[60] Although all groups passed the test, the two weakest contain the vault cash reserve requirements on time deposits, suggesting that, as in Model II, it may not be significant. One notable feature of state reserve requirements was the very low reserve requirements on time deposits. This naturally led state banks to hold a much higher percentage of their liabilities as time deposits than national banks. In 1910 state banks held 36.6 percent of total deposits and 28.6 percent of total liabilities as time deposits, while comparable figures for national banks were 13.9 percent and 12.5 percent respectively.[61] As most state bank requirements on time deposits were vault cash requirements, there was little need to deposit reserves with the predominantly national re-

[58] Multicollinearity occurs when there is strong correlation or collinearity among the explanatory variables. This makes it difficult to obtain very precise estimates. The estimates are still unbiased, but the standard error is larger. Strong correlation of variables may affect the signs of the coefficients, and the estimation may become very sensitive to any changes in the number of observations or model specification. For a more detailed discussion of the issue, see G. S. Maddala, *Econometrics*, pp. 183–191.

[59] Simple correlations among the reserve requirement variables, which are one indication of multicollinearity, ranged from 0.247 to 0.584. These were the highest correlations among all pairwise combinations of variables.

[60] The statistics obtained were: for both total requirements, 36.0; for both vault cash requirements, 39.6; for both demand deposit requirements, 45.4; for both time deposit requirements, 24.4; and for all the reserve requirements, 50.6. The first four pass a 5 percent level of significance as the chi-square distribution with two degrees of freedom has a critical value of 5.99. The last test also passes, as the critical value at 5 percent with four degrees of freedom is 9.49.

[61] Board of Governors of the Federal Reserve System, *All Bank Statistics, United States, 1896–1955*, pp. 40–41 and 44–45.

serve banks. There was thus no hierarchy effect, as in the case of demand deposits, and the sign on the coefficient was positive as expected.

The last interesting aspect of the estimated coefficients is the similarity in magnitude of the estimates for the voluntary and compulsory deposit insurance variables. Equality of value would appear to indicate that the two systems were perfect substitutes for one another in their effect on a bank's choice of charter. A bank could avoid deposit insurance in a voluntary system by not joining, but could also do so with seemingly equal ease in a compulsory system by changing to a national charter. To examine the equality of the two coefficients an approximate t-test using the larger of the two standard errors was performed with the null hypothesis that the coefficients are equal.[62] The null hypothesis could not be rejected for the second and third models, but it could be rejected in the first model where all the variables are present. This may, however, be attributable to multicollinearity, which created problems in the analysis of the reserve requirements.

Government Policy and Membership in the National Banking System

Goodness of fit may be evaluated in another way that will also allow examination of questions about the effects of changes in regulation on the bank population. Probit analysis assumes that a bank's choice of charter is normally distributed. For each class of banks, that is banks subject to the same regulations, there is an estimated critical value, I, obtained by multiplying the values of the independent variables by their respective estimated coefficients, which divides the normal population between those selecting a state and those choosing

[62] For Model I, $t = 2.217$, for Model II, $t = 0.287$, for Model III, $t = 0.747$.

a national charter. This value when plugged into a normal distribution will yield a prediction of the percentage of banks in each class of banks in each state choosing a state charter. These percentages may then be multiplied by the total number of new banks in the state to predict how many will take out state charters.[63]

The estimates from Model I were used because that model had the highest log likelihood ratio statistic, indicating it explained more variation than the other two specifications. The predicted state- and national-bank totals compared very favorably to the actual number. In the period from October 31, 1908, to October 31, 1910, 620 banks (21.6%) took out national charters and 2,242 (78.4%) took out state charters. The model predicted these to be 593 (20.7%) and 2,269 (79.3%) respectively, an error of only 0.9 percent.

Changes in federal regulations to improve the attractiveness of membership in the National Banking System can be evaluated by substituting a vector of alternative regulations for the actual vector to estimate the percentages of banks in each class choosing a state charter. The impact of the Gold Standard Act's provision lowering the minimum capital requirement for national banks from $50,000 to $25,000 in towns with a population under 3,000 may be examined by estimating the number of banks that would have taken out national charters if the capital requirement had been $25,000 greater in the period. This increased the probability of banks taking out state charters. The total effect on the number of banks nationwide is startlingly small; only twenty-seven fewer banks (566 total or 19.8% of all new banks) than predicted would have taken out national charters. This suggests that there was little to gain by lowering the minimum capital requirements for national banks.

At this point it might be objected that the states substantially

---

[63] See Appendix B for a more detailed description of this procedure.

changed their bank regulations in the twenty years prior to
the Federal Reserve Act, at least in part, in response to the
efforts of the Comptroller and the Congress to enlarge the
membership of the federal system. The impact of a lower
national-bank capital requirement would clearly have been
greater if the states' legislation had remained unaltered. The
states' success at whittling away national banks' advantages
may be approximated by substituting the state regulations of
1895 for those of 1909 in predicting the number of banks
choosing state and national charters. If the states had kept
their 1895 legislation, while the national system had reduced
its lowest capital requirement by half, 931, or 32.5 percent,
of the new banks would have taken out national charters and
1,931, or 67.5 percent, state charters. Clearly, the change in
federal regulation would have been more effective if the states
had not reacted by lowering their reserve requirements to
maintain membership in their banking systems.

The effect of the Gold Standard Act on the distribution of
assets between the federal and state banking systems can also
be measured. In 1900, the National Banking System held 61.6
percent of all commercial-bank assets; but by 1913, although
the total assets had risen, its share had fallen to 54.3 percent.
Over the period 1900–1913, when 3,736 new national banks
and 10,867 new state banks and trust companies were organized,[64] the average size of state institutions and national banks
tended to fall, implying that smaller than average firms were
taking out charters. In real terms, the average size of national
banks fell from $1,325,000 to $1,244,000 and that of state
institutions from $662,000 to $503,000.[65] In the absence of

[64] The Comptroller's figures are used instead of Barnett's. Although they
may not be as complete, they are a continuous series, and, as already noted,
they are closely correlated with the alternative series. Employing the other
series would not substantially alter the results. In particular, the differences
in the assets series are very small, indicating that only the smallest institutions
were omitted.

[65] The consumer price index (U.S. Department of Commerce, *Historical*

alternative numbers on the size of new banks, it will be assumed that each new bank brought into the federal system $1,277,000, or the average size of national banks in 1908. This is obviously too high, but it sets a ceiling on the impact of regulatory changes.

If there had been no reduction in the minimum federal capital requirements in the sample period, the National Banking System would in 1910 have had 55.4 percent of all commercial-bank assets, instead of the actual 55.6 percent. The policy appears to have been a complete failure, yet if states had maintained their 1895 capital regulations in the face of lower national-bank requirements, the national system would have had 58.0 percent of all assets in 1910. Over the period 1900–1914, this policy might have slightly helped to increase the federal system's share of banks and assets if the states had not reacted as they did.

What else could the Congress and the Comptroller have done to keep more banks in the national system? One possibility would have been to require all banks to meet federal reserve requirements. Another would have been to permit national banks to lend on real estate. To assess the impact of these regulatory changes on the banking systems, it will be assumed that all banks in the long run selected a banking system on the same basis as new banks did. In 1910, the absence of restrictions on real estate loans would have drawn in 43.3 percent of all commercial banks with 70.0 percent of all commercial-bank assets. This result is sensitive to the size of the state banks transferring their allegiance. If the new national banks were the average size of established state rather than national banks, the National Banking System's share of assets would have been 60.3 percent. If Congress had imposed national reserve requirements on all banks, then 31.0 percent

Statistics, p. 199) was used to deflate the figures. If the wholesale price index were used, it would yield very similar results.

of all banks, instead of an actual 34.9 percent, would have belonged to the federal system, implying a decline in assets. This small loss may be attributed to the hierarchical determination of reserve requirements, which increased the attractions of a national charter, and the low interest rates for the sample period.

The estimation of the number of banks selecting a national charter in the absence of differences in national and state reserve requirements may be somewhat too low for the period 1900–1913. Banks were sensitive to the cost of holding non-interest-bearing reserves. The opportunity cost in the period 1908–1910 may have been a little lower than in the earlier part of the decade. This is suggested by the fact that interest rates on call loans were fairly low in this two-year period. The average annual rates were 1.92, 2.71, and 2.98 percent for the years 1908 through 1910. In contrast the interest rates for the years 1900–1907 were: 2.94, 4.00, 5.15, 3.71, 1.78, 4.44, 6.54, and 7.01 percent.[66] If these on average higher interest rates represented higher costs, then state charters would have been more attractive in the presence of existing reserve requirement differentials. Eliminating these differentials would have then cut more deeply into the state banking system's membership.

It is important to note that these significant regulatory changes would only have stabilized the membership in the National Banking System, whose assets had declined to 54.3 percent of all banks' assets in 1913. They would not have brought a majority of commercial banks into the National Banking System or have greatly increased its total assets. The weakness of these changes may be partly attributable to the fact that they would not have profoundly altered the nation's banking structure. One alternative, increased branch banking, might

---

[66] Ibid., p. 1001.

have had an important impact on both banking structure and membership.

Unfortunately, the counterfactual analysis applied so far cannot be used to examine the effects of removing the severe restrictions on branching. The negative coefficient on the branch banking variable in all estimations indicates that branching decreased the number of new banks. In branching states, the number of bank offices increased through the opening of new branches rather than new banks. More liberal branching laws on the order of state-wide branching would have substantially modified the nation's banking structure so that the type of analysis applied so far is not useful to examine its impact on membership. There is no direct way to do this either, as branching was prohibited to national banks; however, it is possible to gain some insights into the effects of branching on membership by noting that one of the obvious characteristics of national banks was that they were larger than state banks.

This observation is confirmed by an ordinary least squares regression of the percentage of total commercial-bank assets in the National Banking System by state (MEM) on the average size (in millions of dollars) of the commercial banks in each state (SIZE) for 1910. The regression indicates that average bank size was an important factor affecting membership:

$$\text{MEM} = 0.593 + 0.055 \text{ SIZE} \qquad (4)$$
$$(2.854) \quad (4.839)$$
$$R^2 = 0.337 \qquad F_{2,\ 42} = 11.45$$

The coefficient on bank size appears to be reasonable in magnitude, and the t-statistic indicates that bank size did significantly contribute to the percentage of commercial-bank assets in the National Banking System.

The potential importance of branching for membership may be indirectly assessed by examining the contribution of branching to the average size of state banks. An ordinary least squares regression was performed where the average asset size of state banks in millions of dollars (SBSIZE) in 1910 was regressed on the minimum state capital requirements in thousands of dollars (MK), a dummy variable for branch banking (BB, where BB = 1 indicates that some form of branching was allowed), total state reserve requirement on demand deposits (TRR), state vault cash requirements on demand deposits (VCRR), and as a measure of population dispersion the ratio of rural to total population in the state (RPTP). The result was:

$$\begin{aligned} \text{SBSIZE} = 0.531 &+ 0.025\text{MK} + 0.329\text{BB} - 0.005\text{TRR} \\ (1.331) \quad &(4.487) \qquad (1.957) \qquad (-0.419) \\ &+ 0.009\text{VCRR} - 0.835\text{RPTP} \\ &\quad (0.371) \qquad \quad (-1.904) \\ R^2 = 0.574 \quad &F_{5,\,42} = 13.67 \end{aligned} \qquad (5)$$

From this it may be inferred that an increase in the rural population would have decreased the average size of banks in the state and a rise in the minimum capital requirements increased it. The branch banking variable indicates that on average some form of branching contributed $329,000 to the average size of state banks. This is not a negligible amount, given that the average size of these banks was $503,000 in 1913.

Unfortunately, the results here are biased against the potential effect of branching because branching was measured with a dummy variable. Those states in which branching was permitted on a state-wide basis were therefore treated the same as those in which it was more severely limited. If all the states that did allow branching had permitted it on a state-wide basis, the contribution of branching to average bank size undoubtedly would have been greater. Free nationwide branching would have led to the rise of fewer larger banks which very probably would have been members of the federal banking system. However, given the strong unit banking lobbies in Washington and the state capitals, it was politically infeasible to offer increased branch banking as a solution to the National Banking System's problems.

The Limits on Membership in the National Banking System

The efforts of the Comptroller of the Currency and the Congress to maintain the dominance of the National Banking System were stymied by several factors. Financial innovation tended to weaken any special advantages conferred on national banks, as evidenced by the development of deposit banking which circumvented the state banks' inability to issue bank notes and by the rise of the trust companies, which created their own special advantages not open to national banks. Attempts by the federal authorities to reduce the advantages of the state-chartered institutions by easing national-bank requirements were met by a reduction in state requirements to maintain the attractions of state charters. The lower capital requirements and weaker portfolio restrictions helped to create a large number of small, mostly rural state banks. These smaller, commercial banks formed anti-branch-banking lobbies which successfully blocked increased branching at the federal level and in many states. The National Banking System was thus deprived of another means of augmenting its membership.

The Federal Reserve Act sought to reverse the National Banking System's declining fortunes and strengthen the banking system as a whole. Member banks' reserve requirements were reduced, new areas of activity were open to them, and they were provided with advantages such as access to the discount window. The founders of the Federal Reserve were optimistic that these changes would revive the federal system, but the experience of the National Banking System should have warned them about the problems inherent in the dual banking system. As long as membership was still voluntary and the states were able to charter and regulate banks, there was little chance, as will be seen in Chapter 3, that the Federal Reserve System could succeed where the National Banking System had failed.

2

Federal Banking Reform and the Evolution of the Federal Reserve System

The Motives for Reform

BEFORE the panic of 1907, banking reform was primarily the concern of big-city bankers and federal officials, but that financial crisis, which traumatized the nation, made reform a political imperative. Legislative proposals in Congress to restructure the banking system awakened the interest of the entire banking community. The conflicts already apparent between national banks and state-regulated institutions were heightened, and the tensions between country, reserve-city, and New York banks grew as each feared that the others would secure more favorable legislation. The Federal Reserve Act of 1913 reflected an attempt to accommodate the diverse banking interests and secure their support for reform. The Federal Reserve System was, thus, not patterned after the European central banks. Instead, it was modeled on the clearinghouses, institutions familiar and acceptable to most bankers. The number of Federal Reserve banks, their control by bankers, and the absence of any alteration in the federal laws restricting branching are testimony to the successful opposition of most banks to the creation of a centralized institution either operated by the government or dominated by the nation's largest banks.

One of the principal objectives of the Federal Reserve Act was to substantially reduce correspondent banking. It was widely held that the banking system was vulnerable to crises because banks' reserves, which were supposed to protect convertibility, were scattered about in individual banks' vaults and kept on deposit at correspondent banks. The aim of the act was to pool reserves in regional reserve banks where they could be used to make rediscounts to member banks, as the clearinghouses had done to a limited extent. Banking reformers felt that this would eliminate the pyramiding of reserves in correspondent balances and deprive the New York banks of the use of these funds in the stock market, whose oscillations, it was believed, induced frequent financial crises. Furthermore, the establishment of the reserve banks as federal clearinghouses was intended not only to increase the efficiency of clearing processes but also to eliminate the need to hold balances with correspondents for clearing purposes.[1] However, the Federal Reserve was not successful in diminishing the role of correspondent banking in the nation's financial system or in securing the entry of more than a fraction of the state banks and trust companies. It did establish a central bank in name, if not in substance, which discounted the commercial paper of member banks. Yet even this was a qualified success. The Federal Reserve's actions in the 1920s were strongly colored by the real bills doctrine and the normative judgments about how money markets ought to function that had shaped the Federal Reserve Act. These help to explain the Federal Reserve's preoccupation with the stock market and its failure to comprehend quickly how the various instruments of monetary control could best be employed and what their effects on the economy were. This chapter treats the progress of banking reform and the evolution of the Federal Reserve System as a struggle between different interests in the banking

[1] Leonard L. Watkins, *Bankers' Balances*, pp. 8–9.

community. The success of the Federal Reserve System is evaluated from the point of view of its framers' objectives. These goals are seen as continuing to exert a major influence on the Federal Reserve's conduct in the first decade and a half of its operation, in spite of the changes the system underwent.

Correspondent Banking before the Federal Reserve Act

Correspondent banking was one important feature of the pre–Federal Reserve banking system on which most critics focused their attention. The pyramiding of bankers' balances in New York City, where a portion was invested in the stock market, occasioned a legitimate concern about the ability of banks to realize their interbank deposits in a panic and presented a situation that fueled the public's fear of speculation. Regarded as a major weakness of the banking system, correspondent banking was largely the product of restrictive legislation passed by the state legislatures and the Congress in the second half of the nineteenth century. The widespread limitations on branch banking and low capital requirements created a system in which unit banks were dominant. Correspondent banking arose out of the need to clear payments between individual banks and to bridge local and regional money markets. By the late nineteenth century, correspondent banking had evolved into a fairly efficient system of transferring and allocating funds across the nation. The post-1907 reform legislation did not attempt to alter the laws that had produced this banking structure, as these regulations also created a constituency that fought to preserve the unit bank. The unit banking lobby opposed any extension of branching, pressed for deposit insurance, and defeated the effort of the Federal Reserve System to impose universal par clearance.[2]

---

[2] For an analysis of the struggle over branching and nonpar clearance, see Chapter 3. State-sponsored deposit insurance is treated in Chapter 4.

In spite of contemporary criticism, the correspondent banking system and the clearinghouses served the financial needs of the nation well. Correspondent banking developed very early out of the need to clear interbank payments.[3] The legislation restricting branching and encouraging the formation of unit banks ensured that the nation's consumers and producers would have their means of payment supplied by thousands of banks. Trade between economic agents using different banks required the development of a mechanism to clear payments between banks that would minimize the costly transfer of coin and currency from bank to bank. The collection, or presentation for payment in legal tender, of checks, drafts, notes, bills, and other instruments of credit was facilitated by the development of correspondent banking and the clearinghouses, which increased clearing, or the offsetting of mutual claims and payment of the difference.[4]

Correspondent banking was particularly important for the nation's country banks. Many of these banks operated in small isolated towns and depended on their correspondent banks to assist with out-of-town collections. When a country bank received an instrument drawn on an out-of-town bank or had a note, bond, or acceptance from such a bank fall due, it would send the item to a city correspondent which could arrange for collection. In return, the country bank would collect items for its correspondent. To simplify payments to and from correspondents, banks maintained deposits, or bankers' balances, with their correspondent to which items could be credited or debited. When necessary, banks would clear claims against one another by means of bank drafts or other instruments.[5]

The growing use of personal checks increased the need for

---

[3] Walter Earl Spahr, *The Clearing and Collection of Checks*. This book provides a detailed study of the business of clearing and collection.

[4] Ibid., pp. 77 ff.

[5] John A. James, *Money and Capital Markets in Postbellum America*, pp. 99–100 and Watkins, *Bankers' Balances*, p. 103.

banks to clear and expanded the correspondent system. Matters were complicated by exchange charges that many banks levied on checks or other instruments remitted to them by out-of-town banks. These charges usually took the form of a discounted payment. Banks that imposed these service charges were said to engage in nonpar clearing. Banks would sometimes designate a correspondent through which they would accept checks at par, and checks then followed circuitous routes to reach these "par points," delaying the collection of checks.[6] The complex system of clearing and collection allowed banks a larger reserve base than they would have had with a less roundabout means for the presentation of checks. Banks counted items in the process of collection as part of their reserves as soon as they were mailed to a bank. In the early years of the twentieth century, this float was estimated to be between $300 million and $500 million.[7] Pointing to circuitous routing of checks and the large float, critics of banking attacked the nation's system of clearing payments as wasteful and inefficient.

Bankers' balances were not peculiar to any group of banks. All classes of national banks and their state-chartered rivals held interbank deposits. These were heavily concentrated in the large national banks in the major financial centers. The desirability of holding deposits with banks was enhanced by the form in which required reserves were to be held. The National Banking Act of 1864 allowed country banks to hold three-fifths and reserve-city banks one-half of their required reserves on deposit at reserve-city and central-reserve city banks respectively. State banking laws usually allowed state banks to hold some portion of their reserves in this form. For any bank, the alternative of holding reserves in the form of interest-bearing deposits, instead of vault cash, was an attrac-

---

[6] Watkins, *Bankers' Balances*, pp. 103–105.
[7] James, *Money and Capital Markets*, p. 112.

Table 2.1
Bankers' Balances, 1902–1914
(in millions of dollars)

	1902	*1903*	*1904*	*1905*	*1906*
Central-reserve city-banks					
Individual deposits	719	678	716	881	842
Balances due from	125	128	140	157	144
Balances due to	647	615	760	793	748
Reserve-city banks					
Individual deposits	746	776	773	890	964
Balances due from	294	286	328	372	396
Balances due to	462	463	510	589	620
Country banks					
Individual deposits	1,636	1,749	1,825	2,013	2,253
Balances due from	400	388	412	478	507
Balances due to	134	135	143	165	177
Nonnational banks					
Individual deposits	6,007	6,353	6,589	7,568	8,161
Balances due from	743	769	963	975	984
Balances due to	150	264	340	357	354

SOURCE: Leonard L. Watkins, *Bankers' Balances*, pp. 12 and 14.

tive one. All these factors combined to produce a pyramiding of bankers' balances in the central reserve cities.

This concentration of deposits is presented in Table 2.1 where the individual and interbank deposits for the three classes of national banks and state institutions are given for the years 1902–1914. The hierarchy of interbank deposits, in which national country banks and state banks deposited their funds in reserve-city banks and reserve-city banks redeposited some of these funds and their own in the central-reserve-city banks of New York, Chicago, and Saint Louis, changed little in this period. The ratio of central-reserve-city banks' net balances due to other banks to their total individual demand and time deposits rose a little, from 73.5 percent in 1902 to 75 percent in 1914. Reserve-city banks' net balances due to other banks as a percentage of their individual deposits did decline substantially in these years, from 22.5 to 15.6, as a

1907	1908	1909	1910	1911	1912	1913	1914
795	890	1,029	1,080	1,051	1,093	976	1,142
153	154	165	174	202	201	195	190
806	946	1,022	890	1,049	1,031	965	1,047
1,021	1,034	1,180	1,278	1,337	1,421	1,436	1,522
422	429	497	478	567	579	551	558
675	685	790	783	856	884	887	880
2,509	2,454	2,691	2,944	3,092	3,314	3,543	3,624
555	522	581	549	618	645	650	643
204	192	223	227	242	263	269	251
8,778	8,411	9,212	10,002	10,432	11,201	11,531	12,377
1,004	1,132	1,329	1,191	1,412	1,424	1,380	1,482
390	375	447	325	474	454	464	519

NOTE: The figures are for midsummer call dates.

result of a tremendous expansion in total deposits. National country banks' net deposits due from other banks fell slightly, from 5.3 to 4.5 percent, and the state banks' net deposits due from other banks rose slightly, from 11.3 to 11.9 percent.

New York was the chief guardian of bankers' balances. Together with Chicago and Saint Louis, it held approximately 50 percent of all correspondent balances, accounting for about 70 percent of central-reserve-city balances by itself. Within New York City a small group of banks held most of these balances. In 1912, eight New York City banks held about 60 percent of the city's interbank deposits.[8] This concentration of bankers' balances in New York placed the major banks of the city in a key position of influence and responsibility for the proper functioning of the banking system. In a system in which there was no lender of last resort, they were vulnerable

[8] Watkins, *Bankers' Balances*, pp. 20–22.

to any concerted demand by interior banks to convert their deposits to cash. A panic, such as occurred in 1907, could easily disrupt this system. Between August 22 and December 3, 1907, country banks increased their cash by 23.4 percent and reduced their correspondent balances by 13.5 percent while cutting loans by 3.5 percent. This strained the reserve-city banks, which lost 14.6 percent of their cash and responded by drawing their interbank deposits down by 17.3 percent and reducing loans by 4.7 percent. In the center of this maelstrom, New York City banks lost 19.1 percent of their cash, as their correspondents drew down on their balances, but like a central bank, the New York banks attempted to prevent a breakdown of financial intermediation and increased their loans by 9.0 percent.[9]

New York's efforts to halt the crisis reflected its position as the center for interbank lending in normal times. Interbank borrowing had a seasonal character, following the financing needs of agriculture. The height of borrowing by country banks occurred in the planting and harvesting seasons when they borrowed from New York and other cities to accommodate their customers. In the slack seasons they invested their surplus of investable funds in the money markets of financial centers. The heaviest borrowers were rural national and state banks, and movement of the cotton crop was the most important generator of borrowing needs. Correspondent balances played a key role in establishing lines of credit. The size of a loan was dependent on a bank's record and the maintenance of a satisfactory average balance. The common practice was to provide loans up to five times the bank's average annual deposits with the lender.[10] It is difficult to determine the extent of interbank borrowing in the pre–Federal Reserve era, as many bankers attempted to conceal loans from other banks on the grounds that depositors and other cred-

[9] Ibid., pp. 32–33.
[10] James, *Money and Capital Markets*, pp. 150–153.

Table 2.2
National-Bank Borrowings, 1902–1926
(in millions of dollars)

Year	Central-Reserve-City Banks	Reserve-City Banks	Country Banks
1902		5	18
1903		7	22
1904		5	25
1905		6	21
1906		8	29
1907		8	31
1908		7	35
1909		5	29
1910		9	60
1911		4	42
1912		9	50
1913		11	61
1914		11	78
1915	3	6	87
1916	1	12	55
1917	191	96	74
1918	164	344	326
1919	317	602	497
1920	558	807	553
1921	193	537	623
1922	64	107	330
1923	169	285	308
1924	31	47	259
1925	129	116	218
1926	93	155	241

SOURCE: Leonard L. Watkins, *Bankers Balances*, pp. 156–157 and 168–169.
NOTE: The figures are for midsummer call dates.

itors would take this as a sign of weakness.[11] The borrowings of national banks as given by loans, discounts, and bills payable, but not overdrafts or repurchase agreements, are given in Table 2.2.

Bankers' balances not only facilitated clearances, they also

[11] Oliver C. Lockhart, "The Development of Interbank Borrowing in the National Banking System, 1869–1914," pp. 140–148.

offered country banks easier access to the nation's money markets. Country banks obtained many services from their correspondents in New York, Chicago, Saint Louis, or other cities.[12] Although there was a variety of investment opportunities open to banks sending funds to the major financial centers, the most liquid and secure investment was in call loans. These were payable on demand and backed with stocks or bonds as collateral. The very active New York and Chicago call money markets offered banks a very liquid secondary reserve asset. If local loan demand was slack, two alternatives were open to the country banker. He could place his surplus funds on deposit with his correspondent for the interest offered and let the latter bear the cost of investing these funds, or he could obtain the assistance of his correspondent to invest them directly in the market. When the call rate was high, country banks tended to invest in the market directly; and when it was low, they preferred to invest in bankers' balances.[13] The call loans of New York City banks on their own account and on the account of their correspondents and the call money rates for 1908–1912 are given in Table 2.3.

Although the banking system had difficulty in handling liquidity crises, it had to a large degree overcome the obstacles to clearing payments and integrating money markets created by the severe state and federal restrictions on branch banking. However, most contemporary criticism failed to appreciate why this particular banking structure had emerged and thus erred in its analysis of the system's defects. The concentration of banking resources in New York City was taken as evidence of a highly cartelized industry, when actually it was quite competitive. Reserve-city banks vigorously solicited business by circulars, letters, and traveling salesmen, offering interest on

---

[12] For a summary of how the correspondent system worked see James, *Money and Capital Markets*, pp. 237–243.

[13] Ibid., p. 104.

Table 2.3
Call Loans of New York City Banks 1908–1912

Date	Loans (in millions of dollars)		Call Money Interest Rates
	On Own Account	For Accounts of Correspondents	
1908			
Jan. 1	361	107	4.75%
July 1	552	89	1.22
Nov. 1	501	85	1.75
1909			
Jan. 1	587	104	1.81
July 1	629	122	2.06
Nov. 1	531	169	4.65
1910			
Jan. 1	552	208	4.72
July 1	514	160	2.41
Nov. 1	495	125	3.23
1911			
Jan. 1	512	144	3.18
July 1	615	129	2.36
Nov. 1	503	143	2.72
1912			
Jan. 1	521	141	2.42
July 1	649	141	2.88
Nov. 1	526	241	6.38

SOURCE: U.S. Congress, House of Representatives, *The Money Trust Investigation before the Subcommittee on Banking and Currency*, pt. 16, pp. 1192–1193.

deposits and a variety of services.[14] It was true that at times the New York Clearing House attempted to eliminate the payment of interest on demand deposits, but these efforts were always frustrated by a handful of opposed banks.[15] Critics charged that New York banks protected themselves in times of crisis and shortchanged their correspondents. The opposite was, in fact, true, and central-reserve-city banks' loans

[14] Ibid., pp. 110–111.
[15] Fritz Redlich, *The Molding of American Banking: Men and Ideas*, vol. 2, p. 284.

rose in these periods, providing assistance to the interior banks. Interest rates on these loans did rise, but that was what any sound institution, commercial bank or central bank, would do in a panic.[16]

The Clearinghouses and the Panic of 1907

While correspondent banking established bilateral relations between banks, the clearinghouses harmonized the multilateral transactions between banks in the cities. The establishment of clearinghouses was the product of close cooperation between banks to reduce the high cost of clearing and collection. The problems of collection that led to the formation of correspondent relations were even more intense in the cities, where banks serving large-scale industrial and commercial enterprises found themselves burdened by the constant need to clear claims with one another. Until the 1850s, the more than sixty New York City banks were still clearing checks and other items with one another through bankers' balances and a system of messengers. It was not uncommon for a large bank to maintain balances of $2,000 to $3,000 with thirty other banks, a costly arrangement for any institution.[17] Although Albert Gallatin had written a pamphlet in 1831 describing how to set up a clearinghouse based on British models, it was not until 1853 that the New York City banks assembled to establish one. The New York Clearing House was incorporated in 1854 with fifty-two member banks.[18] It was an exclusive club. Membership required a minimum capital of $500,000—or two and one-half times the minimum that would be required for national banks in New York City. A prospective member bank's books were open to the close scrutiny of

16 Oliver C. Lockhart, "The Development of Interbank Borrowing in the National Banking System," pp. 232–235.
17 James Graham Cannon, *Clearing Houses*, pp. 150 ff.
18 Ibid., pp. 151–154.

the clearinghouse, and it needed the consent of three-quarters of the membership to join. The manager appointed by the governing committee oversaw the clearing of interbank claims and the end-of-the-day settlements between banks with coin certificates. These certificates were recognized as legal tender by the National Bank Act and could thus be counted as vault cash without requiring the physical transfer of specie.[19] This arrangement substantially reduced messenger costs and the amount of coin needed for settlement of interbank claims. Fees to pay for the clearinghouse's services were assessed on a pro-rata basis on the volume of each bank's clearings.[20]

The success of the New York Clearing House led banks in other financial centers to establish clearinghouses. These were set up in Boston (1855), Philadelphia (1858), Baltimore (1858), Cleveland (1858), Chicago (1865), and Saint Louis (1868).[21] By 1913 there were 162 clearinghouses in the United States whose clearings totaled $173.8 billion. Activity was still concentrated in the largest clearinghouses. New York accounted for clearings equal to $98.1 billion; Chicago, $16.0 billion; Philadelphia, $8.6 billion; Boston, $8.3 billion; and the next eleven largest, $22.0 billion.[22]

The desire to lower the costs of clearing and collection had driven the New York City banks to cooperate in the formation of the first clearinghouse. Its success depended on the members remaining solvent and sufficiently liquid to ensure continuous clearing. This recognized interdependence led mem-

[19] Spahr, *The Clearing and Collection of Checks*, p. 138.
[20] Ibid., p. 383.
[21] Ibid., p. 71.
[22] U.S. Comptroller of the Currency, *Annual Report*, 1913, pp. 788–790. The largest clearinghouses attained a high degree of financial sophistication. The ratio of the balances held at the clearinghouses by member banks to clearings fell steadily, reflecting a reduction in the cost of operations to banks. Balances were not allowed to stand idle. Banks lent and borrowed these funds on an overnight basis in a manner reminiscent of the Federal Funds market. In Boston, the interest rate on these funds was approximately equal to the call rate. See Cannon, *Clearing Houses*, pp. 230–240.

bers of the clearinghouse to aid one another in times of crisis. In 1857, New York country bankers found themselves in tight liquidity positions and refused to redeem their notes in New York City with coin. In lieu of this the members of the clearinghouse agreed to accept certificates paying 6 percent interest with loans made by the country banks as collateral. Several prominent city bankers realized how this type of arrangement might be used to fend off panics, and they set up a committee to examine the idea. The New York Clearing House accepted the proposals, which provided for the issuance of short-term clearinghouse loan certificates in times of stress. Any clearinghouse member was permitted to deposit with a designated house committee an amount of its bills receivable, U.S. stocks, Treasury notes, or stock of New York State and receive certificates of deposit equal to 75 percent of the face value of the items deposited and bearing interest of 7 percent per annum. These certificates could then be used for settling balances at the clearinghouse for thirty days.[23] These certificates allowed members to substitute secondary reserves for primary reserves in interbank settlements. In effect, the clearinghouse offered banks an opportunity to rediscount their assets to gain additional liquidity which could be used within the clearinghouse. This freed lawful money for other purposes. The clearinghouse could not act as a central bank and create legal tender, but it went as far as it could in this direction. The New York Clearing House, like a central bank, also enforced acceptance of its certificate issue and once suspended a bank's right to its facilities for three months for failing to accept another's loan certificate.[24]

Although limited in use, the clearinghouse loan certificates enjoyed a fair degree of success in combating liquidity crises. A panic was averted in New York City in 1860 by this means and a pooling of clearinghouse member-bank reserves. Loan

[23] Redlich, *The Molding of American Banking*, vol. 2, pp. 161–168.
[24] Spahr, *The Clearing and Collection of Checks*, p. 143.

certificates were issued in 1861, though they did not prevent a panic. They were employed again in 1863 and 1864. The use of clearinghouse loan certificates spread to other cities. During the panic of 1873, the clearinghouses of New York, Philadelphia, Boston, Baltimore, Saint Louis, and Cincinnati issued certificates worth $42,030,000. Coupled with the Treasury's purchase of bonds, this helped to ease the crisis.[25] Local liquidity problems in New Orleans in 1879 were eased by the issuance of $54,000 of loan certificates. New York issued them in 1884, and New York, Boston, and Philadelphia used the issue of loan certificates to calm money markets in 1890.[26]

Responding to the panic of 1893, at least twelve clearinghouses issued over $68 million of loan certificates, of which New York accounted for $41.5 million. This crisis was marked by a new development: loan certificates were issued in small denominations and circulated outside of the clearinghouses as banks used them to pay their customers. This occurred primarily in Georgia and South Carolina, although the Cincinnati, Chattanooga, and Birmingham clearinghouses were known to have issued certificates in very small denominations.[27] This inconvertible paper was without sanction of law and should have been subjected to the 10 percent tax imposed on currency issued by institutions other than national banks. However, owing to the usefulness of such currency in preventing a worse crisis and its immediate retirement once legal tender began to circulate again, the government made no attempt to enforce the law.[28]

During the panic of 1907, this practice spread across the whole country. The seasonal shift of funds in 1907 to the South and the Midwest was preceded by European central banks raising their discount rates. This coincided with a turn

[25] Ibid., pp. 140–145.
[26] Ibid., pp. 141–146.
[27] Ibid., pp. 149–155.
[28] Ibid., p. 164.

in the business cycle and money became very tight in New York City. When liquidity problems forced Knickerbocker Trust Company, the second largest trust company in New York, to suspend payments, a run on other institutions began.[29] From the outset there was extensive hoarding of cash by the public and country banks. The public stored much of its increased holdings in safety deposit boxes, and the southern and western country banks augmented their vault cash.[30] To ease the liquidity position of their members, the clearinghouses began issuing clearinghouse loan certificates. The crisis was, however, sufficiently severe to cause the Secretary of the Treasury to deposit over $25 million of federal funds in New York banks. Even so, New York banks were eventually forced to restrict payments of currency.[31] These restrictions spread throughout the country as banks found they could no longer draw on their balances in New York. Bank holidays were declared in some states, and several state banking superintendents told their chartered banks to limit payments in currency and coin.[32]

The issuance of clearinghouse certificates matched the magnitude of the crisis. Afterward, A. Piatt Andrew found that $238 million of large-denomination clearinghouse loan certificates had been issued, compared to $69 million in 1893. In addition to this, he discovered that $23 million of small-denomination loan certificates and $12 million in clearinghouse managers' checks were issued for circulation outside of the clearinghouses. Supplementing this substitute currency was $14 million in cashiers' checks and $47 million in manufacturers' paychecks, not redeemable for cash but marked

[29] Charles E. A. Goodhart, *The New York Money Market and the Finance of Trade 1900–1914*, pp. 111–120.

[30] A. Piatt Andrew, "Hoarding in the Panic of 1907."

[31] Milton Friedman and Anna J. Schwartz, *A Monetary History of the United States, 1867–1960*, pp. 159–163.

[32] A. Piatt Andrew, "Substitutes for Cash in the Panic of 1907," pp. 497–505.

"payable to the bearer," "payable in clearing house funds," or "payable only through the clearing house." All of this inconvertible paper money totaled $334 million, and Andrew believed that upward of $500 million had been issued.[33]

The issuance of these currency substitutes injected a substantial amount of liquidity into the banking system. Near the height of the crisis in December 1907, high-powered money in the United States was $3,069 million, of which $1,208 was held as reserves by banks and $1,861 million as currency by the public.[34] If the large-denomination clearinghouse loan certificates uncovered by Andrew are treated as bank reserves, their emission raised reserves to $1,446 million. If other types of clearinghouse instruments are considered as additions to currency, the quantity held in the hands of the public stood at $1,958 million in December 1907. Clearly, banking liquidity was substantially increased, and "currency," legal and illegal, in the hands of the public increased somewhat. If Andrew's figures are wrong, they err on the volume of small clearinghouse instruments which were harder to detect but would have increased the amount of currency in the hands of the public. The monetary contraction would undoubtedly have been more severe if no clearinghouse certificates had been issued and banks had been forced to cut back even more on their loans. Issuance of small clearinghouse instruments in conjunction with restrictions on currency payments helped diminish the pressure of the panic.

In spite of the large issuance of emergency certificates, the clearinghouses were poor substitutes for a full-fledged central bank as they could not freely expand the monetary base. Even in their surrogate role, their ability to cope with a crisis depended on the mutual trust and cooperation that was fostered by their daily exchanges. The exclusive character of the clearinghouses promoted cooperation in the face of crises, yet the

[33] Ibid., pp. 510–516.
[34] Friedman and Schwartz, A Monetary History of the United States, p. 800.

proliferation of national and state banks and trust companies to meet the growing demand for banking services threatened their ability to cope with the extraordinary needs for increased liquidity in bad times.

The clearinghouses were most effective if they prompted banks to cooperate in quick preemptive actions. One notable example of this activity, which forestalled a panic, occurred in 1905 in Chicago. Three Chicago banks controlled by John R. Walsh failed. The Chicago Clearing House under the leadership of James Forgan took the initiative. Rather than have these banks' depositors bear the cost of insolvency, the clearinghouse banks absorbed it in the belief that it would be better to prevent a breakdown of confidence and bear the cost of the bank's losses than risk a larger crisis precipitated by a panic in which the costs to all banks would be high.[35] There was considerable opposition to this action, but within the narrow confines of the clearinghouse, pressure could be put on recalcitrant banks to take joint action.

One problem that did not emerge in this situation which plagued other crises was that banks needed to recognize their interdependence to act effectively. If they failed to do so and each tried to safeguard its own position, taking a *sauve qui peut* course of action, they would be unable to prevent a crisis. If the clearinghouse banks were strong relative to the rest of the affected banks, they could extend sufficient credit; but as the number and resources of outside banks increased, corrective measures by the clearinghouse banks became less effective, as they were unable to increase the monetary base. The tremendous growth of commercial banks before 1914 could only serve to hinder the actions of the clearinghouse banks to avert crises. In addition to the integration of money markets, which furthered banks' interdependence, this was one of the factors

[35] Redlich, *The Molding of American Banking*, vol. 2, pp. 285–286. What the Chicago banks did is very similar to the actions taken by the Federal Deposit Insurance Corporation on behalf of failed banks.

behind the growing sensitivity of the banking system in financial crises. Oliver M. W. Sprague concluded in his study, *Crises of the National Banking System* that the crises were becoming worse. He wrote about the panic of 1907: "It is impossible to escape the depressing conclusion that the banking situation was handled less skillfully and boldly than in 1893 and far less so than in 1873."[36]

The unfolding of the 1907 crisis offers some insights into the problems and weaknesses of the clearinghouse acting as a lender of last resort. Since the late 1890s the national and state banks in New York City had experienced particularly keen competition from the newly developing trust companies whose financial innovations and lower reserve requirements had allowed them to penetrate the commercial banking market.[37] The trust companies engendered considerable hostility owing to their unequal advantages, and they were kept at arm's length by the banking establishment. The New York Clearing House was unwilling to include the trust companies among its members. In 1903 the clearinghouse ruled that if trust companies wanted to clear through member banks, they would have to raise their level of required reserves. Most trust companies angrily stopped their indirect clearing arrangements with clearinghouse members, severing a very important tie with their rival commercial banking institutions.[38] The link that might have ensured that cooperation would overrule competition in times of crisis was broken. The clearinghouse's membership, which should have expanded as institutions multiplied, remained limited, circumscribing its ability to deal effectively with a panic.

The events of 1907 bear this out. When money markets became very tight in October, eight banks sought and received assistance from the New York Clearing House when they

---

[36] Oliver M. W. Sprague, *Crises of the National Banking System*, p. 319.
[37] Larry Neal, "Trust Companies and Financial Innovation," pp. 35–45.
[38] Sprague, *Crises of the National Banking System*, pp. 251–253.

found themselves in illiquid positions. Their adverse balances and a weakening in the stock market forced Knickerbocker Trust, one of the few trust companies still clearing through member banks, to seek a loan from its clearing agent at the clearinghouse, the National Bank of Commerce.[39] The news of the national bank's refusal started a run on the trust company, which was forced to suspend cash payments. The panic spread to other trust companies and then to the banks, until on October 22 the New York Clearing House offered assistance to all institutions.[40] However, by then events were beyond the control of the clearinghouse. Even support of the Treasury and a fund organized by J. P. Morgan were insufficient, and the panic was only halted by a general restriction of cash payments. Summing up for the National Monetary Commission, Sprague argued that had Knickerbocker been a member of the clearinghouse, it would have received the needed loan and the crisis would have been prevented.[41] The clearinghouse quickly moved to correct its error and invited several trust companies to join. The year 1913 found the clearinghouse membership composed of thirty-one national banks, seventeen state banks, and fifteen trust companies.[42]

The rivalry between state and federal authorities for the control and regulation of banks, explored in Chapter 1, thus affected the ability of the clearinghouses to prevent or halt liquidity crises. The efforts of the states to whittle away the attractions of national-bank membership by lowering minimum capital and reserve requirements helped to atomize the banking system even further, making interbank cooperation in times of crisis exceedingly difficult. The state and federal limitations on branching were perhaps the most important factor in creating a banking structure in which the seasonal

[39] Ibid., pp. 252–253.
[40] Friedman and Schwartz, *A Monetary History of the United States*, p. 159.
[41] Sprague, *Crises of the National Banking System*, p. 251.
[42] U.S. Department of the Treasury, *Annual Report*, 1913, pp. 35–38.

regional movement of funds took place between institutions who competed but did not cooperate with one another. Aware of the difficulties experienced by the clearinghouses in controlling crises, the founders of the Federal Reserve were concerned with ensuring that the new system's coverage would be broad. The efforts to obtain a large membership for the Federal Reserve, treated in Chapter 3, were directed at establishing the Federal Reserve banks as superclearinghouses.

The Development of the Reform Movement

Correspondent banking and the clearinghouses offered a combination of competitive and cooperative solutions to the pre–Federal Reserve banking system's major defects which were the result of restrictions on branching and the absence of a central bank able to increase liquidity in times of crisis. These two institutions also provided a frame of reference for bankers and reformers that shaped the course of banking reform. Given the reserve-city banks' position of vulnerability and responsibility, it is not surprising that the leaders of the earliest reform movements came from the reserve-city bankers. The reform movement was centered in Chicago where banking was growing rapidly around the turn of the century. The midwestern reserve-city bankers devoted time and energy to organizing and running the American Bankers Association (ABA), and they dominated its executive positions. The country bankers' interests were still focused on the state rather than the national level. The great financiers of New York and the other northeastern financial centers also remained fairly aloof from the national organization, leaving the midwestern city bankers to run the show.[43]

One of the first proposals to reform the banking system was presented at the 1894 Baltimore convention of the ABA.

[43] Robert H. Wiebe, *Businessmen and Reform: A Study of the Progressive Movement*, pp. 24–25.

The "Baltimore Plan" was designed by Charles Holmes of the Second National Bank of Baltimore and Alonzo Hepburn of the Third National Bank of New York. It provided for the repeal of the bond-secured note circulation and its replacement by a currency based on bank assets equal to three-fourths of a bank's paid-up capital. To give the new currency the protection previously afforded by bonds, a guarantee fund was proposed. To ward off panics, an emergency circulation subject to a heavy tax was permitted.[44] The plan was supported by the leaders of the midwestern city banks, James Eckels of Chicago and Frank Bigelow of Milwaukee, who hoped to bolster their relative position in the banking system vis-à-vis New York. However, the Baltimore Plan never got off the ground. Distrusting the midwestern city bankers, the politically powerful New York banking community opposed the plan. Support was not forthcoming from the country banks, who also distrusted the midwestern city bankers and were more interested in a reform measure that would recognize rural assets.[45] The plan was never discussed in Congress, as no one on the House Banking and Currency Committee was interested.[46]

After the election of McKinley, the midwestern city bankers regrouped to press for reform, and in 1897, they held the Indianapolis Monetary Convention to which other businessmen and Republican politicians were invited. This conference selected a Monetary Commission to draft a reform bill. Published in 1900, this plan was based on the Baltimore Plan. Its chief author was J. Laurence Laughlin of the University of Chicago. The plan allowed banks to issue notes equal to their paid-up capital less the amount invested in real estate—an item bound not to please country bankers. Note issue above

[44] Robert Craig West, *Banking Reform and the Federal Reserve, 1863–1923*, pp. 43–44.

[45] Wiebe, *Businessmen and Reform*, pp. 62–63.

[46] West, *Banking Reform*, pp. 44–49.

60 percent of a bank's capital was, however, subject to a heavy tax, the intent being to make this an emergency currency. A guarantee fund was also provided for.[47] The proposal was more successful than the Baltimore Plan as the Secretary of the Treasury, Lyman Gage, a former Chicago banker, endorsed a similar bill. But the debate on banking reform was only seriously begun when a reform bill was introduced in Congress by Representative Charles Fowler of New Jersey in 1902.

The Fowler bill was warmly supported by the midwestern city bankers, as it included the features of earlier plans. In addition, it had two novel provisions. It would establish banknote redemption centers in twenty cities. This marked the first step toward some type of central clearinghouse. The plan also would legalize branching to strengthen the banking system and equalize interest rates. The bill's supporters pointed to the stability of the banking system in Canada where nationwide branching was permitted.[48] Academic support came from Oliver M. W. Sprague who argued that branching banks, by virtue of their increased size and geographical diversification, could more easily handle the normal seasonal movement of funds. He also stated that the mutual assistance of branch bank offices would strengthen each bank's ability to withstand liquidity crises.[49]

The officers of the ABA moved to approve the Fowler plan at their annual convention, but it aroused the ire of the country bankers who defeated the motion. In its place a resolution was substituted that condemned branch banking because "individualism in management would cease, local taxes [would] be evaded, [there would be] no home distribution of profits, and local progress [would be] retarded," and attacked an asset-

---

[47] Wiebe, *Businessmen and Reform*, p. 63.

[48] West, *Banking Reform*, pp. 46–50.

[49] Oliver M. W. Sprague, "Branch Banking in the United States," pp. 242–246.

secured currency because it would "further inflate credit, drive our gold abroad . . . and help us into a panic when we are out of one."[50] The leaders of the ABA were only able to prevent this from becoming the association's official stand by a parliamentary maneuver. Undaunted, the country bankers returned home; and at the state banking conventions, they continued their attack on the city bankers' program. The state associations of Kansas, Illinois, Iowa, Minnesota, Missouri, Nebraska, South Dakota, and Wisconsin passed lengthy resolutions condemning the proposed legislation and lashing out at branching and an asset-backed currency.

The country bankers also found support in academic circles. A. Piatt Andrew of Harvard rhapsodically praised the American system of unit banking and the absence of a central bank in an article appearing in the *Quarterly Journal of Economics* on the eve of the 1907 panic. He wrote:

> Nowhere else will one find such equality of importance among the banks, and such absence of any predominant leadership. Nowhere else will one find so large a number of quite disconnected firms, or such mutual independence of action. We have no less than 16,000 separate banking institutions, and among them all, despite considerable variations in size, a certain democratic equality prevails. The largest is not particularly large when judged by English or European standards, and none is in a position, either, because of its dimensions or its privileges to exert an effective control over the rest. They recognize among themselves no headship.[51]

The country bankers' position was defined by Andrew Frame of Waukesha, Wisconsin, one-time president of the Wisconsin Bankers Association and leader of the country bankers in the ABA. Addressing the association's annual conference in 1904 he stated the basic view of the country bankers. The country banks were absolved of all responsibility for financial crises.

[50] Wiebe, *Businessmen and Reform*, p. 63.
[51] A. Piatt Andrew, "The Treasury and the Banks under Secretary Shaw," pp. 556–557.

Frame charged that "national calamities are not born in country towns. Panics are bred in great cities where colossal promotions flourish . . . where the reserves are loaned to stock jobbers that ought to be held to meet the call of the country banks for their deposits to move crops. When the stock jobber is called upon to liquidate, he must attempt to rob Peter to pay Paul, but because of the lack of proper cash reserves generally, stocks decline as forced sales to obtain cash and general liquidation take place."[52]

The distrust of the New York City banks and their relationship with the stock market was widespread. After the panic of 1907, the Money Trust Investigation conducted by a subcommittee of the House Committee on Banking and Currency under the chairmanship of Arsène Pujo of Louisiana blamed the correspondent banks and the New York Clearing House for the crisis. Representing populists and progressives, the subcommittee singled out the huge New York City banks for creating a cartellike club in the New York Clearing House. It charged that the clearinghouse banks, while extending credit to themselves, had cut off credit to their correspondents in the interior when funds became tight.[53] Although these banks actually increased interbank loans, this view was taken up by many bankers and businessmen. What these groups particularly feared was that the large banks and other financiers manipulated the stock market for their own benefit and to the detriment of others. Many regarded commodity and stock speculation as serving no useful purpose, and some legislation was passed by the Congress and the state legislatures to limit it.[54] The solution that Frame put forward to protect the coun-

[52] Andrew Jay Frame, *Address on Panic Panaceas before the Convention of the American Bankers Association*, pp. 10–11.

[53] Redlich, *The Molding of American Banking*, vol. 2, page 287.

[54] Cedric B. Cowing, *Populists, Plungers, and Progressives: A Social History of Stock and Commodity Speculation, 1890–1936*, pp. 167 ff. Twenty-five states followed the example of Kansas in 1911 and passed "Blue Sky laws," which created commissions to judge the soundness of securities before they could

try banks from the dangers of Wall Street speculation and the panics it supposedly engendered was simple and easily appreciated by his fellow bankers. More notes had to be made available to banks in times of crisis. The clearinghouse loan certificates had helped considerably, and Frame proposed to legalize these as temporary clearinghouse national bank notes to be issued with collateral and subject to high interest rates. The natural conservatism of the nation's clearinghouses, he believed, would prevent any unnecessary issue of notes, and the high interest rates would prevent inflation by ensuring quick redemption as soon as the crisis was over.[55]

As the debate over reform heated up, New York City banks and other big eastern banks realized that some type of reform would be instituted. To guard against passage of unfavorable legislation, they answered the Fowler plan with a bill of their own introduced into Congress by Senator Nelson Aldrich of Rhode Island. Aldrich's 1903 bill would have allowed banks to organize voluntary associations which in times of crisis would issue an emergency currency backed by selected state, municipal, and railroad bonds. This program came under immediate attack from the midwestern city bankers, who were for an asset-, not a bond-secured currency, and the country bankers whose portfolios lacked the requisite bonds.[56]

The different interest groups in the banking community continued to generate plans and programs. In 1906, the Currency Commission of the ABA, run by James B. Forgan of Chicago, wrote a bill based on the midwestern bankers' earlier models and presented it to Congress through Representative Fowler. The country bankers under the leadership of Andrew

---

be traded in the state. Even in New York, the home of the stock market, the legislature moved to regulate the stock market's activities. The legislature passed an "anti-bucket shop law" in 1908; and Governor Charles Evans Hughes appointed a committee to investigate the stock market.

[55] Frame, *Address on Panic Panaceas*, pp. 12–13.

[56] Wiebe, *Businessmen and Reform*, pp. 64–65 and West, *Banking Reform*, pp. 49–50.

Frame rallied to defeat the bill, and it died in committee. On their behalf, Leslie Shaw, an Iowa country banker and former Secretary of the Treasury, proposed a highly taxed emergency currency that would be distributed by the federal government through the local clearinghouses. Many country bankers looked favorably on such a plan even though it included government participation because it offered protection from the dominance of the big-city bankers.[57]

The panic of 1907 reaffirmed all interested parties' concern for the weaknesses of the financial system, and the battle over reform was begun with renewed vigor. The opening move was made by Senator Aldrich, who after consultation with J. P. Morgan and other New York financiers, introduced a bill in Congress in January 1908 for an emergency currency based on railroad and local government bonds. Both the midwestern city banks and the country banks attacked the new Aldrich bill for drawing the government in to assist the big-city banks, which held most of the eligible bonds. The Currency Commission of the ABA responded by drafting another bill, but the alienated country banks refused to offer them any support.[58] The crisis still at hand, the House of Representatives passed a bill introduced by Representative Edward Vreeland which compromised on the different reform proposals by adopting elements of each. The final congressional product, the Aldrich-Vreeland Act, was based heavily on the House's version. It created voluntary currency associations which could issue highly taxed emergency currency based on either commercial paper or specific types of long-term bonds.[59] By decentralizing control, excluding railroad bonds, and including commercial paper, the bill found acceptance in most sections of the banking community. The institutions created were, in effect, government-sponsored clearinghouse associations whose

[57] Wiebe, *Businessmen and Reform*, p. 65.
[58] Ibid., pp. 72–74.
[59] West, *Banking Reform*, pp. 50–51.

purpose was to issue loan certificates as an emergency legal tender. This was an expedient act, and these associations never completely replaced the clearinghouses. In the crisis following the outbreak of World War I, 1,366 of the national currency association members received a total of $386 million in emergency currency. But the clearinghouses were not inactive; they had issued loan certificates totaling $212 million by the time the crisis was over.[60] The Aldrich-Vreeland Act was accepted only as a temporary measure to fill the gap while more thorough legislation was being prepared. At the same time, Congress created the National Monetary Commission to study the problems of the banking system. This was an important move for it shifted the focus of reform to a congressional commission. Its chairman, Senator Aldrich, used the commission as a forum to promote the ideas of the eastern financiers, seeking advice principally from Frank Vanderlip of National City Bank, Paul Warburg of Kuhn, Loeb, and Company, and Henry Davidson of the House of Morgan.[61]

The Aldrich Bill

The New York–based reformers believed that the greatest weakness of the American banking system was the absence of a central bank, but they were astute enough to realize that an institution patterned after European central banks was politically unacceptable. This was evident from the strident attacks made on Leslie Shaw when he was Secretary of the Treasury and attempted to increase the central banking functions of the Treasury. Criticism had come from the banking com-

[60] U.S. Comptroller of the Currency, *Annual Report*, 1915, pp. 90–130. Friedman and Schwartz were probably too enthusiastic when they concluded that the Federal Reserve System was unnecessary after the passage of the Aldrich-Vreeland Act. The Aldrich-Vreeland associations did not provide enough additional liquidity in the crisis, as indicated by the emission of clearinghouse loan certificates. See Friedman and Schwartz, *A Monetary History of the United States*, p. 172.

[61] Wiebe, *Businessmen and Reform*, p. 75.

munity and academia for self-aggrandizement and encouraging imprudent banking.[62] Fear of any centralized control meant that the central banking institution would have to be carefully tailored. The two leading theorists of the New York banking community, Paul Warburg and Victor Morawetz, both recognized in their writings on banking reform that a central bank would have to be a decentralized institution. In both their outlines, they suggested the establishment of a modified central bank whose branches would hold bank reserves, providing a reservoir of credit. The regional reserve banks would provide discount facilities for member banks, and some central agency would issue notes.[63]

Recognizing that the successful passage of a bill to establish some form of a central bank required support of the other banking factions, overtures were made to the Currency Commission of the ABA. Forgan and his fellow midwestern city bankers were informed by Aldrich that the bill in gestation would include an assets currency as well as a central bank. The Chicago-based reformers accepted the overture and were consulted on the legislation's progress. This formed an alliance which was made public in 1909 when George Reynolds, a prominent Chicago banker, announced in his ABA presidential address that the best reform package would include a central bank as well as an assets currency.[64] This coalition then sought to win the public over to the idea of a modified central bank. The leaders of the two groups toured the state banking associations to promote the reform package, and they made a concerted effort to outflank the opposition even before the new Aldrich bill was made public.

Aiming to demonstrate the broad support that a central

[62] One vocal critic was A. Piatt Andrew. See Andrew, "The Treasury and the Banks under Secretary Shaw," pp. 558–560. For additional information consult Richard H. Timberlake, Jr., *The Origins of Central Banking in the United States*, pp. 175–185.

[63] West, *Banking Reform*, chapter 3.

[64] Wiebe, *Businessmen and Reform*, pp. 75–76.

bank had, the *Banking Law Journal*, at the instigation of Paul Warburg, polled the bankers on the issue. The journal mailed a letter to all national and state banks and trust companies asking them the question: "Do you favor a central bank if not controlled by 'Wall Street' or any Monopolistic Interest?" Respondents were also asked to give their reasons and suggestions.[65] The question was vaguely worded to allay fears that a central bank would come under control of the "money trust," and analysis of the banking community's disposition toward reform is clouded by this vagueness. The questionnaire failed to ask banks to discriminate between a central bank controlled by the government, one controlled by bankers, or none at all. It also left open the question of its organization and whether it would issue an asset- or bond-based currency. Nevertheless, the poll may be taken as an indication of whether or not bankers favored any type of central bank. Fortunately, the journal printed about 200 of the detailed replies, throwing additional light on the type of institution favored by different bankers.

The journal received 5,613 replies, which represented 28.4 percent of all commercial banks in 1909. Of all national banks, 32.5 percent answered, and 26.3 percent of the state banks and trust companies replied. The banks in the whole sample were 59.3 percent in favor of a central bank of some type, 33.7 percent opposed, and 7.0 percent undecided. National banks were slightly more favorably disposed toward a central bank than state banks or trust companies, with 61.0 percent for, 32.8 percent against, and 6.2 percent undecided. State-chartered institutions recorded 58.2 percent in favor, 34.3 percent against, and 7.5 percent undecided. The strongest regional support came from New England and the Pacific states where 73.0 percent of the banks in each region answered positively. Other regions' positive replies were: the

---

[65] "The Central Bank Question."

mid-Atlantic states, 61.3 percent; the South, 60.0 percent; the West, 59.3 percent; and the Midwest, 58.9 percent.

The approximately 200 published responses offer further insights into banker opinion. Most of the country bankers who responded negatively stated that they believed that it was either impossible to keep Wall Street from controlling the proposed institution or that it would fall prey to the whims of the politicians. M. Lauritsen, president of the First State Bank of Tyler, Minnesota, for example, wrote to the journal, "No, there is no way possible to keep a central bank free from Wall St., without it, couldn't be a success, again you can't keep it out of the hands of Monopolists and politics, a central bank means concentrating wealth at the expense of small banks."[66] H. V. Temple, president of the First National Bank of Lexington, Nebraska, just wanted a modified Aldrich-Vreeland Act to add more elasticity to the currency.[67] So strong was some country bankers' fear of the influence of Washington and New York that 2 percent of those polled specifically stated that the new institution should be located in the West.[68] The most common position was expressed by J. E. Boyce, president of Cotton Belt Savings and Trust Company of Pine Bluff, Arkansas, who replied, "Yes, I think that it should be made a bankers' bank or a national clearing house, under government supervision, to discount for banks, preferably, stock to be owned in small units only by all banks in the United States, state as well as national banks."[69]

The most divisive issue was whether bankers or the government should control the institution. Some believed that a banker-controlled institution was necessary to keep the central bank free from politics, while others feared this would lead to control by Wall Street and favored some government reg-

[66] Ibid., p. 960.
[67] Ibid., p. 964.
[68] Ibid., p. 962.
[69] Ibid., p. 943.

ulation. As M. B. Lane, president of Citizens' and Southern Bank of Savannah, Georgia, argued, "I am heartily in favor of a Central Bank and believe the only Central Bank that can be successfully put in operation and controlled will be through the Treasury Department in Washington, by Managers whose term of office would not be subject to termination by any changes in national administration."[70] The issue of retaining a modified bond-secured currency versus implementing an asset-based currency was quite secondary to the concern over who would control the institution. No doubt these replies fortified the New York bank reformers' conviction that the new institution would have to be cast in the framework of a clearinghouse to make it politically acceptable to the majority of bankers.

Having sounded out the banking community, Aldrich and his advisers, Davidson, Warburg, A. Piatt Andrew, and Vanderlip, assembled to draw up a bill. The new Aldrich bill of 1911 proposed the creation of a National Reserve Association with a paid-in capital of $100 million, wholly owned by subscribing banks. There were to be fifteen regional districts, and local associations of banks would select the board of directors of each district's branch. The head office overseeing the branches was to be located in Washington, but the government would not be represented in the new institution. Membership was voluntary for state institutions but required of national banks. The authors appealed to the banking community, stressing that the National Reserve Association would function like a clearinghouse. Speaking to the ABA convention in 1911, Senator Aldrich stated, "The organization proposed is not a bank, but a cooperative union of all banks of the country for definite purposes and with very limited defined functions. It is, in effect an extension, an evolution of the Clearing House plan modified to meet the needs and requirements of an entire people."[71]

[70] Ibid., p. 947.
[71] West, *Banking Reform*, pp. 72–73.

The composition of the board of directors was intended to please all groups. Small banks were given a voice in the selection of directors, and large banks' votes had additional weight, measured by their subscription to the association's stock. The National Reserve Association's branches were to rediscount notes and bills of exchange endorsed by members on agricultural, industrial, or commercial transactions of not more than twenty-eight days' maturity. This was supposed to impart sufficient elasticity to the currency according to the principles of the real bills doctrine. The Aldrich bill forbade the discounting of bills drawn to carry stocks, bonds, or other investment securities in order to sever the relation between banking and the stock market.[72]

To gain broader public acceptance for the bill, the National Citizens' League was founded in 1910 at the behest of Paul Warburg. Emphasizing its supposed national character, the league was headed by J. Laurence Laughlin who had previously been the moving force behind many of the midwestern bankers' proposals. Joined by H. Parker Willis and others, Laughlin began a propaganda campaign for the new bill, emphasizing its responsiveness to the needs of the entire business and banking community.[73] The chief organ of the league's campaign was its publication *Banking Reform*. The campaign was successful in securing the endorsements of the ABA, twenty-nine of the forty-six state banking associations, and many business groups.[74]

The Federal Reserve Act

The ground had been carefully prepared for the Aldrich bill; but just as it was reported to Congress, the Democrats gained control of the House of Representatives in the elections of 1910. Their opposition killed the bill's chances of passage.

---

[72] Ibid., pp. 72–79.
[73] Ibid., pp. 79–82.
[74] Wiebe, *Businessmen and Reform*, p. 77.

The victory of Woodrow Wilson in 1912, and the Democrats' capture of both houses of Congress put the Democrats in charge of banking reform. The chairmanship of the House Committee on Banking and Currency was taken over by Representative Carter Glass, who immediately hired H. Parker Willis as his financial expert.[75] The issues of control, centralization, and backing for the new currency were again opened, even though the new Democratic reform bill drew heavily on its Republican predecessor. The first draft of the new act differed little from the Aldrich bill. Both had a decentralized system coordinated by a central board, and the discount provisions were essentially the same. Neither had the government playing a significant role; banking was left to the bankers.[76] However, once debate on the bill began, the Democrats made it clear that they thought bankers had too much power and that the bill went too far in the direction of centralized control by the governing board. The solution to these complaints, which made the bill politically acceptable, was provided by President Wilson, who wanted the Federal Reserve Board made up entirely of presidential appointees.[77] As the Federal Reserve System emerged from the House and Senate conference, it remained a decentralized institution; but while bankers retained control of the Federal Reserve banks, the government gained some control over the Board of Governors. Also the type of bills acceptable for discount was broadened and their maturity increased.

The Democrats' reworking of the bill split apart the delicately balanced alliance of bankers Aldrich and his associates had formed. Among the New York bankers, Vanderlip denounced the presidential appointments to the Federal Reserve Board, but Hepburn and Warburg were more conciliatory. Warburg remained in contact with Glass and Willis as the new

[75] West, *Banking Reform*, pp. 89–92.
[76] Ibid.; see chapter 5 for a complete comparison.
[77] West, *Banking Reform*, p. 112.

bill moved through Congress. The reform-minded Chicago bankers split into two factions, each side taking some other reserve-city bankers along with them. James Forgan denounced the new bill as unworkable and criticized the injection of the government into the new system. His cross-town rival George Reynolds wrote to Glass and tried to influence him. Similarly, the country bankers took sides. Antagonists like Andrew Frame disliked both the Aldrich and the Glass bills and wanted nothing more than a continuation of the Aldrich-Vreeland Act. Many others felt that some reform, even if flawed, was needed and asked for the inclusion of rural assets in the definition of paper eligible for rediscount and a lowering of reserve requirements. Both of these features were incorporated into the Federal Reserve Act. Representative Glass, Senator Robert L. Owen, and Secretary of the Treasury William G. McAdoo courted the conciliationists. When it became evident that the Democratic Congress would have its way, some of the hard-liners relented. Hepburn and Vanderlip encouraged banks to enter the system, and even Forgan admitted the beneficial aspects of the Glass bill. Another olive branch was extended to the predominantly Republican bankers when Wilson named no Bryan Democrats to the Federal Reserve Board and selected Paul Warburg and Henry Wheeler, a popular businessman from the Chicago Association of Commerce.[78] For the country banks, fearful of monopoly, twelve reserve districts were created and their locations fixed in early 1914.

Apart from the organizational aspects, the basic provisions of the Federal Reserve Act of 1913 were: (1) All member banks were to subscribe an amount equal to 6 percent of their paid-up capital and surplus to the stock of their Federal Reserve Bank, one-half of which was to be paid in and the other half on call. (2) All state-chartered members had to conform

[78] Wiebe, *Businessmen and Reform*, pp. 129–137.

to the minimum capital requirements of national banks. (3) Reserve requirements on demand deposits for all member banks were reduced from the levels established by the National Banking Act to 18 percent for central-reserve-city banks, 15 percent for reserve-city banks, and 12 percent for country banks on demand deposits, and 5 percent on time deposits for all classes of banks. These reserves were eventually to be kept on deposit, without interest, at the Federal Reserve banks, although for an interim period part of the reserve could be carried in vault cash. (4) No member bank was permitted to keep on deposit with a nonmember a sum in excess of 10 percent of capital and surplus. (5) All members were required to submit twice yearly to examinations by the Comptroller of the Currency; and every Federal Reserve bank could, at its own discretion, make special examinations. (6) Extended to all members was the privilege of rediscounting at the Federal Reserve banks notes, drafts, and bills of exchange arising out of actual transactions for agricultural, industrial, or commercial purposes. These instruments could not be used to carry stocks or bonds, except those of the United States government, and they were limited to a maturity of ninety days, except for agricultural bills which were allowed a maturity of six months. Paper for a firm or individual worth more than 10 percent of the bank's capital and surplus was prohibited. Bank acceptances, based on the import or export of goods, with maturities up to three months were discountable, provided they did not exceed 50 percent of a bank's capital and surplus. (7) Federal Reserve banks were to receive from their members on deposit, at par, checks and drafts drawn upon any of the depositories of the Federal Reserve banks. The Federal Reserve banks were also empowered to act as clearinghouses for member banks. (8) The act provided for gradual retirement of national bank notes to ensure that the prices of bonds used by national banks to secure their issue would not be depressed.[79]

These provisions contained many items intended to please various sections of the banking community. The real bills doctrine was to be implemented for the midwestern city bankers, but rural assets were given special treatment to conciliate the country bankers. Furthermore, the whole institution was cast in the framework of a network of clearinghouses, giving it a familiar appearance. In spite of these and many other provisions, including a lowering of reserve requirements, bankers did not display much enthusiasm for the new system. The national banks were required to join, but state and trust-company membership remained voluntary. Bankers would henceforth vote on the Federal Reserve System with their feet in addition to applying pressure in Congress. The continued struggle for a larger membership is the subject of Chapter 3; the remainder of this chapter is concerned with the Federal Reserve's fulfillment of the banking reformers' objectives.

Correspondent Banking under the Federal Reserve System

The critics of the pre–Federal Reserve banking system focused their attention on the pyramiding of reserves and the difficulty of interior banks trying to realize their reserves on deposit with reserve-city and central-reserve-city banks in a crisis. Banking reformers had hoped to reduce the role of the correspondent banks, replacing them with the Federal Reserve banks, which would take over the process of clearing and collection and impart elasticity to the currency by providing discount facilities but would not invest their reserves in the stock market.

H. Parker Willis, one of the intellectual fathers of the Fed-

---

[79] Charles S. Tippetts, *State Banks and the Federal Reserve System*, pp. 32–38.

eral Reserve System, argued that "the massing of funds in New York and other financial centers, of which so much has been said in recent years is largely due to the present reserve requirements of national banks."[80] The solution the Federal Reserve was supposed to effect was to transfer these reserves to the Federal Reserve banks where they would be safe from the speculative fluctuations of the money markets. According to Willis, "The presumed effect of this plan will be to end the placing of reserves with Central Reserve City banks for use in stock market operations, to keep reserves in some measure at home, and to require speculators to get funds they need in their operations either by directly borrowing them from persons who hold them and want to loan cash for that purpose or else borrowing from banks in places where the operations are to be carried on."[81]

The idea of reducing bankers' balances naturally upset reserve-city bankers who had favored the Aldrich Plan under which they could have retained a greater degree of control. Many country bankers distrusted the reserve-city bankers' motives, but they had sided with them when it appeared that the Democrats were going to prohibit the deposit of funds with correspondents. Glass tried to offer a compromise, allowing banks to place 5 percent of their deposits with correspondents; but the banking community denounced this move. Even though many bankers were suspicious of the operations of the major-city correspondent banks, they recognized this as a threat to the functioning of the banking system. The result of a campaign by the ABA and other bankers' associations was that these plans were dropped. The only limitation was the amount a member bank could carry with a nonmember. In 1917, Congress acted to enhance the attractiveness of membership in the Federal Reserve System by further lowering reserve requirements. Member banks were thereafter required to hold

[80] Henry Parker Willis, *The Federal Reserve System*, p. 174.
[81] Ibid., p. 175.

a reserve of 3 percent against time deposits, and central-reserve-city banks were to keep 13 percent, reserve-city banks 10 percent, and country banks 7 percent against demand deposits.

Appraisal of the effect of the Federal Reserve System on bankers' balances is clouded by this reduction in reserve requirements and the wartime monetary expansion. However, it is clear the Federal Reserve failed to replace completely the correspondent banks. Some idea of the effect of the Federal Reserve System on bankers' balances may be gained by comparing Table 2.4, which shows the hierarchy of interbank deposits from 1915 to 1926, with Table 2.1, which covers the period 1902–1914. Before World War I the central-reserve-city banks' net deposits due to other banks as a percentage of individual deposits had risen rapidly to 88.9 in 1909, and fallen to 74.7 in 1914. Net deposits due to other banks from reserve-city national banks experienced a secular increase but remained at slightly over 20 percent of individual deposits. Net deposits due from other banks to country banks also grew steadily in this period, although as a percentage of individual deposits they too declined. A similar pattern is shown by the growth of state banks' interbank deposits for the years 1902–1914; however, the structure of deposits cannot be analyzed owing to the lack of data disaggregated by bank location.

After 1914, bankers' balances for the most part continued to grow; but as a proportion of other deposits, their importance diminished considerably. Overall, bankers' balances as a percentage of total deposits declined from 33.6 in 1915 to 16.3 in 1926. The net balances due to banks from central-reserve-city banks fell from almost 75 percent of individual deposits in 1914 to 30 percent in 1926. The reserve-city net balances due to other banks also dropped below 20 percent falling to 13.4 percent in 1926. The country banks' and all nonnational banks' net balances due from other banks declined to less than 5 percent of individual deposits. The most

Table 2.4
Bankers' Balances, 1915–1926
(in millions of dollars)

	1915	1916	1917	1918	1919
Central-reserve-city banks					
Individual deposits	1,262	1,834	2,073	2,213	2,908
Balances due from	159	202	237	207	213
Balances due to	1,167	1,357	1,433	1,378	1,362
Reserve-city banks					
Individual deposits	1,672	2,041	2,451	2,746	3,308
Balances due from	553	616	605	612	612
Balances due to	815	1,051	1,211	1,120	1,267
Country banks					
Individual deposits	3,631	4,250	5,090	5,223	6,157
Balances due from	564	719	795	643	756
Balances due to	225	305	382	290	345
State member banks					
Individual deposits	—	—	—	4,939	6,897
Balances due from	—	—	—	444	546
Balances due to	—	—	—	482	677
Nonmember banks					
Individual deposits	12,635	14,749	16,783	12,836	13,942
Balances due from	1,640	2,005	2,294	1,481	1,727
Balances due to	575	751	888	311	229

SOURCE: Leonard L. Watkins, *Bankers' Balances*, pp. 52–53, 55.
NOTE: Until 1918, the figures for state members of the Federal Reserve are

notable feature of these decreases is that the most precipitous declines occurred, not in the period of transition when reserve requirements were being reduced (1914–1918), but afterward. The years 1920–1926, when there was no change in federal reserve requirements and little alteration in state requirements, cover most of the decline in the relative size of bankers' balances. The other factors that may be responsible for this decline are the spread of branch banking, which absorbed correspondent bank functions, and the growth of other types of liquid assets like government bonds, which provided alternatives to investing in bankers' balances.[82]

[82] See Chapter 3 for an analysis of the spread of branch banking.

1920	1921	1922	1923	1924	1925	1926
3,157	2,817	3,210	2,673	3,358	3,666	3,745
163	136	114	118	183	160	132
1,314	1,028	1,137	1,050	1,348	1,230	1,286
3,732	3,216	3,597	3,909	4,053	4,626	4,811
531	366	498	447	568	554	585
1,192	864	1,067	1,029	1,147	1,266	1,232
7,247	6,709	6,908	7,715	7,992	8,623	9,042
700	514	629	641	694	786	765
318	241	279	306	300	360	348
8,242	8,208	9,224	10,189	11,217	12,456	13,118
432	338	406	392	497	519	500
636	556	642	800	1,026	1,123	1,071
15,452	14,650	14,833	15,953	17,027	18,133	18,865
1,687	1,487	1,575	1,732	1,817	2,098	2,050
228	102	110	401	80	362	361

included with the figures for the nonmember banks. All figures are for the midsummer call dates.

Although the Federal Reserve may have had some impact on the decrease in bankers' balances, it did not disrupt the structure of the system. The pyramiding of balances continued, although on a relatively smaller scale, as evidenced by Table 2.4. The hierarchy of interbank deposits remained unchanged. In 1913, New York City national banks held over 72 percent of central-reserve-city bankers' balances; and in 1926, they still had 73 percent of these deposits.[83]

Bankers' balances continued to play an important role in facilitating the functioning of the banking system. The Federal Reserve System did not substantially reduce correspond-

[83] Watkins, *Bankers' Balances,* p. 59.

ent banking because it still served the needs of integrating
money markets and facilitating clearance of payments between banks in the absence of extensive branching. The opening of the Federal Reserve's discount window did have an
important impact on the pattern of interbank borrowing, but
it did not entirely remove correspondent banks from the picture.

Banks did not have to join the Federal Reserve to gain access
to the discount window when they could borrow from other
banks that were members. New York City banks borrowed
almost exclusively from the Federal Reserve, as did banks in
other major financial centers. The farther banks were from
a financial center, the more then tended to depend on their
correspondents.[84] Banks in the South, the Midwest, and the
West continued to be the largest borrowers from correspondent banks.[85] The Federal Reserve's eligibility requirements,
designed according to the precepts of the real bills doctrine
to promote the use of short-term high-quality, "self-liquidating" paper tended to exclude the smaller rural banks from
using the window. The major-city banks serving the largest
industrial and commercial enterprises possessed the desired
commercial paper. Discounting was easy for them, and it was
convenient and profitable for them to assist member and nonmember banks that did not have the best collateral to obtain
funds indirectly from the discount window by intermediation.
Correspondent banks accepted a hodgepodge of paper, using
their high-quality paper to obtain funds from the discount
window. Not surprisingly, the rates on interbank loans were
usually above the discount rate, reflecting the intermediation
taking place.[86] The hierarchy of interbank borrowing was not
interrupted by the operation of the Federal Reserve, as can

[84] Ibid., pp. 174–177.
[85] Ibid., pp. 186–188.
[86] Ibid., pp. 187–193.

be seen in Table 2.2. Central-reserve-city and reserve-city banks continued to act as interbank intermediaries, but now they had the additional resources of the Federal Reserve available to meet the demands of their correspondents.

City correspondents continued to serve as agents for their respondents' investments. The enormous wartime increase in government securities, which flooded the financial market, offered an excellent form of secondary reserves for banks. Federal Reserve open market operations promoted the liquidity of government securities, giving banks another alternative to investments in call loans. These assets were often purchased by New York banks for their respondent banks. Bankers' balances were still an attractive form of reserves for nonmembers whose state regulations still permitted them to hold part of their reserves on deposit at reserve agents and for member banks who desired to hold excess reserves. A 1917 investigation found that 233 of the 612 New York banks were paying interest of 1 to 4 percent on bankers' deposits. Faithful to the intentions of the Congress, the Federal Reserve Board made it clear that it regarded this interest as an attack on the deposits of other banks. The New York Federal Reserve Bank was able to persuade the members of the New York Clearing House to tie their interest rate on interbank deposits to the discount rate, but it failed to eliminate it entirely or to extend this convention to other clearinghouses.[87] The bankers' balances gathered by correspondent banks in the major financial centers continued to be invested in call loans on collateral of securities, contrary to Carter Glass's expressed expectations. Correspondent banks offered a much wider variety of services to country banks than did reserve banks. By these services and the bootlegging of credit to banks that did not have the appropriate collateral or the right of access to the discount window, correspondent banks were able

[87] Ibid., pp. 263–265.

to maintain their position and function in the nation's financial system.[88]

In the eyes of many banking reformers, one of the most certain failures of the Federal Reserve Act was the continued investment of banks' funds in loans on call to the stock market. J. Laurence Laughlin believed that country banks and even New York City banks did not really want to invest in call loans. He looked to the Federal Reserve to provide greater liquidity for banks so that they would not have to put their funds into this market. The Federal Reserve's impact was negligible, as is readily seen by comparing the volume of call loans for 1908–1912, in Table 2.3, with the levels of 1917–1926, in Table 2.5. The volume of loans made by New York City banks on their own account using balances due banks and loans on account of their correspondents both continued to rise.[89] What surely shocked reformers even more was the increased investment in these short-term loans at even lower interest rates. Whereas a call rate of 4.7 percent elicited New York bank loans of $552 million on their own account and $208 million on their correspondents' accounts in January 1910 and $574 million and $220 million in January 1919, these loans stood at $1,084 million and $1,067 million in November 1925. To any banking reformer who believed in the real bills doctrine, this must have seemed a dangerous trend. Distrust of speculation and the stock market had not evaporated; and the frequent concern of the Federal Reserve with the stock market in the 1920s has its basis in the origins of the banking reform movement.

---

[88] Tippetts, *State Banks*, pp. 199–201.

[89] The figures for call loans from the Money Trust Investigation and the Federal Reserve Board are not directly comparable. The Pujo Commission's sample contained twenty-nine to thirty-two national and state banks and trust companies, while the Federal Reserve Board had forty-three member and nonmember banks. Both series include the major correspondent banks; and hence, although they contain different numbers of banks, they can be compared to give some idea of the changes in the volume of call loans before and after the Federal Reserve Act.

Table 2.5
Call Loans of New York City Banks, 1917–1926

Date	Loans (in millions of dollars) On Own Account	For Accounts of Correspondents	Call Money Interest Rates
1917			
Nov. 2	671	164	4.17%
1918			
Jan. 4	505	128	4.10
July 5	511	142	5.63
Nov. 1	572	211	5.85
1919			
Jan. 3	574	220	4.78
July 3	772	503	6.55
Nov. 7	782	736	11.06
1920			
Jan. 2	715	635	8.19
July 2	437	501	8.29
Nov. 5	381	574	7.90
1921			
Jan. 7	346	440	6.71
July 6	340	385	5.60
Nov. 2	409	394	5.03
1922			
Jan. 4	547	398	4.55
July 5	847	524	3.86
Nov. 1	884	717	4.89
1923			
Jan. 3	938	652	4.32
July 5	741	632	5.06
Nov. 7	499	631	4.81
1924			
Jan. 2	712	620	4.39
July 2	875	590	2.10
Nov. 5	926	703	2.42
1925			
Jan. 7	1,142	838	3.32
July 1	1,157	1,135	4.09
Nov. 4	1,084	1,067	4.74
1926			
Jan. 6	1,285	1,622	4.33

SOURCE: Board of Governors of the Federal Reserve System, *Banking and Monetary Statistics, 1914–1941*, pp. 495–497.

The Clearinghouse Functions of the Federal Reserve Banks

The authors of the Federal Reserve Act and those who headed the early Federal Reserve System were eager to establish a national system for clearing payments and checks to reduce the costs to banks and the public. The provision of clearing facilities by the Federal Reserve banks was intended to reduce further the motive for holding bankers' balances. More rapid clearing would also decrease the float and make reserve requirements more effective. It was considered essential that the new clearing system operate on the basis of par remittance; otherwise the Federal Reserve banks would be faced with absorbing or attempting to pass on exchange charges. The Federal Reserve Act permitted the Federal Reserve banks to receive on deposit checks and drafts from members; and in 1916, the Federal Reserve Board mandated clearance at par. In the early years of operation a small charge, 0.9 percent on the dollar, was levied to cover expenses; but the Federal Reserve banks' earnings on their portfolios began to grow, and this charge was eliminated in 1918.[90]

The Federal Reserve enjoyed some success in taking over the business of clearing and collection. As shown in Table 2.6, the clearings at the Federal Reserve rose swiftly from nothing to approximately one-third of all clearings by the clearinghouses and the Federal Reserve banks. The Gold Settlement Fund served to unify the system by facilitating interdistrict clearances. The Federal Reserve System campaigned vigorously to force par collection of checks until its efforts were blocked by the courts.[91] The Federal Reserve followed in the footsteps of the Boston Clearing House, which had been able to force all banks in its area to remit at par before 1914.[92]

[90] Tippetts, *State Banks*, pp. 270–271.
[91] For a more detailed account of the struggle over nonpar clearance, see Chapter 3.
[92] Spahr, *The Clearing and Collection of Checks*, pp. 127–128.

Table 2.6
Clearings at the Clearinghouses and the Federal
Reserve Banks, 1914–1929
(in millions of dollars)

Year	Clearings at All Clearinghouses	Clearings at the Federal Reserve Banks
1914	163,849	—
1915	162,777	5,442
1916	242,236	12,538
1917	303,997	51,593
1918	321,461	121,511
1919	387,366	136,493
1920	462,920	179,505
1921	374,825	130,482
1922	380,492	160,472
1923	412,195	207,719
1924	438,778	219,832
1925	505,906	258,611
1926	533,077	272,945
1927	543,955	278,399
1928	614,219	301,703
1929	713,762	367,215

SOURCES: U.S. Comptroller of the Currency, *Annual Report*, 1914–1929 and Board of Governors of the Federal Reserve System, *Annual Report*, 1915–1929.

The Federal Reserve Bank of Boston went one step further and took over the operations of the Boston Clearing House. In New York, the New York Federal Reserve Bank was elected a limited member of the clearinghouse and coexisted with that institution.[93]

While absorbing a considerable portion of clearings and collections, the Federal Reserve System still left most of the clearinghouses intact. In 1920, the clearings of all the clearinghouses providing information to the Comptroller of the Currency were $462,920 million; while the clearings at the Federal Reserve banks amounted to $179,505 million, or 27.9

[93] Ibid., p. 169.

percent of the total. This proportion changed little over the decade. The Federal Reserve banks accounted for 32.9 percent of the total clearings in 1928. The Federal Reserve in its efforts to unify the process of clearing required items to be presented according to very strict rules. Many banks avoided this burden by continuing to clear through their correspondents and the clearinghouses. As with bankers' balances, changes in the volume and pattern of clearings did not depend solely on the distribution of activity between the private and federal agents. Increased branch banking by internalizing clearings could reduce their volume.

The relationship between clearings at the Federal Reserve banks and the clearinghouses, and branch banking was examined, using data for the years 1920–1936. Information on the extent of branching and bank debits was lacking for earlier years, but the results of the regressions offer considerable insight into the relationships of the 1920s. The model employed posits that annual clearings through all clearinghouses or through the Federal Reserve banks would increase as the value of checks debited to the accounts of bank customers, that is, bank debits, increased. This was simply intended to show that as the banks' supply of the means of payment increased so did the need to clear interbank payments. The volume of bank debits was used because it is a flow variable (bank deposits are not), as are clearings. Furthermore, it was hypothesized that clearings would decrease as branching increased, as this would internalize the clearing process. Three measures of branching were used: (1) the ratio of branching banks to all commercial banks, (2) the ratio of branch bank offices to all commercial-bank offices, and (3) the ratio of branch bank loans and investments to all commercial-bank loans and investments.[94] The results of the regressions for

[94] Data for branching banks came from the Board of Governors of the Federal Reserve System, *Banking and Monetary Statistics, 1914–1941*, p. 297. Commercial bank data were obtained from Board of Governors of the Federal

the clearinghouses are reproduced in Table 2.7 and for Federal Reserve banks in Table 2.8.[95]

All equations explaining the variation of the dependent variable were significant, as indicated by the F-statistic. The percentage of variation explained, measured by the R^2, was high. The coefficients on the bank debit variable for the clearinghouse data were consistently estimated to be around 0.67 and for the Federal Reserve bank's clearings to be around 0.32. This follows from the fact, obvious from a casual examination of the data, that the Federal Reserve obtained and kept approximately one-third of the clearing business. If bank debits rose by $1 billion, this would result in Federal Reserve clearings increasing by over $300 million and clearinghouse clearings by about $670 million.

For the clearinghouse regressions, the branching variables were all negative and significant, giving a clear indication that the expansion of branching reduced the volume of clearings. For example, in Table 2.7, for Model I, a 1 percent increase in the ratio of branch bank offices to all commercial-bank offices would reduce clearings by $3.875 billion. This same powerful effect of branching on clearings is registered by the other two branching variables. Interestingly, the increase in branching did not detract from the use of the Federal Reserve banks as clearinghouses. In all three models of Federal Re-

---

Reserve System, *All Bank Statistics, United States, 1896–1955*. The volume of bank debits is given in U.S. Department of Commerce, *Historical Statistics of the United States*, p. 1001. Various issues of the U.S. Comptroller of the Currency's *Annual Reports*, 1920–1936, yielded the clearings for the clearinghouses, and the Board of Governors of the Federal Reserve System's *Annual Reports*, 1920–1936, provided the needed information on the Federal Reserve banks' clearings.

[95] In both cases the Durbin-Watson statistic in the original ordinary least squares regression indicated the possible presence of autocorrelation. Using the Durbin Two-Stage Procedure, the autocorrelation was determined to be second order and the appropriate adjustment was made. For an exposition of the Durbin Two-Stage technique, see G. S. Maddala, *Econometrics*, pp. 277–284.

Table 2.7
Determinants of Clearings at the Clearinghouses Corrected for
Autocorrelation by the Durbin Two-Stage Procedure, 1920–1936

	Model I	*Model II*	*Model III*
Independent Variables			
Intercept	120.28	202.11	114.45
	(2.81*)	(4.52*)	(2.19*)
Ratio of branch bank offices to all commercial-bank offices	−387.50 (−2.16*)		
Ratio of branching banks to all commercial banks		−2,063.30 (−3.76*)	
Ratio of loans and investments by branching banks to those by all commercial banks			−185.28 (−1.54†)
Bank debits	0.67 (13.24*)	0.67 (20.24*)	0.67 (10.71*)
Coefficients for Second-Order Autocorrelation			
r_1	0.458	0.112	0.601
r_2	−0.401	−0.564	−0.355
Goodness of Fit			
R^2	0.942	0.976	0.907
F-statistic	114.9*	293.1*	69.0*
Durbin-Watson statistic	1.835	1.536	1.949

NOTE: The dependent variable is annual clearings through all clearinghouses in billions of dollars. The numbers in parentheses are *t*-statistics.
  * Significant at the 0.05 level.
  † Significant at the 0.10 level.

serve bank clearings, a rise in the branching variable increased the volume of clearing activity. In Model I in Table 2.8, a 1 percent increase in the ratio of branch bank offices to all commercial-bank offices would lead to a $2.607 billion increase in Federal Reserve bank clearings. This is not surprising, as it is well known that the larger banks made more extensive use of Federal Reserve facilities.[96] The overall effect

[96] Tippetts, *State Banks*, chapter 6 and R. Alton Gilbert, "Utilization of

Table 2.8
Determinants of Clearings at the Federal Reserve Banks Corrected for
Autocorrelation by the Durbin Two-Stage Procedure, 1920–1936

	Model I	*Model II*	*Model III*
Independent Variables			
Intercept	195.49	247.23	9.39
	(0.98)	(1.06)	(0.41)
Ratio of branch bank	260.70		
offices to all commercial-	(2.65*)		
bank offices			
Ratio of branching banks		928.93	
to all commercial banks		(1.66†)	
Ratio of loans and invest-			133.43
ments by branching			(2.50*)
banks to those by all			
commercial banks			
Bank debits	0.32	0.32	0.31
	(11.91*)	(9.99*)	(11.48*)
Coefficients for Second-Order			
Autocorrelation			
r_1	0.509	0.388	0.562
r_2	−0.314	−0.126	−0.306
Goodness of Fit			
R^2	0.911	0.884	0.903
F-statistic	72.8*	54.2*	66.2*
Durbin-Watson	1.915	1.592	1.942
statistic			

NOTE: The dependent variable is annual clearings through the Federal Re-
serve banks in billions of dollars. The numbers in parentheses are *t*-statistics.
   * Significant at the 0.05 level.
   † Significant at the 0.10 level.

of an increase in branching would lead to a net decrease in
clearings. For the bank office variable, total clearings would
fall by $1.269 billion as they decreased for the clearinghouses
and rose for the Federal Reserve banks. The same is true for
the other measures of branching. More branching created
larger banks, which absorbed and internalized the clearing

Federal Reserve Bank Services by Member Banks: Implications for the Costs
and Benefits of Membership."

process and proceeded to clear between each other through the Federal Reserve banks.

This evidence supports the contemporary studies of Leonard Watkins and Oliver M. W. Sprague, and the modern work of John James, all of whom view the correspondent banking system and clearinghouses as the means by which the financial system integrated money markets and facilitated clearings of interbank payments in the presence of strong legislative restrictions on branching. Increased branch banking would probably have reduced bankers' balances substantially. Some evidence is available for examining the relation between bankers' balances and branching. The correlation between the ratio of bankers' balances to all commercial-bank deposits by state on June 30, 1925, and the ratios of branch bank offices to all commercial-bank offices and branching banks to all commercial banks in each state for that year were found to be -0.462 and -0.467 respectively.[97] This suggests that even an increase in intrastate branching could have reduced bankers' balances. The results indicate that if the Federal Reserve Act had included some extension of branching on an intrastate or interstate basis, the objectives of the banking reformers would have been furthered. Bankers' balances held for the purposes of clearing would have been reduced as more interbank intermediation would have taken place within larger, more geographically diversified, banks. Banks might also have been strengthened by more branching. Chapter 4 offers evidence

[97] The data for deposits were obtained from the Board of Governors of the Federal Reserve System, *All Bank Statistics*, and for branching banks from the Board of Governors of the Federal Reserve System, *Banking and Monetary Statistics*, p. 298. The idea for this test came from an article, "More on Correspondent Banking," in which the anonymous author examined the Spearman rank correlation coefficient of branch bank offices as a percentage of all commercial-bank offices to interbank deposits as a percentage of total demand deposits and found them to be negatively related. A rank correlation test was used because the observations were on Federal Reserve districts for December 1964 and offered too few observations to use ordinary correlation techniques.

that there was an inverse relationship between various measures of branching and bank failures in the 1920s.

An expansion of branching, through its effects on clearing and on membership, as shown in Chapter 3, would certainly have strengthened the Federal Reserve System. But federal legislation to increase branching was not forthcoming in 1913. The forces arrayed against it were too strong. Any attempt to attach provisions to allow national banks to branch would have alienated the powerful country bankers' lobby, upset the balance of political support, and threatened to obstruct the passage of the Federal Reserve Act.

The Evolution of Monetary Policy

In addition to dismantling the correspondent banking system, the framers of the Federal Reserve Act aimed to strengthen the banking system by increasing the currency's "elasticity" to ensure that increased seasonal demands for money did not generate financial crises. The motivating monetary theory behind the Federal Reserve Act was the real bills doctrine. This theory held that banks should invest primarily in short-term commercial bills, representing real transactions or production. If banks followed this prescription, the requirements of trade and industry would regulate the supply of credit without causing inflation or deflation.[98] Two of the architects of the Federal Reserve Act, J. Laurence Laughlin and H. Parker Willis, promoted the new system on the grounds that it would create an environment in which the real bills doctrine would come into operation.[99] According to Willis's description of the Federal Reserve System's operation in his 1923 book, the system ensured that no note would be issued without a transaction to call for it and no commercial transaction would occur

[98] West, *Banking Reform*, p. 138.
[99] Ibid., p. 147.

that could not obtain a note to facilitate it.[100] However, this theory largely ignored how the American financial system actually functioned. The "self-liquidating" short-term, two-name commercial paper held to be the key to the success of the real bills doctrine was not, in fact, the most common financial instrument. These bills had declined from 69 percent of national-bank loans and investments in 1880 to 35 percent in 1914.[101] If the new institution would discount only these bills, banks had to be encouraged to use them. Yet in the eyes of the strict real bills banking reformers, the Federal Reserve would succeed simply by passively accommodating banks by discounting this type of bill. Increasing the liquidity of this type of asset, it was believed, would lead banks to use them more. The stability of the credit markets would thus be assured.

Not all reformers adhered to this strong interpretation of the real bills doctrine. One prominent dissenter was Paul Warburg, a banker with strong ties to European banking. In his volume on rediscounting in Europe, prepared for the National Monetary Commission, Warburg emphasized that discounting was not a passive process. Central banks used this instrument to regulate the volume of credit.[102] There were also academics like A. Piatt Andrew and Oliver M. W. Sprague who pointed to the fact that credit creation often raised prices. The extension of credit might appear justified by the real bills criterion, but it could contribute to inflation.[103] Nevertheless, critics of the doctrine, like Warburg and Sprague, supported the idea of the Federal Reserve because they believed that liquidity was not an intrinsic characteristic of real bills. They believed that an institution like a central bank was necessary to ensure bank liquidity in times of financial stress, as occurred

[100] Henry Parker Willis, *The Federal Reserve*, pp. 254–255.
[101] West, *Banking Reform*, pp. 155–162.
[102] Ibid., pp. 148–149.
[103] Ibid., pp. 150–151.

during high seasonal demands for money and when a panic shook the banking system.[104] Owing to their different interpretations of how the Federal Reserve would function, theoretical opponents could agree on the legislation, believing that it would impart the needed elasticity to the currency by one means or another.

Putting the monetary theory of the Federal Reserve Act into practice, the new Federal Reserve System did not adhere closely to the strict real bills doctrine as propounded by Laughlin and Willis. The consensus of the Federal Reserve Board is revealed in its first *Annual Report*. The report states that it was the duty of the system "not to await emergencies but, by anticipation, to do what it can to prevent them."[105] The views of Warburg, a member of the Board of Governors, were espoused. The board rejected a completely passive role, stating that at times "the great weight of their [the Federal Reserve banks'] influence should be exerted to secure a freer extension of credit and an easing of rates. . . . There will just as certainly, however, be other times when prudence and a proper regard for the common good should be pursued and accommodations curtailed."[106] This went beyond the idea of a clearinghouse that would provide currency in an emergency, and represented a move toward a more European style of central bank management.

The Federal Reserve Board did adhere more strictly to the act's limitations on the type of paper that would be considered eligible for discounting. Governor W.P.G. Harding reaffirmed this in 1916: "It is clear that the intent of the Act is to safeguard the self-liquidating character of acceptances, as securities of an investment nature are barred and provision is made that the transactions should be based upon an actual

[104] Ibid., p. 152.
[105] Board of Governors of the Federal Reserve System, *Annual Report*, 1914, p. 17.
[106] Ibid., p. 18.

sale of goods."[107] By allowing only nonspeculative loans to be rediscounted at the Federal Reserve, it was hoped that the link between the banking system and the stock market through call loans would be severed, thereby strengthening the banking system.

The Federal Reserve did not, however, have the opportunity to put these principles into operation. World War I and the tremendous borrowing demands of the government put pressure on the Federal Reserve to join the war effort and serve as a conduit for the sale of government securities. Secretary of the Treasury McAdoo decided to finance war borrowing at rates below those prevailing on the market. To assist this policy, the Federal Reserve was pressed into service. A policy of offering a preferential discount rate on loans to banks to buy government bonds was adopted.[108] This meant the Federal Reserve had to abandon an independent monetary policy to support the Treasury's inflationary financing of the war.

World War I altered the conditions under which the Federal Reserve operated. Co-opted by the Treasury, the Federal Reserve's discounts on commercial paper almost disappeared, to be replaced by credit for government debt. By May 1919, 95 percent of the Federal Reserve banks' discounts were backed by government securities. These discounts declined after the war but remained a large portion of the Federal Reserve's discounts. The portfolios of the Federal Reserve banks grew quickly with the purchase of government bonds. As a percentage of all investments, these securities rose from a negligible 4.3 in April 1917 to 55.1 in April 1918.[109] These changes loosened the Federal Reserve from its real bills moorings, and legitimized operations using government securities. More im-

---

[107] West, *Banking Reform*, p. 184.
[108] Elmus R. Wicker, *Federal Reserve Monetary Policy 1917–1933*, pp. 8–12.
[109] West, *Banking Reform*, p. 188.

portant, the rapid wartime inflation emphasized that the volume of credit was at least as important as its quality.

The process of coming to grips with the use and effects of discounting and open market operations was slow and painful. The Federal Reserve Board harbored no doubts that permissive credit was causing the postwar inflation. The governors' desire for higher discount rates was finally agreed to by the Treasury in 1919. The Federal Reserve then abruptly halted the expansion of credit, resulting in the crash of 1920–1921. Once the downswing began, there was no immediate reduction in the Federal Reserve's discount rates, increasing the severity of the crisis. This insensitivity has been attributed by Friedman and Schwartz and Lester V. Chandler to the Federal Reserve's concern with its gold reserve; but it may be, as Elmus Wicker has argued, that it was also worried about reducing the "redundant" money supply and restoring the "proper" relationship between prices and output by decreasing the loans to banks to carry public debt.[110]

Even in the early 1920s, there was no overall conception of a monetary policy. True, the Federal Reserve accommodated seasonal needs, but there was little coordination of the Federal Reserve's various activities. The failure to comprehend the importance of open market operations demonstrates this vividly. Once the Federal Reserve banks had been organized and had begun operation, they started to buy and sell acceptances and securities. There was no coordination of this activity by the different reserve banks and their competition frequently spoiled the market. Early in 1916, the Governor of the New York Federal Reserve bank, Benjamin Strong, recognized the need to coordinate these activities, but his pleas were ignored by the other banks.[111] Finally, in May 1922, the Governors'

---

[110] Friedman and Schwartz, *A Monetary History of the United States*, pp. 237–238, 249; Lester V. Chandler, *Benjamin Strong, Central Banker*, pp. 183–185; Wicker, *Federal Reserve Monetary Policy*, pp. 47–50.

[111] Chandler, *Benjamin Strong*, pp. 76–80.

Conference was persuaded to establish a committee to organize this activity and coordinate the discount rate. The Federal Reserve Board surprised the governors in 1923 by dissolving this committee and creating the Open Market Investment Committee to carry out the purchase and sale of securities.[112] This aggrandizement was probably fortunate, for the governors appear not to have understood how to coordinate the use of the discount rates with open market operations. In their October conference in 1922, when monetary ease was needed, they voted to decrease open market purchases in proportion to their increased discounts, pointedly failing to understand the effects of the various monetary instruments.[113]

The Federal Reserve Board's *Tenth Annual Report* of 1923 is usually cited as the turning point in the Federal Reserve's thinking on monetary policy. This report proposed two criteria, one qualitative and the other quantitative, for monetary policy. The qualitative test, which emphasized the need to ensure that credit was used for productive, as opposed to speculative, purposes made obeisance to the real bills doctrine but also served to underline the Federal Reserve's very real concern with the stock market. The quantitative test proposed to limit "the volume of credit within the field of its appropriate uses to such amount as may be economically justified—that is, justified by a commensurate increase in the nation's aggregate productivity."[114] The report reflected the experience gained by the board in 1922 and 1923, when open market purchases were used to reduce discounting and open market sales were used to increase it. This explicit recognition of the importance of coordinating the two instruments provided a rationalization for the creation of the Open Market Invest-

[112] Ibid., pp. 202–234.
[113] Wicker, *Federal Reserve Monetary Policy*, p. 71.
[114] Ibid., p. 65.

ment Committee.[115] Open market operations were henceforth conducted so as to make the discount rate "effective."

While the *Tenth Annual Report* marked the Federal Reserve's acknowledgment of the role and importance of open market operations, the theory behind the use of this instrument was still colored by real bills notions and may have slowed the board's reaction to events. Although the Federal Reserve apparently failed to identify the turning point in the next business cycle and did not respond quickly to declining interest rates and indices of prices and production, the Open Market Investment Committee did eventually begin open market purchases in December 1923. This simultaneously met the Federal Reserve's goals of lessening the recession, increasing the Federal Reserve banks' investment portfolios, aiding sterling, and creating a favorable market for the flotation of foreign bonds. As the recession deepened in early 1924, the committee increased its purchases and the New York Federal Reserve Bank lowered its discount rate to 4 percent in April. However, most of this effort was directed toward reducing member-bank indebtedness. The problem was that hesitation impeded recovery because sales of securities in the previous boom delayed the money markets' response to the change in demand for bank credit. Getting banks out of debt was necessary to speed up the market response to a contraction.[116]

The Federal Reserve's hesitancy to act may be partly explained by the fear that a reduction in the discount rate or purchase of securities would stimulate stock market speculation rather than business. Several Federal Reserve banks took this view, and argued that open market purchases should be made only to meet the expenses and dividends of the individual banks. While Governor Benjamin Strong and board member Adolph Miller vigorously and, for the most part, successfully supported the use of these monetary instruments,

[115] Friedman and Schwartz, *A Monetary History of the United States*, p. 251.
[116] Wicker, *Federal Reserve Monetary Policy*, pp. 82–93.

few Federal Reserve officials outside of New York and Washington regarded open market purchases as a means to counter a recession.[117] Concern over the stock market did affect the use of open market operations, as the Federal Reserve Board treated the purchase of commercial bills and government securities differently. From Warburg, who sat on the board in the years before World War I, to Governor Owen Young in 1929, the board members regarded the purchase of bills as aiding genuine business transactions and the purchase of securities as providing money to all sorts of activities, including the stock market.[118] This invalid distinction between the effects of buying the two different financial instruments led to futile attempts to direct economic activity by buying bills rather than securities and helped to justify policies of direct pressure to prevent investment in stocks.[119] Apparently, only Benjamin Strong firmly eschewed any role for the Federal Reserve as an arbiter of the stock market.[120]

Both the board and the Federal Reserve Bank of New York agreed that security speculation was a cause for concern. As early as 1919, the board refused to raise the discount rate to reduce member-bank borrowing and instead applied "direct pressure" to discourage banks from making speculative investments. The threat behind direct pressure was that banks refusing to cooperate would be denied access to the rediscount window—a position that conflicted with most of the Federal Reserve banks' belief that this was interference with the member-bank "privilege" of borrowing.[121]

Congressional concern over investment by member banks in loans on stocks and bonds did not stop with the passage of the Federal Reserve Act. Worries about speculation increased,

---

[117] Ibid., p. 84.
[118] Friedman and Schwartz, *A Monetary History of the United States*, p. 226.
[119] Ibid., p. 267.
[120] Chandler, *Benjamin Strong*, pp. 423–427.
[121] Ibid., pp. 254–257.

when, in 1926, the Federal Reserve Board decided to begin publication of the weekly totals of New York City brokers' loans in the *Federal Reserve Bulletin*. This provided a barometer of banking involvement in the stock market; and a subcommittee of the Senate Committee on Banking and Currency, headed by Senator Robert La Follette, began an investigation into speculation in 1928. H. Parker Willis testified to the menace that stock market speculation presented but despaired that any legislation could control it.[122] Senator Smith Wildman Brookhart of Iowa, a committee member, complained that the stock market was drawing off funds from his home state which was suffering from a dearth of credit. To prevent speculative investments by banks he recommended a bill that would establish 100 percent reserve requirements.[123] The only witness at the hearings to deny consistently that brokers' loans were dangerous was Oliver M. W. Sprague, who blamed the growing distress in the nation's agricultural areas on a local depression in agriculture and too many small banks. Sprague, a defender of branch banking, stated that call loans were the safest, most liquid type of commercial loan and contrasted these with the poor investment opportunities offered by loans to agriculture.[124]

Federal Reserve policy ignored the rising number of bank failures in the South and the West. The Federal Reserve Board strongly believed that bank failures resulted only from poor bank management. Omitted from almost all discussions of policy is any reference to bank suspensions. This seems strange, as one of the salient features of the banking system in the 1920s was a higher rate of suspensions than any earlier period. The Federal Reserve did collect figures on the suspensions and noted the higher rates of failures among nonmembers located in agricultural regions but failed to see any connection

[122] Cowing, *Populists, Plungers, and Progressives*, pp. 132–138.
[123] Ibid., p. 138.
[124] Ibid., pp. 139–140.

between these and banking and monetary policy. In 1926, when the agricultural depression was well under way, the consensus of the Governors' Conference was that "the chief factors which have resulted in failures during the past several years have been bad management and economic conditions which have resulted from the War."[125] This myopia is another example of the Federal Reserve's failure to see the connections between banking structure and monetary stability.

Given congressional pressure and the continued influence of real bills notions, it is not surprising that the Federal Reserve persisted in applying qualitative measures of credit control. This points to a more basic misunderstanding of the mechanism of monetary control than most historians have attributed to the leaders of the Federal Reserve System. From experience, they had gained a greater understanding of the means of monetary control, but Friedman and Schwartz's strong conclusion that "the new monetary mechanism offered a delicate yet effective means of smoothing economic fluctuations, and that its operators knew how to use it toward that end"[126] seems unwarranted. Congressional pressure and the concern of many Federal Reserve bankers over speculation continued to influence policy. Robert West's argument that by 1923 the real bills theory was seriously weakened is essentially correct, but some elements of the theory continued to influence the formation of policy.[127] The Federal Reserve's ability to control economic fluctuations through the appropriate use of monetary instruments had clearly increased; yet as the lengthy policy debates in Congress, at the Federal Reserve Board, and at the Federal Reserve banks make clear, the view that discounting of the wrong kind of bills could fuel the fires of speculation persisted. Elmus Wicker's conclusion that the performance of Federal Reserve officials in the first twenty years

---

[125] Friedman and Schwartz, *A Monetary History of the United States*, p. 270.
[126] Ibid., p. 296.
[127] West, *Banking Reform*, chapter 11.

was constrained by their attachment to specific economic goals, imperfect understanding of the tools of monetary management, and imprecise knowledge of how a central bank can influence the level of economic activity seems much closer to the mark.[128] The suspicion of correspondent banking and the almost universal condemnation of bankers' balances reveal a failure to appreciate how the banking system integrated financial markets. The political impossibility of promoting branching, which would have diminished the role of correspondent banks and conferred a larger role on the Federal Reserve banks, represents the true failure of reform to change the system. The preservation and perpetuation of unit banking and the essential structure and functioning of the pre-1914 banking system were primarily attributable to the political power of the smaller unit banks. In spite of this, the Federal Reserve did manage to evolve from a clearinghouse type of institution operating on the principles of the real bills doctrine toward a central bank with discretionary powers; but, owing to conceptual constraints, the transformation was incomplete.

[128] Wicker, *Federal Reserve Monetary Policy*, p. ix.

3

The Dual Banking System in the Early Years of the Federal Reserve System, 1914–1929

The Survival of the Dual Banking System

THE DECLINE in the membership of the National Banking System after 1900 deeply concerned banking reformers, and it served to direct their efforts to change the banking system. By passing the Federal Reserve Act, Congress hoped to strengthen the system, but no attempt was made to reshape it completely. The dominance of unit banking was not challenged, and the Federal Reserve System was grafted on to the National Banking System. The founders of the Federal Reserve earnestly desired all banks to enter the new system; but, while they required all national banks to join, state-bank membership remained voluntary. This was another victory for the country-bank lobby which had successfully opposed the creation of a European-style central bank and now was assured that the dual banking system would not be dissolved.[1] The struggle between the federal and state authorities to charter

---

[1] Robert Craig West, *Banking Reform and the Federal Reserve, 1863–1923*. For a detailed discussion of the political evolution of the Federal Reserve Act, see chapters 5–7.

and regulate commercial banks was thus inherited by the new system. The willingness of banks to join the federal system continued to depend on the relative costs and benefits of membership. Like its predecessor, the new federal system encountered the greatest difficulty in persuading the smaller unit banks to join. As long as Congress tolerated the chartering and regulation of banks by the states and maintained the legal constraints on the banking structure, the Federal Reserve System was unable to realize anything like nationwide coverage.

The lessons of the National Banking System apparently were not evident to the founders of the Federal Reserve System, who were confident that the new attractions of membership would suffice to induce banks to join. The federal program for banking reform first began to take shape under Senator Nelson W. Aldrich, chairman of the National Monetary Commission. This bipartisan commission had been set up by Congress in the wake of the panic of 1907 to investigate the weaknesses of the American banking system and to explore the operation of other countries' banking systems. Upon completion of the National Monetary Commission's investigation, Aldrich published *A Suggested Plan for Monetary Reform* in January 1911. The Federal Reserve System appeared in embryo form here as a National Reserve Association with membership limited to national banks. Aldrich intended to expand the federal system's coverage of the banking system by creating two new classes of national banks. One new class would be permitted to make loans secured by real estate with lower reserve requirements against time deposits, and the other would be the federal system's equivalent of trust companies with all the privileges the states usually granted these institutions. These changes recognized that excluding national banks from these two types of financial intermediation had caused the federal system to lose ground to the state banking systems. Aldrich's plan would have granted only a few new powers to existing national banks. For these institutions, reserve requirements were to remain the same and branching would still be prohibited. The only substantial concession made to national banks was to allow them to conduct business in foreign countries, a privilege previously limited to trust companies.[2]

This ambitious, but ill-conceived scheme establishing parallel institutions to increase membership in the federal system rather than augmenting the functions of existing ones was changed in the bill presented to Congress that became known as the Aldrich bill. Aldrich and his advisers decided to try to co-opt the existing state institutions.[3] In order not to put the national banks at a disadvantage vis-à-vis state banks and trust companies, the state organizations joining the National Reserve Association were required to meet the same capital and reserve requirements as national banks. All member institutions were to enjoy equal privileges and to be subject to examination by the National Reserve Association. Once a member of the system, a bank could only exit by self-liquidation. Member banks were to be allowed to offer loans on real estate up to 30 percent of time deposits, provided the bank was not in a reserve city; and banks were allowed to organize companies to conduct business in foreign countries.[4] As the restrictions on members of the new federal system were not greatly eased, the authors of the Aldrich bill seem to have put great faith in the National Reserve Association's discounting of commercial paper to attract state institutions.

The election of Woodrow Wilson and a Democratic Congress in 1912 killed any chance for the passage of the Republican Aldrich bill. Yet this change in government did not

[2] Nelson W. Aldrich, *A Suggested Plan for Monetary Reform.*
[3] West, *Banking Reform*, pp. 70–72.
[4] Ibid., pp. 75–79.

substantially alter the direction of banking reform. In spite of the Democrats' condemnation of Republican plans, the Federal Reserve Act drew heavily on the Aldrich bill. Provisions for discounting and organization were similar, except that the Federal Reserve System rejected the idea of a centralized system of regional banks under the authority of its shareholding bankers in favor of an apparently more decentralized system subject to the control of the federal government.[5] Banking reform's new congressional steward was Representative Carter Glass, chairman of the House Committee on Banking and Currency. The new Democratic majority was also interested in securing as large a membership as possible for the new system. The new plans for reform required state banks and trust companies joining the system to comply with national-bank capital and reserve requirements. Reserve requirements on demand deposits for all member banks were reduced from the levels prescribed in the National Banking Act to 18 percent for central-reserve-city banks, 15 percent for reserve-city banks, 12 percent for country banks, and 5 percent on time deposits for all classes of banks. After an interim period, these reserves were to be kept on deposit without interest at the Federal Reserve banks. The powers of the national banks were expanded to maintain the membership of the National Banking System within the Federal Reserve. To the consternation of trust companies and state banks, national banks were permitted to act as trustees, executors, and administrators of stocks and bonds, and to receive savings deposits subject to a 5 percent reserve requirement.[6]

While the banking community had, for the most part, given its approval to the Aldrich Plan, they attacked the Glass bill.

[5] Ibid., chapters 5 and 6.
[6] Charles S. Tippetts, *State Banks and the Federal Reserve System*, p. 22. For a more detailed account of the act's provision, see the section on the Federal Reserve Act in Chapter 2.

The American Bankers Association and the state banking associations objected that the Federal Reserve System allowed for too much government interference and diminished the influence of member bankers. Although they gave bankers an opportunity to voice their objections, the bill's Democratic sponsors ignored them and made no changes in the Federal Reserve Act. It became law on December 23, 1913.[7]

The founders of the Federal Reserve System were certain that its success would depend on the entry of all banks. Benjamin Strong, president of the New York Federal Reserve Bank, was adamant: "No reform of the banking methods in this country will be complete and satisfactory until it includes all banks."[8] Conscious that the state banks and trust companies were suspicious of the new federal system, the Federal Reserve Board drew up specific regulations for state members with an eye to allaying these fears. State institutions entering the system were allowed to exercise their charter rights so long as they did not conflict with the provisions of the Federal Reserve Act, and they were allowed to withdraw upon twelve months' written notice.[9]

In spite of warnings from the banking community, the authors of the Federal Reserve Act were confident that the new system would draw the state institutions into its fold. This belief was rudely shattered by the almost universal refusal of state banks and trust companies to join. The additional privileges given to national banks led few state institutions to take out national charters. Fewer state banks took out affiliate status. By June 1917, only fifty-three state-chartered firms had entered the system. This was disappointing, and the subsequent fortunes of the dual banking system, registered in the changing allegiances of banks, are presented in Table 3.1.

[7] Ibid., pp. 22–38.
[8] Lester V. Chandler, *Benjamin Strong, Central Banker*, p. 80.
[9] Tippetts, *State Banks*, pp. 41–45.

Surveying the problem in 1915, the New York Federal Reserve agent wrote:

> Many of the banks in large cities are unable to take full advantage of the lowered reserve requirements, but in spite of the loss of interest on their reserve balance, most of them understand what the system in its larger aspects means for American banking and generally give it their support. While the same may be said of many of the country banks, yet it is among the country banks as a class that most of the apathy and hostility to the Federal Reserve System which still persists is found. Their opportunities and earnings are relatively small, and in order to live they must figure closely. They feel the loss of interest on reserve deposits; the absence, as yet, of dividends on their capital contribution; and the prospective loss or decrease of the exchange they generally charge on remitting checks drawn upon them . . . they believe that they will, in fact, be required to carry even larger reserves than heretofore in order to obtain collection services for notes, drafts and nonmember bank checks and the various other services now rendered by their reserve agents. . . . Few of them, as yet, conceive of the reserve bank as their active reserve agent performing all the services which go with the relationship. . . . The rediscounting privilege has been little availed of and the larger functions of the Federal Reserve System, such as influencing domestic rates and international gold movements through the development of a discount market and by dealing in foreign bills appear remote from their spheres of activity. They feel that the system has few advantages to offer in return for the cost it entails upon them.[10]

The Federal Reserve agent pinpointed the major problem facing the Federal Reserve in its pursuit of universal membership—its inability to attract small, mostly rural, banks.

Lacking the support of the American Bankers Association and other banking associations, the Federal Reserve System was greeted with suspicion by state bankers. Although some state bankers supported the system, there were many who raised their voice against it. At the 1916 meeting of the Iowa

[10] Board of Governors of the Federal Reserve System, *Annual Report*, 1915, pp. 178–179.

Table 3.1
The Dual Banking System, 1914–1929

Year	National Banks		State-Chartered Member Banks		State-Chartered Nonmember Banks	
	Number	Total Deposits (in millions of dollars)	Number	Total Deposits (in millions of dollars)	Number	Total Deposits (in millions of dollars)
1914	7,518	8,560	0	0	17,992	8,830
1915	7,597	8,817	17	77	18,260	9,099
1916	7,571	10,872	34	261	18,611	10,946
1917	7,599	12,767	53	629	19,178	12,488
1918	7,699	14,015	513	4,939	19,244	9,030
1919	7,779	15,935	1,042	6,897	19,037	9,906
1920	8,024	17,159	1,374	8,242	19,688	10,713
1921	8,150	15,142	1,595	8,208	20,043	9,637
1922	8,244	16,323	1,648	9,224	19,566	9,558
1923	8,236	16,899	1,620	10,189	19,345	10,637
1924	8,080	18,349	1,570	11,217	18,722	11,090
1925	8,066	19,912	1,472	12,456	18,320	12,095
1926	7,972	20,644	1,403	13,118	17,860	12,491
1927	7,790	21,778	1,309	13,615	17,050	12,388
1928	7,685	22,645	1,244	13,405	16,401	13,165
1929	7,530	21,586	1,177	14,279	15,797	13,170

SOURCES: Board of Governors of the Federal Reserve System, *All Bank Statistics, United States, 1896–1955*, pp. 39–41. Board of Governors of the Federal Reserve System, *Banking and Monetary Statistics, 1914–1941*, pp. 22–23.
NOTE: All figures are for June 30.

Bankers Association, the president of the association warned: "I believe I am not suggesting anything out of the way in saying that the state and savings banks of this state, should they ever desire or feel that they should belong to the Federal Reserve bank, would find it a great mistake and a calamity for them."[11] This opposition was not confined to the financial hinterland. The editor of the *Financial Age* of New York City, F. Howard Hooke, who traveled to the same convention told the assembled bankers that the Federal Reserve Act was "fundamentally unsound, structurally wrong and unpracticable in its operation."[12]

Above all what state bankers feared were the additional powers of examination and control granted to the Federal Reserve Board and the Comptroller of the Currency. Comptroller John Skelton Williams was arrogant and high-handed in his conduct, belittling the state banks and pushing for forced nationalization of all state banks. The president of the American Bankers Association attacked the Federal Reserve Act for conferring "upon one of our government officials an extraordinary power and discretion, unwarranted by the spirit of our institutions and repugnant to republican principles."[13]

In this climate of opinion, it was not surprising that relatively few state banks and trust companies were persuaded to join the federal system. It appears that the close ties between city correspondents and country banks tended to inhibit the latter from joining. The city correspondents feared a loss of business in clearing operations and loans to banks in their hinterlands and often advised country banks not to enter the new system. Furthermore, the principal advantage of membership touted by the Federal Reserve, discounting, did not attract many country bankers, who often lacked the eligible paper. In the relatively easy credit conditions preceding and

---

[11] Howard H. Preston, *History of Banking in Iowa*, p. 209.
[12] Ibid., pp. 209–210.
[13] Tippetts, *State Banks*, p. 66.

during World War I, most banks found it easy to borrow when necessary from their city correspondents.[14] A few far-sighted individuals recognized that in spite of the prohibition on member-bank borrowing for nonmembers, as long as banks could borrow from correspondents who were members of the Federal Reserve, membership was not essential to obtain the benefits of the discount window.[15]

The Guaranty Trust Company of New York conducted a nationwide investigation of country banks' complaints in 1916. At the top of the list were objections that the subscription to Federal Reserve stock and the required reserves on which no interest was paid were both too high.[16] The state legislatures abetted their chartered institutions' hesitancy by only gradually granting permission to join the Federal Reserve System. Without state legislation or a favorable judicial ruling, state banks and trust companies were not allowed to count reserves at the Federal Reserve banks toward meeting state requirements. By the end of 1915, only twenty-five state legislatures had passed the necessary legislation.[17]

Concerned that the success of the Federal Reserve System depended on a broad membership, some officials considered legal compulsion. In his private correspondence, Benjamin Strong recommended this course of action to Pierre Jay in 1916: "After the state institutions [have] been given every opportunity to form their own judgment of the System, if they then do not take membership, I think the Federal Reserve Board and the Federal Reserve Banks should join in asking Congress to force them in."[18]

Under pressure from the American Bankers Association to

[14] Ibid., pp. 70–75.
[15] Ibid., p. 24. Charles Conant's testimony to the House Committee on Banking and Currency makes this point.
[16] Ibid., pp. 77–100.
[17] Ibid., p. 87.
[18] Chandler, *Benjamin Strong*, pp. 81–82.

make membership more acceptable, the Federal Reserve Board proved to be more conciliatory. The first step in this direction was the Act of September 7, 1916. This authorized the Federal Reserve banks to receive on deposit from member banks all checks and drafts that were payable on presentation, thus extending the clearing and collection system. It also allowed the Federal Reserve Board to permit member banks to carry in the Federal Reserve banks any portion of reserves required to be held in their own vaults, and restrictions on discounting agricultural, livestock, and two-name paper were eased.[19]

Major revisions in the Federal Reserve Act were enacted in an amendment of June 21, 1917, which removed many of the state institutions' objections. State members could now leave the Federal Reserve with only six months' notice, and the amount of Federal Reserve stock that could be canceled in any one year was raised from 10 to 25 percent. State banks and trust companies were to retain their full charter and statutory rights under state law upon entrance, giving legal affirmation to the Federal Reserve Board's 1915 regulations. The Federal Reserve Act imposed on state member banks the national-bank restrictions on the amount that could be lent to any firm or corporation. The 1917 amendment allowed state institutions to offer loans of more than 10 percent of capital and surplus, but then prohibited Federal Reserve banks from rediscounting the paper of any bank that was liable for an amount greater than 10 percent of its capital or surplus. The Comptroller also lost the right to examine state members, who, thereafter, were subject only to examination by the Federal Reserve Board or their Federal Reserve banks. Perhaps the most significant change affecting the attractiveness of Federal Reserve membership was the reduction of required reserves. National and state member country banks were now required to hold 7 percent of demand deposits on reserve at

19 Tippetts, *State Banks*, pp. 106–107.

the Federal Reserve (not in their vaults); reserve-city banks, 10 percent, and central-reserve-city banks, 13 percent. The reserve requirement for all classes of banks on time deposits was reduced to 3 percent. The Federal Reserve Board argued that, with the passage of this act, the major objections to state membership had been removed.[20]

The effects of the 1917 amendment are difficult to discern. The United States' entry into World War I was accompanied by a big drive urging state banks to join the system. Although no other major legislative alterations were enacted, there was an intense patriotic appeal. The American Bankers Association, which had previously kept its distance from the Federal Reserve System, now pleaded with its members to join and thereby strengthen the nation's financial system. The Iowa Bankers Association, whose officers had roundly condemned the system a few years before, now praised the Federal Reserve as a "proven tower of strength to the nation," invited Federal Reserve Governor W.P.G. Harding to its convention, and urged its members to join.[21]

Beginning in 1918, a substantial number of state institutions joined the Federal Reserve System, as can be seen in Table 3.1. Between 1917 and 1919, the number of member state banks and trust companies rose from 53 with deposits of $629 million to 1,042 with deposits of $6,897 million; while non-members fell in number from 19,178 to 19,037, with their deposits declining from $12,488 million to $9,906 million. This was still only a partial success. The country bankers, for the most part, did not find the Federal Reserve noticeably more attractive. Typical of the opinion of small-town bankers were the sentiments voiced by a Tennessee banker at the American Bankers Association in November 1917: "I do not think it is any more necessary for me to join the Federal Reserve System to show my patriotism than it is for me to go

[20] Ibid., pp. 108–114.
[21] Preston, *History of Banking in Iowa*, pp. 211–212.

down to one of these hotels and let them charge me three and a half dollars for a plate of soup."[22] Moreover, many states kept in place the legal obstructions that prevented state banks from joining. By 1919, no enabling legislation had yet been passed by the legislatures of Alabama, Arizona, Arkansas, Colorado, Delaware, Illinois, Indiana, Kansas, Maryland, North Carolina, Oklahoma, Tennessee, Utah, Vermont, West Virginia, and Wyoming.[23]

Although patriotism may have moved some banks to join the Federal Reserve, increased enrollment after World War I suggests that the amendments to the Federal Reserve Act had made membership more attractive. After the war, all the Federal Reserve banks campaigned vigorously to increase their membership, publishing testimonials of satisfied banks. The slump of 1919–1920 provided further proof of the value of membership, as member banks found it easy to borrow at the Federal Reserve banks when credit was tight.[24] State members grew in number from 1,042 in 1919 to 1,648 in 1922, and their deposits swelled from $6,897 million to $9,224 million. Nonmembers, who numbered 19,037 in 1919, increased slightly to 19,566 in 1922; however, their total deposits declined from $9,906 million to $9,558 million. Total deposits in 1922 were almost equal for members and nonmembers, indicating that the campaign to augment membership had been most successful among the largest state banks.

The years 1921–1922 marked the high point for the number of commercial banking institutions and for the rapid growth of the Federal Reserve System. After this time, the total number of banks began to decline. The admission of banks to the Federal Reserve System dropped off, and banks began to withdraw from the system.

Throughout the 1920s, the banking system continued to

[22] Tippetts, *State Banks*, p. 118.
[23] Ibid., pp. 132–133.
[24] Ibid., pp. 139–145.

grow. Its assets rose, but the number of banks declined. Between 1920 and 1929, the number of national banks fell from 8,024 to 7,530, a decline of 6.2 percent, even as total national bank deposits rose 25.8 percent. In the same period, state members of the Federal Reserve System fell in number from 1,374 to 1,177, or 14.3 percent, while their deposits rose 73.2 percent. Nonmember banks fell in number from 19,688 to 15,797, a decline of 19.8 percent, with total deposits rising 22.9 percent. The relative positions of these three classes of commercial banks were also altered. In 1920, national banks represented 27.8 percent of all commercial banks, with 47.5 percent of all deposits; state members 5.1 percent, with 22.8 percent of deposits; and nonmembers 67.1 percent, with 29.7 percent of all commercial-bank deposits. By 1929, national banks represented 31.2 percent of the institutions, with 44.0 percent of deposits; state members 4.7 percent of the banks, with 29.1 percent of deposits; and nonmembers 64.0 percent of the banks, with 26.9 percent of deposits. The Federal Reserve System appears to have gained little ground in this period, as the percentage of banks and deposits outside the system declined while that of member banks rose from 32.1 to 36.0 percent, and their deposits increased from 70.3 to 73.1 percent. The Federal Reserve remained deeply concerned about its membership. Its relative gains are attributable more to the greater weakness of nonmember banks than to its own strength. Until 1921, the number of banks in the United States had been growing; but, after that date, the number of nonmember banks began to decrease. Two years later, the number of state member and national banks began to fall as well, a trend that continued through the 1920s.

The sources of change in the bank population are presented in Table 3.2. The greatest sources of decline in the number of banks were suspension and voluntary liquidation. These accounted for 41.1, 27.8, and 58.1 percent of the decrease in national, state member, and nonmember banks respectively.

Table 3.2
Sources of Change in the Number of National and State Banks, 1920–1929

	Number	%
National Banks		
Total increase	*1,419*	*100.0*
New banks	817	57.6
Converted from state membership	144	10.1
Converted nonmember banks	365	25.7
Other	93	6.6
Total decrease	*2,140*	*100.0*
Suspensions and voluntary liquidations	879	41.1
Consolidations and absorptions	1,104	51.6
Converted to state membership	22	1.0
Converted to nonmember banks	135	6.3
State Members of the Federal Reserve		
Total increase	*624*	*100.0*
Admission of nonmembers	566	90.7
Converted from national banks	22	3.5
Other	36	5.8
Total decrease	*986*	*100.0*
Suspensions and voluntary liquidations	274	27.8
Consolidations and absorptions	270	27.4
Converted to national banks	144	14.6
State bank withdrawals	298	30.2
State-Chartered Nonmember Banks		
Total increase	*3,931*	*100.0*
New banks	2,680	68.2
Converted from national banks	135	3.4
State bank withdrawals	298	7.6
Other	818	20.8
Total decrease	*8,359*	*100.0*
Suspensions and voluntary liquidations	4,855	58.1
Consolidations and absorptions	2,589	31.0
Converted to national banks	349	4.2
State banks joining the Federal Reserve	566	6.7

SOURCE: Board of Governors of the Federal Reserve System, *Banking and Monetary Statistics, 1914–1941*, pp. 52–53.

Consolidations and absorptions led to decreases for each class of banks of 51.6, 27.4, and 31.0 percent. Consolidations and absorptions were primarily a means by which banks acquired branches. These changes therefore constituted no loss, in terms of assets, to the banking system. If these are eliminated as a source of decrease, and assuming the banks so amalgamated would have stayed within the system, national banks actually increased by 383, or 4.7 percent, state members fell by 92, or 6.2 percent, and nonmembers declined by 1,839, or 9.4 percent. The small gains of the Federal Reserve System appear then to be attributable to the higher rates of suspension and voluntary liquidation among nonmembers. The failing commercial banks were mostly located in the West and the South where the deepening agricultural depression closed many banks. Although more national and state member banks were dissolved in these areas of the country, nonmembers suffered the most as they were more often small banks heavily engaged in loans on real estate. In the period 1920–1929, 30 nonmember banks with deposits of $66 million closed in the Northeast, 308 with deposits of $101 million in the Midwest, and 85 with deposits of $36 million in the Pacific states. In the South 1,468 banks with deposits of $358 million went out of operation, and 2,525 in the West with deposits of $514 million closed their doors. Deposits lost to national banks, $361 million, and state members, $127 million, were less than the total loss to nonmembers of $1,078 million.[25] The decline of nonmembers attributable to banks joining the Federal Reserve System, 915, was small in relation to the number, 4,855, that closed by suspension and liquidation.

The Federal Reserve found to its dismay that new banks still preferred to take out state charters, and relatively few of them joined the federal system. Between 1920 and 1929, 2,680 banks took out state charters, representing 68.2 percent of the total increase in banks. This includes 244 existing private banks, whose numbers continued to decline from 799 with assets of $213 million to 291 with $156 million of assets.[26]

[25] Board of Governors of the Federal Reserve System, *Banking and Monetary Statistics, 1914–1941*, pp. 286–289.

[26] U. S. Comptroller of the Currency, *Annual Report*, 1920–1929. The figures are for June 30.

This decline may be traced to the continued pressure of state legislatures to force them to enter the state banking systems. By January 1919, sixteen states required private banks to submit to the same regulations and supervision as state banks; and many other states applied other types of coercion.[27]

The Federal Reserve System did not match the attractions offered to new banks by the state systems. There were 365 conversions of state and private banks to national charters and 817 new formations. The system also lost 298 state members that withdrew and 135 national banks that took out state charters to leave. The Federal Reserve System had lost its early momentum and was not succeeding in attracting new members or reducing the size of the state banking systems.

The Federal Reserve's inability to entice state institutions to join was a consequence of the federal system's continuing struggle with the state legislatures for control and regulation of banks. Many state legislatures responded to the Federal Reserve Act's easing of restrictions on national banks by lowering requirements to retain their hold on state banks. The federal regulatory authorities were put in a difficult position. In order to draw state institutions into the new system, they had, while compelling national banks to join, made the terms of entry more generous for state banks and trust companies. To overcome the state institutions' opposition to membership in the 1920s, the obvious option was to dilute the entrance requirements. However, if the reduced requirements were not also applied to national banks, there was a danger that they would abandon their national charters.

Reserve Requirements

The rivalry between Congress and the state legislatures is most clearly seen in the determination of reserve requirements. The Federal Reserve Act substantially reduced reserve

[27] Preston, *History of Banking in Iowa*, p. 167.

requirements and eliminated the right to let balances held
with correspondent banks serve as legal reserves. The lowered
requirements were intended to enhance the attractiveness of
membership, preserve the hierarchy of the National Banking
System, and reduce correspondent balances. The greatest gain
for member banks was in the differentiation between demand
and time deposits which previously had been lumped together. According to the National Monetary Commission's
survey of 1909, many states already distinguished between
these two types of deposits. Thirty states either did not require
reserves to be held against time deposits or set them lower
than the National Banking Act's 15 percent.[28] This undoubtedly played a part in determining what liabilities different
banks issued. In 1910 national banks held 14 percent of their
total deposits as time deposits, while state banks held 37 percent. In his study of state banks and the Federal Reserve
System, Charles Tippetts noted that after the passage of the
Federal Reserve Act, there was an effort by large banks to
persuade their customers, especially large businesses, to hold
time instead of demand deposits in order to gain the benefits
of the reduced reserve requirements.[29] By 1925, the proportion of time deposits that both held had risen; the gap had
narrowed a little, with national banks holding 30 percent and
state banks 47 percent of their total deposits as time deposits.[30]

Aware of the implications of the Federal Reserve Act for
membership in the state-chartered banking systems, state legislatures reacted quickly, and by 1915 fifteen states had lowered their reserve requirements. The Federal Reserve Board
was naturally upset by this trend which reduced the attractiveness of membership. In its *Annual Report* for 1915 it mor-
alized:

[28] Samuel A. Welldon, *Digest of State Banking Statutes*, Tables A, B, and C.
[29] Tippetts, *State Banks*, pp. 232–233.
[30] Board of Governors of the Federal Reserve System, *All Bank Statistics,
United States, 1896–1955*, pp. 35–45.

It is unfortunate that in some of the states reserve requirements have been materially lowered by legislative enactment since the adoption of the Federal Reserve Act. . . . This is an element of danger in the banking system, because weakening of the reserves of state banks and trust companies makes them more vulnerable in times of emergency. . . . The Board is firmly of the opinion that the states themselves should, instead of permitting a reduction in the reserves of State banks and trust companies, require them to maintain reserves higher than the reserves of national banks. . . . It is scarcely necessary to say that the credit resources of the country would be greatly enlarged and strengthened with corresponding benefit to business and to all the people of the country were the State banks and trust companies joined together with national banks in the homogeneous and well-organized bank system provided by the Federal Reserve Act.[31]

The changes in state reserve requirements after the passage of the Federal Reserve Act can be seen in Table 3.3. By 1917, every state except South Carolina required its chartered banks to hold some minimum portion of deposits as reserves. Between 1910 and 1917, when the Federal Reserve reduced its requirements, many states added reserve requirements to their statute books for the first time. Their requirements were, on the whole, higher for country banks; but the onus was substantially reduced as all states allowed banks to continue to hold a sizable fraction of their reserves in interest-bearing deposits with reserve agents. Many banks apparently considered this one of the main benefits of remaining outside the Federal Reserve, and the refusal of the Federal Reserve to pay interest on reserves was frequently cited as one of the major reasons banks were reluctant to join the system.[32]

The trend toward lowering state requirements continued, and by 1928 twelve states had again reduced their requirements. Only three states moved in the other direction. South

[31] Board of Governors of the Federal Reserve System, *Annual Report*, 1915, pp. 13–14.
[32] Tippetts, *State Banks*, pp. 208 ff.

Table 3.3
Legal Reserve Requirements, 1909–1929

	Year Effective	Country Bank		Reserve-City Bank		Central-Reserve-City Bank	
		Demand Deposits	Time Deposits	Demand Deposits	Time Deposits	Demand Deposits	Time Deposits
National Banks	1909	15 (3/5)	15 (3/5)	25 (1/2)	25 (1/2)	25 (0)	25 (0)
Federal Reserve Member Banks	1913	12 (0)	5 (0)	15 (0)	5 (0)	18 (0)	5 (0)
	1917	7 (0)	3 (0)	10 (0)	3 (0)	13 (0)	3 (0)

	Year Effective	Country Bank		Reserve Agent		Central Reserve Agent	
		Demand Deposits	Time Deposits	Demand Deposits	Time Deposits	Demand Deposits	Time Deposits
Nonmember Banks							
Alabama	1909	15 (3/5)	none	designated	none	—	—
Arizona	1909	15 (3/5)	15 (3/5)	designated	designated	—	—
	1922	15 (2/3)	15 (2/3)	20 (2/3)	20 (2/3)	—	—
Arkansas	1909	none	none	none	none	—	—
	1913	15 (any)	15 (any)	20 (3/5)	20 (3/5)	—	—
California	1909	15 (3/5)	15 (3/5)	20 (3/5)	20 (3/5)	—	—
	1915	12 (2/3)	12 (2/3)	15 (2/3)	15 (2/3)	18 (2/3)	18 (2/3)
Colorado	1909	none	none	none	none	—	—
	1915	20 (4/5)	20 (4/5)	25 (4/5)	25 (4/5)	—	—
Connecticut	1909	15 (11/15)	none	designated	designated	—	—
Delaware	1909	10 (2/3)	10 (2/3)	15 (2/3)	15 (2/3)	—	—
	1921	10 (2/3)	5 (2/3)	10 (2/3)	5 (2/3)	—	—
Florida	1909	20 (3/5)	20 (3/5)	designated	designated	—	—

State	Year						
Georgia	1909	25 (all)	none	designated	none	—	—
Idaho	1920	15 (all)	5 (all)	designated	designated	—	—
	1909	15 (1/2)	15 (1/2)	designated	designated	—	—
	1915	15 (3/5)	15 (3/5)	designated	designated	—	—
	1919	15 (4/5)	15 (4/5)	designated	designated	—	—
Illinois	1909	15 (3/5)	15 (3/5)	25 (1/2)	25 (1/2)	—	—
	1924	15 (any)	15 (any)	15 (any)	15 (any)	—	—
Indiana	1909	15 (any)	15 (any)	designated	designated	—	—
	1917	12.5 (any)	12.5 (any)	12.5 (any)	12.5 (any)	—	—
Iowa	1909	none	none	none	none	—	—
State banks	1915	10 (3/4)	10 (3/4)	15 (3/4)	15 (3/4)	—	—
Trust cos.	1915	15 (3/4)	8 (3/4)	20 (3/4)	8 (3/4)	—	—
All firms	1924	15 (17/20)	8 (17/20)	20 (17/20)	8 (17/20)	—	—
Kansas	1909	20 (3/4)	20 (3/4)	25 (3/5)	25 (3/4)	—	—
State banks	1915	12 (8/12)	5 (8/12)	15 (10/15)	5 (10/15)	—	—
Trust cos.	1915	25 (8/12)	10 (8/12)	25 (8/12)	10 (8/12)	—	—
State banks	1919	7 (8/12)	3 (8/12)	10 (10/15)	3 (10/15)	—	—
State banks	1927	15 (1/2)	5 (1/2)	25 (8/12)	10 (8/12)	—	—
Kentucky	1909	15 (1/3)	none	25 (1/3)	none	—	—
	1914	12 (2/3)	5 (2/3)	15 (2/3)	5 (2/3)	—	—
	1924	7 (2/3)	3 (2/3)	10 (2/3)	3 (2/3)	13 (2/3)	3 (2/3)
Louisiana	1909	25 (8/25)	none	designated	none	—	—
	1915	20 (7/10)	none	designated	none	—	—
Maine	1909	15 (2/3)	none	designated	none	—	—
Maryland	1909	none	none	none	none	—	—
Massachusetts	1915	15 (2/3)	none	designated	none	—	—
	1909	15 (3/5)	none	15 (1/2)	none	—	—
	1915	15 (3/5)	none	20 (1/2)	none	—	—

Table 3.3 (cont.)

		Country Bank		Reserve Agent		Central Reserve Agent	
		Demand Deposits	Time Deposits	Demand Deposits	Time Deposits	Demand Deposits	Time Deposits
Michigan	1909	20 (3/4)	20 (3/5)	designated	designated	—	—
	1915	15 (1/2)	15 (1/2)	20 (1/2)	20 (1/2)	—	—
	1921	12 (1/2)	12 (1/2)	20 (1/2)	20 (1/2)	—	—
Minnesota	1909	20 (1/2)	20 (1/2)	designated	designated	—	—
	1915	12 (3/4)	5 (3/4)	15 (3/4)	5 (3/4)	—	—
Mississippi	1909	none	none	none	none	—	—
	1915	15 (any)	7 (any)	25 (any)	10 (any)	—	—
Missouri	1909	15 (any)	none	designated	none	—	—
State banks	1915	15 (3/5)	none	15 (3/5)	none	—	—
Trust cos.	1915	15 (3/5)	none	18 (11/18)	none	—	—
All firms	1927	15 (4/5)	3 (any)	15 (3/5)	3 (any)	18 (11/15)	3 (any)
Montana	1909	15 (any)	15 (any)	25 (any)	25 (any)	—	—
	1921	10 (any)	10 (any)	15 (any)	15 (any)	—	—
Nebraska	1909	15 (3/5)	15 (3/5)	20 (3/5)	20 (3/5)	—	—
	1915	15 (2/3)	15 (2/3)	20 (2/3)	20 (2/3)	—	—
Nevada	1909	15 (2/3)	15 (2/3)	25 (2/3)	25 (2/3)	—	—
New Hampshire	1909	none	none	none	none	—	—
	1915	15 (2/3)	15 (2/3)	15 (2/3)	15 (2/3)	—	—
New Jersey							
State banks	1909	15 (3/5)	none	15 (3/5)	none	—	—
Trust cos.	1909	15 (4/5)	none	15 (4/5)	none	—	—
New Mexico	1909	15 (3/5)	15 (3/5)	15 (3/5)	15 (3/5)	—	—
	1915	12 (3/5)	12 (3/5)	12 (3/5)	12 (3/5)	—	—

	Year						
New York							
State banks	1909	15 (3/5)	none	20 (1/2)	none	25 (2/5)	none
Trust cos.	1909	10 (6/10)	none	13 (6/13)	none	15 (1/3)	none
State banks	1915	12 (2/3)	none	15 (1/3)	none	18 (1/3)	none
North Carolina	1909	15 (3/5)	5 (3/5)	15 (3/5)	5 (3/5)	—	—
North Dakota	1909	20 (3/5)	10 (3/5)	20 (3/5)	10 (3/5)	—	—
Ohio							
State banks	1909	15 (3/5)	15 (11/15)	15 (3/5)	15 (11/15)	—	—
Trust cos.	1909	15 (3/5)	10 (7/10)	15 (3/5)	10 (7/10)	—	—
Oklahoma	1909	20 (2/3)	20 (2/3)	25 (2/3)	25 (2/3)	—	—
	1915	15 (2/3)	15 (2/3)	20 (2/3)	20 (2/3)	—	—
	1926	15 (2/3)	15 (2/3)	25 (2/3)	25 (2/3)	—	—
Oregon	1909	15 (2/3)	15 (2/3)	25 (2/3)	25 (2/3)	—	—
	1915	15 (2/3)	10 (2/3)	15 (2/3)	10 (2/3)	—	—
	1920	15 (3/4)	10 (3/4)	15 (3/4)	10 (3/4)	—	—
Pennsylvania	1909	15 (2/3)	15 (2/3)	15 (2/3)	15 (2/3)	—	—
	1915	15 (2/3)	7.5 (2/3)	15 (2/3)	7.5 (2/3)	—	—
Rhode Island	1909	15 (3/5)	15 (3/5)	25 (3/5)	25 (3/5)	—	—
South Carolina	1909	none	none	none	none	—	—
	1922	7 (any)	3 (any)	7 (any)	3 (any)	—	—
South Dakota	1909	20 (1/2)	20 (1/2)	25 (1/2)	25 (1/2)	—	—
	1917	17.5 (any)	17.5 (any)	20 (any)	20 (any)	—	—
Tennessee	1909	none	none	none	none	—	—
	1915	10 (any)	none	10 (any)	none	—	—
	1927	10 (any)	3 (any)	10 (any)	3 (any)	—	—
Texas	1909	25 (1/3)	25 (1/3)	25 (1/3)	25 (1/3)	—	—
	1914	15 (3/5)	15 (3/5)	20 (3/5)	20 (3/5)	—	—

Table 3.3 (*cont.*)

		Country Bank		Reserve Agent		Central Reserve Agent	
		Demand Deposits	*Time Deposits*	*Demand Deposits*	*Time Deposits*	*Demand Deposits*	*Time Deposits*
Utah	1909	15 (any)	15 (any)	20 (any)	20 (any)	—	—
	1915	15 (7/8)	15 (7/8)	20 (7/8)	20 (7/8)	—	—
Vermont	1909	none	none	none	none	—	—
	1915	15 (2/5)	3 (2/5)	15 (2/5)	3 (2/5)	—	—
Virginia	1909	15 (3/5)	15 (3/5)	15 (3/5)	15 (3/5)	—	—
	1915	12 (7/12)	5 (7/12)	12 (7/12)	5 (7/12)	—	—
	1924	10 (any)	3 (any)	10 (any)	3 (any)	—	—
Washington	1909	20 (any)	20 (any)	20 (any)	20 (any)	—	—
	1915	15 (any)	15 (any)	15 (any)	15 (any)	—	—
West Virginia	1909	15 (3/5)	none	15 (3/5)	none	—	—
	1925	10 (4/5)	5 (4/5)	10 (4/5)	5 (4/5)	—	—
Wisconsin	1909	15 (any)	15 (any)	25 (any)	25 (any)	—	—
	1915	12 (any)	12 (any)	20 (any)	20 (any)	—	—
Wyoming	1909	none	none	none	none	—	—
	1915	20 (any)	10 (any)	20 (any)	10 (any)	—	—

SOURCES: George Barnett, *State Banks and Trust Companies since the Passage of the National-Bank Act.* Board of Governors of the Federal Reserve System, *Annual Report,* 1915, pp. 104–113. Board of Governors of the Federal Reserve System, *Federal Reserve Bulletin,* 4 (October 1917), pp. 768–795, 10 (March 1924), pp. 154–181, 14 (November 1928), pp. 778–805.
NOTE: Reserve requirements are in percentages. The number in parentheses is the portion of reserves that could be held on deposit with reserve agents.

Carolina finally imposed its first reserve requirements, Arizona raised its requirements for reserve-city banks, and Tennessee increased the requirements for time deposits. By lowering reserve requirements, the Federal Reserve had hoped to draw more state-chartered institutions into the federal system, but the states' reduction of reserve requirements served to undermine these efforts. The overall effect may have been, in many instances, to set reserve requirements below the level that banks would have held had regulation not imposed any requirements. Further obstruction to the drive for members came from the refusal of fifteen states to pass legislation allowing state banks to count as vault cash for state requirements their deposits at the Federal Reserve banks, creating an additional burden for state member banks in these states.[33]

Correspondent Banking and the Discount Window

The Federal Reserve was also partly frustrated in its attempt to reduce the role of correspondent banks and lower the volume of correspondent balances. Federal Reserve banks were supposed to take over the two primary functions of city correspondents. They were charged with offering short-term loans to country banks and developing a nationwide mechanism for clearing payments between banks. Discounting was to provide banks with a new source of credit, and each Federal Reserve bank was to become a clearinghouse for its members, with the clearances between Federal Reserve banks being settled through the Gold Settlement Fund. The replacement of private institutions by government-organized ones was intended to strengthen the financial system, eliminating the pyramiding of reserves.[34]

[33] Ibid., p. 234. These states were Connecticut, Florida, Illinois, Indiana, Kansas, Kentucky, Louisiana, Minnesota, Nebraska, North Dakota, Oklahoma, Rhode Island, South Dakota, Virginia, and Wyoming.

[34] See "Correspondent Banking before the Federal Reserve Act" in Chapter 2 for a more detailed discussion of this point.

The Federal Reserve's clearing system failed to dislodge the correspondent banks from their position of eminence in the banking system. Member banks were required to transfer only their legal reserves to Federal Reserve banks, and they were free to continue holding correspondent balances. Nonmember banks and trust companies were, of course, unaffected. One provision of the Federal Reserve Act was designed to ensure the eminence of member banks as correspondents. This permitted no member institution to carry deposits greater than 10 percent of its capital and surplus with any nonmember bank. The Federal Reserve Board interpreted this provision very strictly, declaring that items sent by a member to a nonmember for collection must be considered as on deposit. This meant effectively that only member banks could serve as correspondents for member banks. Partly as a consequence of this and the established prominence of member banks in financial centers, approximately 90 percent of all bankers' balances were held in member banks.[35]

The efforts of the founders of the Federal Reserve System to have the Federal Reserve banks absorb the functions of the correspondents was partially undermined by the need to make joining the system more attractive. The substantial lowering of reserve requirements for all classes of banks and the distinction between demand and time deposits set off a large expansion of deposits that prevented an abrupt dissolution of correspondent relations. Leonard Watkins, in his study *Bankers Balances*, observed that "had reserve requirements remained unchanged, the shifting would most certainly have contributed to a heavy reduction in the reserve part of the balances."[36]

Similarly, the opening of the Federal Reserve's discount window did have an important impact on the pattern of in-

[35] Tippetts, *State Banks*, p. 201.
[36] Leonard L. Watkins, *Bankers' Balances*, p. 83.

terbank borrowing, but it did not entirely remove correspondent banks from the picture. Discounting was supposed to have attracted banks to the federal system; yet, as argued in Chapter 2, banks did not have to join to gain access to funds from the discount window when they could borrow from other banks who were members. The banks in New York City and other major financial centers could borrow from the Federal Reserve. Once in a more liquid position, they could offer loans to nonmembers. This intermediation was particularly important for the smaller, more rural banks who lacked the eligible paper required for discounting at the Federal Reserve banks.[37]

The exclusion of many country banks from direct access to the discount window concerned Congress. On the basis of evidence presented by the joint commission studying the problems of agriculture and agricultural credit, Congress passed the Agricultural Credits Act in 1923. This act attempted to make membership more attractive to country banks and to put the remaining nonmembers at a greater disadvantage. In an effort to broaden the definition of eligible paper to include high-quality agricultural paper, the act extended the limit of maturity of notes, drafts, and bills of exchange for agricultural products and livestock eligible for rediscount at Federal Reserve banks from six to nine months. The act also prohibited the Federal Reserve banks from rediscounting agricultural or livestock paper bearing the signature or endorsement of any nonmember bank that met the Federal Reserve's minimum capital requirements for membership.[38] While the intention was to induce more country banks to join, it is unlikely that the more restrictive clause was very effective, given the fact that banks as intermediaries could easily shuffle their assets and liabilities, taking on the paper themselves and borrowing with their own eligible paper from the Federal Reserve.

[37] Ibid., pp. 187–193.
[38] Ibid., pp. 162–163.

The Federal Reserve Banks and Nonpar Clearing

The Federal Reserve System experienced similar difficulties in its attempt to take over the other primary functions of the correspondent banking system, clearing balances. To replace correspondent banks as the channels for clearing and collection, Federal Reserve banks were to act like regional clearinghouses for their members to settle the claims between banks. The Federal Reserve faced a mammoth task in its efforts to unify the existing piecemeal system of clearing. Correspondent banks that sought to attract funds to invest in the money markets had done so by absorbing collection and exchange charges and offering interest on interbank deposits. At times, the clearinghouses had endeavored to eliminate interest on bankers' balances and exchange charges; but competition for funds caused these efforts to fail. The Federal Reserve also tried to end interest payments and nonpar clearance, which it regarded as costly and wasteful.

Banks that did not clear at par were, in effect, placing a service or exchange charge on the bearers of their checks. For example, a depositor of a downstate Illinois bank paid a Chicago merchant for $1,000 worth of goods with a check. The merchant would deposit the check with his Chicago bank. That city bank would then return the check to the downstate bank which would remit $999 to the city bank while charging its customer's account $1,000. A profit for the country bank would thus be made on this exchange charge. Depending on the customary procedure, the city bank or its customer would bear the cost. Exchange charges were a source of profit to many country banks. City banks sometimes sought to avoid them by remitting checks via circuitous routes to banks that had agreements with the country banks to clear at par. This practice swelled float, or remitted checks in the mails. Items such as these in the process of collection were counted as reserves as soon as they were in the mail, thus reducing the cost of reserves for banks.[39]

The question of nonpar clearance often confused contemporaries, and their arguments often betrayed their origins in heated debate. There are several possible explanations for the banks' desire to continue nonpar clearance apart from the fact that it reduced the burden of reserve requirements. Since the late nineteenth century, banking and financial intermediation had been rapidly developing through the division of labor and specialization of function. Banks that had checks remitted to them charged the remitting banks. This could be done by an explicit price or discount such as an exchange charge or by maintaining an agreed compensating balance on deposit. The latter became standard practice in major cities. Very frequent exchanges among banks led them to hold balances with one another. Banks in the country remitted checks to financial centers more intermittently, and city banks did not hold balances at country banks for the purpose of paying for remitted checks. Therefore, country banks probably preferred an explicit exchange charge. Higher volumes of remittances from distant banks led to specialization in city banks and probably lowered the cost per remitted check. Costs may have been higher for country banks with less specialized facilities. Forcing country banks with infrequent remittances and higher costs to remit at par meant greater costs per check, and this may account for the resistance the Federal Reserve encountered to universal par clearance.[40]

The Federal Reserve banks were quite successful in developing clearinghouse operations and spreading the practice of par clearance. In 1916 there were already 15,679 banks, including nonmembers as well as members, on the Federal Reserve's par list. Any nonmember could use the Federal Reserve's services, but it had to clear at par and pay a small

[39] Ibid., pp. 264–268.
[40] Walter Earl Spahr, *The Clearing and Collection of Checks*, pp. 230 ff.

Table 3.4
Federal Reserve Par List, 1916–1929

Year	Banks on the Par List	Banks Not on the Par List
1916	15,679	not available
1917	17,228	not available
1918	18,997	10,247
1919	25,565	3,996
1920	28,745	1,775
1921	27,881	2,263
1922	27,681	2,288
1923	26,499	2,896
1924	25,032	3,647
1925	24,132	3,970
1926	23,170	3,913
1927	22,281	3,910
1928	21,480	3,911
1929	20,567	3,754

SOURCE: Board of Governors of the Federal Reserve System, *Banking and Monetary Statistics, 1914–1941*, pp. 54–55.

charge. The total number of banks on the Federal Reserve's par list for the years 1916 to 1929 is found in Table 3.4. Some national banks protested being forced to clear at par, but none apparently gave up its charter solely because of this requirement. Eager to establish nationwide coverage, the Federal Reserve Board and the Federal Reserve banks began a campaign to apply pressure on all banks to get on the par list. It was not entirely a propaganda campaign. Some Federal Reserve banks apparently used coercive methods, such as accumulating checks to be presented at one time to nonpar banks. By 1920, 28,745 of the nation's commercial banks were on and 1,775 were off the par list. This campaign engendered great hostility in some regions. Southern bankers began to organize resistance, forming the National and State Bankers Protective Association in 1920, whose purpose was to lobby for nonpar banks in Washington and the state capitals. This lobby successfully obtained laws in Alabama, Florida, Georgia,

Louisiana, Mississippi, North Carolina, South Dakota, and Tennessee legalizing exchange charges against the Federal Reserve banks.[41]

A series of law suits was brought against Federal Reserve banks for their coercive methods; and although none of the charges was ever proven, the Supreme Court ruled in 1923 that it was beyond the power of the Federal Reserve to force par collection of checks by nonmembers. The Court also ruled that the Federal Reserve System had not been charged with establishing a nationwide system of par clearance. The Federal Reserve Board responded to this by issuing Regulation J in 1923 forbidding any Federal Reserve bank from accepting for collection any check drawn on a nonmember that could not be collected at par.[42]

The number of banks on the par list declined throughout the 1920s, although the number of nonpar banks stabilized at around 3,900. The banks desiring nonpar clearance were strongest in the Richmond, Atlanta, and Minnesota districts. The issue was of little interest to banks in the Boston, New York, Philadelphia, and San Francisco districts. In the Boston district, for example, the practice had died out by itself. The major banks had established par clearance by refusing to accept exchange charges from the few banks that persisted in this practice. Nonpar clearance remained viable in the regions in which nonpar banks were the most numerous and the correspondent banks consented to abide by this practice. It was the small country banks in the South and the West that spurned membership in the Federal Reserve System and offered the stoutest resistance to nationwide par clearance. Their resolve and the prohibition on clearing the checks of nonpar banks through a Federal Reserve bank helped to strengthen the correspondent banking system.

[41] Tippetts, *State Banks*, p. 48.
[42] Ibid., pp. 296–315.

The Battle over Branch Banking

To a great extent the need for institutions, public or private, to facilitate the clearing of payments or discounting for banks derived from the unit banks' dominance of the banking system. Under the National Banking System, branch banking was relatively unimportant. The National Banking Act of 1864 and the widespread state prohibitions on branching coupled with low capital requirements encouraged the growth of small unit banks to meet the nation's growing needs for banking facilities. Whereas a system of branching banks could have internalized much of the clearing process and shuttled credit between bank offices, the preeminence of unit banks required the establishment of formal institutions to facilitate these necessary operations.

Branch banking began to grow rapidly in the second decade of the twentieth century as more states allowed some form of it. Branching was forbidden to national banks, and branching privileges made state charters increasingly attractive. In the struggle to attract members, the issue of branching played an important role, replacing the pre-1913 rivalry between the state and federal authorities over capital requirements. The Federal Reserve Act preserved the minimum capital requirements for national banks and required state member banks to conform to them as well.

In contrast to their actions concerning reserve requirements, virtually no states altered their capital requirements after 1913. As the federal system did not threaten their almost universally lower requirements, there was no need to change. However, the failure of small banks to join did elicit the concern of the federal authorities. In June 1923, the Federal Reserve Board determined that of the 19,345 nonmember banks only 9,633 were eligible under the Federal Reserve Act's capital requirements; the rest lacked sufficient capital. One provision of the Agricultural Credits Act of 1923 attempted to ease the entry of smaller banks into the federal system by allowing nonmembers to join with 60 percent of the required capital, if they brought it up to the required levels within five years. This increased the number of banks eligible for membership in that year by 3,965.[43] However, a very few of these small banks, less than a dozen, ever entered the Federal Reserve System on these terms. There was little reason to hope that this provision would augment membership. Since banks could voluntarily increase their capital before entering, it could only speed up the process. Apparently, areas in which these banks were located could not support much larger firms. The only other change in federal regulations was that state banks in cities with a population over 50,000 and possessing less than $200,000 capital were permitted to join. This also had a small impact, as most large city banks had a capital greater than this minimum. More important for the struggle for members was the bitter fight over branching.

The Federal Reserve, the Comptroller of the Currency, and the state banking authorities were not the only ones interested in the issue of branching. Banking reformers were eager to promote it, and the unit bank lobbies aimed at obstructing its spread. Branching permitted banks to grow in size, acquire a greater deposit base, and obtain more loan customers, which enabled them to realize some economies through the division of labor and specialization.[44] Branching was particularly attractive to banks in large cities which saw additional opportunities to grow in size, but it frightened the small-town banks which feared they would be absorbed. As a result of this diversity of interests, the legal sanction of branching spread

---

[43] Ibid., pp. 166–167.

[44] Almost all studies of financial institutions have found that there are significant economies of scale. For a review of the literature, see George Benston, "Economies of Scale in Financial Institutions." Historical evidence is offered by John A. James in his article "Cost Functions of Postbellum National Banks."

Table 3.5
Legal Status of Branch Banking, 1909 and 1924

	State-wide Branching Permitted	Limited Branching Permitted	Branching Prohibited by State Law	Law Silent, Judicial or Administrative Prohibition
1909	Arizona California Delaware Florida Georgia Oregon Rhode Island Tennessee Washington	Louisiana Maine Massachusetts New York	Colorado Connecticut Mississippi Missouri Nevada Pennsylvania Texas Wisconsin	Alabama Arkansas Idaho Illinois Indiana Iowa Kansas Kentucky Maryland Michigan Minnesota Montana Nebraska New Hampshire New Jersey New Mexico North Carolina North Dakota Ohio Oklahoma South Carolina South Dakota Utah Vermont Virginia West Virginia Wyoming
1924	Arizona California Delaware Georgia Maryland North Carolina Rhode Island South Carolina Tennessee Virginia	Louisiana Maine Massachusetts New York Ohio Mississippi Pennsylvania Kentucky Michigan	Alabama Arkansas Colorado Connecticut Florida Idaho Illinois Indiana Minnesota Missouri Nevada New Mexico Oregon Texas Utah Washington Wisconsin	Iowa Kansas Montana Nebraska New Hampshire New Jersey North Dakota Oklahoma South Dakota Vermont West Virginia Wyoming

SOURCES: Frederick A. Bradford, *The Legal Status of Branch Banking in the United States* and Board of Governors of the Federal Reserve System, *Federal Reserve Bulletin*, 10 (December 1924), pp. 929–940.

Table 3.6
Growth of Branch Banking, 1900–1930

Year	Number of Banks Operating Branches			Total Number of Branches
	National	*State*	*Total*	*of Branches*
1900	5	82	87	119
1905	5	191	196	350
1910	9	283	292	548
1915	12	385	397	785
1920	21	509	530	1,281
1925	130	590	720	2,525
1930	166	585	751	3,522

Branching Banks as a Percentage of All Commercial Banks	Branch Bank Offices as a Percentage of Total Bank Offices	Branching Banks' Loans and Investments as a Percentage of All Commercial-Bank Loans and Investments
0.7	1.6	1.8
1.0	3.0	5.9
1.2	3.4	8.9
1.4	4.2	12.2
1.7	5.7	18.6
2.5	10.5	35.2
3.2	15.7	45.5

SOURCES: Board of Governors of the Federal Reserve System, *Banking and Monetary Statistics, 1914–1941*, p. 297. Board of Governors of the Federal Reserve System, *All Bank Statistics, United States, 1896–1955*, pp. 34–35.

slowly and erratically. Table 3.5 shows the change in state banking statutes. In 1909, only nine states and territories allowed state-wide and four limited branch banking. The remaining states prohibited it either by law or by administrative practice. Table 3.6 shows the effects of these laws in restraining the growth of branching. In 1910, there were only 292 banks, or 1.2 percent of all commercial banks, engaged in branching; these operated 3.4 percent of all bank offices and handled 8.9 percent of loans and investments.

The Federal Reserve Act left intact the restrictions on national-bank branching. In 1915, national banks operated only

26 of the 785 branch banks.[45] These were offices opened when some banks had state charters before the Civil War, which they were allowed to retain when they changed their charter. On the other hand, several more states began to open the door to branching. When the Federal Reserve Board surveyed state legislation in December 1924, it found eleven states allowed state-wide branching and nine permitted some limited form of branching. The remaining states imposed legal or administrative prohibitions on branching. The most important legal change occurred in 1909 when California passed a new banking law in response to the crisis of 1907–1908. This law, its amendments, and the administrator of the state banking department all encouraged branching on a state-wide basis, by permitting the opening of new branches and the consolidation of banks with no addition to capital. Full advantage of the law was taken by the Bank of Italy (later the Bank of America). Its enterprising president, Amadeo P. Giannini, used the law to build the largest West Coast bank, providing an example that other bankers soon followed.[46] The growth of branch banking in California was impressive. A year after the passage of the law in 1910, there were 45 branches in the state. These grew to 179 in 1920, placing California third after New York with 229 and Michigan with 218 branches.[47]

The 1920s saw a remarkable expansion of branch banking, the consequence of a few states easing their prohibitions on branching. By 1925, 720 banks were operating 2,525 branches. These accounted for 10.5 percent of all banking offices and 35.2 percent of all commercial-bank loans and investments. The state banks with 2,207 branches led the way.

The success of branching state banks concerned the Federal

[45] Ray B. Westerfield, *Historical Survey of Branch Banking in the United States*, pp. 18–19.

[46] Ibid., pp. 19–22.

[47] Board of Governors of the Federal Reserve System, *Banking and Monetary Statistics*, p. 298.

Reserve, which was worried about the unequal status of its national- and state-bank members. In 1915 the Federal Reserve Board recommended that national banks be allowed to open branches in their main-office city or county. The American Bankers Association, dominated by unit banks, reacted violently to this proposal and adopted hostile resolutions. The political heat was too great, and the Federal Reserve Board was forced to retreat.[48] In spite of this opposition, national banks slowly began to branch. Congress provided them with one loophole in the National Bank Consolidation Act of 1918. This opened the door to national-bank branching in states where branching was legal by permitting a national bank to consolidate with a state bank and keep the separate office and any attached branches. Despite the awkwardness of this method, the number of national-bank branches rose from 26 in 1915 to 318 in 1925.

Sensitive to the disadvantages that national banks had to cope with and frustrated by congressional indifference, Comptroller D. R. Crissinger (1921–1923) ruled that national banks could open intracity offices for the purposes of deposit but not for loans or discounts where this did not conflict with state statutes. Flexing their muscles, the country bankers pushed a resolution through the American Bankers Association's annual convention that stated: "We regard branch banking or the establishment of additional offices by banks as detrimental to the best interest of the people of the U.S. Branch banking is contrary to public policy, violates the basic principles of our government and concentrates the credits of the nation and the power of money in the hands of a few."[49] In spite of this and the opposition of Crissinger's successor Henry Dawes, the Attorney General ruled there was nothing contrary to law in the establishment of these offices.

[48] Ross Robertson, *The Comptroller and Bank Supervision, An Historical Appraisal,* p. 101.

[49] Gerald C. Fisher, *American Banking Structure,* p. 45.

A direct challenge by national banks to the right of states to regulate their branching activities was repelled in 1924 when the Supreme Court ruled against the defendant in the case of the *First National Bank in St. Louis* v. *The State of Missouri.* This national bank had, contrary to state law, opened a branch, and, in so doing, presented a challenge to all state antibranching legislation. The case focused considerable attention on the issue of branching, and many briefs were filed in this case by the friends and enemies of branching as amici curiae. The Justice Department filed on behalf of the national bank, arguing that the provisions of the National Banking Act were unworkable in light of modern banking practices. Fifteen states entered briefs siding with the state of Missouri in defending unit banking.[50]

Branching raised another concern for the Federal Reserve. It was still worried that differences in regulations favoring state members would lead national banks to abandon their charters. In a move toward equalizing these differences, the Federal Reserve Board adopted a resolution in November 1923 stipulating that state banks and trust companies could only open new branches with the express permission of the board and that no more branches outside a bank's home city would be permitted. New state institutions joining the Federal Reserve would have to relinquish their offices outside their home-office city. This change pleased no one. National banks gained nothing, and state members found themselves at a disadvantage vis-à-vis nonmember state banks.[51]

The fight over branching was heating up, as branching made further inroads into the banking system. Even as the total number of banks was declining, the number of branch offices rose from 2,525 in 1925 to 3,522 in 1930. The loans and investments of branching banks as a percentage of all bank loans and investments increased from 35.2 to 45.5. Dur-

[50] Ibid., pp. 47, 63.
[51] Howard H. Preston, "Recent Developments in Branch Banking," p. 454.

ing those same five years, the proponents of branch banking believed that increased branching would strengthen the system at a time when bank failures were on the rise. Its opponents saw it as spreading the big city banks' monopoly power into the countryside.

The conflict forced many more states to take a stand on the legal status of banking within their jurisdictions. Many passed antibranching laws. By the end of the 1920s, twenty-two states forbade branching, and nineteen allowed some form of it within their borders. The number of states in which there was no law regulating branching had dropped to seven by 1929. Overall, only one more state made branching legal. Even in the stronghold of state-wide branching, California, unit bankers' political clout was felt. In 1923, they forced the State Superintendent of Banks to agree to review the opening of any new branch office. Henceforth, the Superintendent exercised discretionary authority over the opening of new branches.[52]

In 1924, a bill was drafted under the supervision of Comptroller of the Currency Dawes and introduced in Congress by Chairman Louis T. McFadden of the House Banking and Currency Committee to expand the branching powers of the national banks and halt their conversion to state charters. In an effort to kill the bill, Congressman Morton D. Hull of Illinois introduced amendments, known as the Hull amendments, that would have forbidden national banks and state members from ever opening branches in states that at the time of the bill's passage did not authorize branches even if the states subsequently altered their legislation. These amendments received the support of the American Bankers Association in 1924. A bitter fight ensued in Congress, with the House of Representatives passing the bill with the amendments and the Senate passing it without them. Each house

[52] Westerfield, *Historical Survey of Branch Banking*, pp. 20–22.

refused to alter its version of the bill. The conflict only moved toward a resolution when at its annual conference in 1926 the American Bankers Association reversed its position on the Hull amendments. However, the association was not unanimous in its vote, and the State Bank Division refused to support the bill without the amendments. Opposition in the House of Representatives began to weaken; and after some logrolling, the McFadden bill was passed without the amendments. It was signed into law by the President on February 25, 1927.[53]

The McFadden Act amended the Federal Reserve Act and affirmed that state banks joining the system could retain all branches in existence at the time of the act's approval but could not keep any out-of-town branches opened after the date of the bill's signing. No member bank could open any branches beyond the corporate limits of the town or city in which its home office was located. National banks were allowed to retain existing branches and acquire branches as provided for in the National Bank Consolidation Act. Furthermore, national banks were permitted to establish new full service branches in their home-office cities if state law granted this to state banks. These branches were, however, limited in number. They were forbidden in towns with a population less than 25,000, restricted to one in towns with a population of 25,000 to 50,000, and limited to two in cities with a population between 50,000 and 100,000. In cities over 100,000, the number of branches permitted was to be determined by the Comptroller of the Currency.[54] The act represented a compromise between expanding the freedom of the national banks to branch and forcing the state members to adhere to national bank regulations. The danger in the act was that it placed member banks at a disadvantage vis-à-vis nonmembers who still could branch, where permitted by state law, outside their home-office cities. In spite of these weaknesses, the bill did create favorable conditions for increasing membership. Until this

[53] Tippetts, *State Banks*, pp. 350–353.
[54] Ibid., pp. 353–355.

time most national-bank branches were restricted to accepting deposits and cashing checks. Shortly after the passage of the act, in March 1927, the largest branching bank in the United States, the Bank of Italy, a state member with branches throughout the state of California, took out a national charter. This brought almost 300 branches into the national system, and the Bank of Italy was followed by the Los Angeles First National Trust and Savings Bank which brought in another 100 branches.[55] The McFadden Act helped to end the erosion of the national system and put national banks and state members on an equal footing.

State Deposit Insurance and Membership

The attractions of a national bank charter were probably also increased by the decline of the state deposit guarantee systems in the 1920s. By 1918, Kansas, Mississippi, Nebraska, North Dakota, Oklahoma, South Dakota, Texas, and Washington had created deposit insurance systems designed to pay depositors of failed banks with funds obtained from assessments on solvent, subscribing state institutions. The decline in agricultural prices and the consequent rise in bank failures bankrupted these funds. Banks dropped their membership or took out national charters to avoid heavier assessments required to pay for the rising amount of liabilities for which the insurance funds became responsible.[56] These deposit guarantee funds, which had brought additional security to their member institutions before the 1920s, now created additional burdens in the form of higher assessments.

Federal and State Supervision of Banking

It is difficult to assess how differences between federal and state supervision affected a bank's membership decision. Fed-

[55] Ibid., p. 335.
[56] See Chapter 4 for a more detailed discussion of state deposit insurance.

eral supervision improved markedly after the passage of the
Federal Reserve Act, and throughout the next two decades
state supervision also improved. The act corrected the defective method of paying examiners by providing them with fixed
salaries and compensation for their expenses rather than compensating them on the basis of the number of banks visited,
as the National Banking Act had specified. The act also multiplied the number of supervisory authorities for most banks.
The Comptroller of the Currency was charged with twice-
yearly examinations of all the national and state member banks.
The Federal Reserve Board was empowered to examine members at its discretion, and the twelve Federal Reserve banks
were allowed to make special examinations of members in
their own districts. It soon became apparent that unless there
was some cooperation among these authorities in their over-
lapping jurisdictions, banks would be saddled with compiling
redundant reports. State members faced the prospect of being
subject to four different examining bodies. This was not immediately or amicably resolved for the Office of the Comptroller was in the possession of J. Skelton Williams, who was
prepared to defend what he considered to be the prerogatives
of the office. Williams began the confrontation by instructing
his examiners not to provide the Federal Reserve banks with
all the information they collected. He made many enemies,
and several bills surfaced in Congress that proposed to abolish
the Office of the Comptroller. A 1917 amendment to the
Federal Reserve Act removed state member banks from the
jurisdiction of the Comptroller, leaving them subject only to
the state supervisors whose standards were less exacting. Relations between the Federal Reserve and the Comptroller were
finally improved when a former Comptroller, D. R. Crissinger, became head of the Federal Reserve System in 1923 and
supervisory authority was shared on a rational basis.[57]

[57] Robertson, *The Comptroller*, pp. 107–113.

Out of this confusion higher standards of federal examination emerged. Although state authorities often lagged behind federal norms, the post-1914 period was one of improved enforcement of bank regulation. The more lax state supervision may have been an additional attraction of the state systems; on the other hand, the knowledge that Federal Reserve members were more strictly supervised may have attracted more depositors and thus worked the other way.

The Determinants of Membership in the Federal Reserve System

To sum up, the factors influencing a bank's decision to join the Federal Reserve System were numerous: minimum capital requirements, reserve requirements, portfolio restrictions, limitations on branching, supervision, par clearance, and deposit insurance. While the determinants of membership have been subjected to extensive empirical analysis for the years after World War II, little work has been done on the 1920s. Of the studies discussed in Chapter 1, only Frodin's covers this period. Frodin found that changes in net cost to member banks strongly affected the trends in membership. In her study net costs were defined as costs less benefits, where costs were reserves less the float plus Federal Reserve stock, and benefits were the value of borrowing at the Federal Reserve and the free services of check collection, coin and currency handling, wire transfers, and safekeeping of securities. A 1 percent increase in net costs produced a 2.22 percent decline in member-bank deposits and a 2.14 percent fall in member-bank capital.[58] Frodin explains the inability of the Federal Reserve System to expand its membership in the 1920s by the increasing net cost per dollar of member-bank deposits, which

[58] Joanna Haywood Frodin, "The Tax/Subsidy Relation between Member Banks and the Federal Reserve System," p. 111.

rose from 10 percent in 1923 to 15 percent in 1929. The swelling of the Federal Reserve's ranks in the 1930s is attributed to a large net subsidy to member banks in that decade.[59] This approach does, however, omit some of the important factors cited above that affected membership.

The analysis of the Federal Reserve's membership problem used here applies the same method used in Chapter 1 for the National Banking System. It includes more determinants and emphasizes the key feature of the dual banking system—the competition between state and federal banking authorities. Most studies like Frodin's handle the membership question by looking at the cost imposed on member banks without investigating the alternative costs imposed on nonmember banks. The objective of this approach is to compare the costs of regulation under both systems, using opportunity cost as the determinant of membership. The question of membership is again analyzed from the point of view of a profit-maximizing firm entering the market. Any prospective financial institution intending to go into the business of commercial banking in this period was confronted with the decision of whether or not to join the Federal Reserve. Firms made their decisions on the basis of whether their expected profits would be higher inside or outside the system. The statistical model used is probit where the dependent variable, reflecting a bank's choice, can take on two values, zero or one, representing respectively entering or remaining outside the Federal Reserve System.[60]

The sample chosen for examination includes all national banks and state-chartered commercial banking institutions (state banks and trust companies) that opened between October 31, 1923, and October 30, 1925. This represents two reporting periods for the Comptroller of the Currency, who was responsible for chartering national banks. This period was chosen because the Federal Reserve's basic regulations and policy

[59] Ibid., p. 106.
[60] For a description of probit and its application, see Appendix B.

had been hammered out and no changes were made. A two-year period was selected because many states issuing biennial reports did not indicate the date of each bank's opening. The *Federal Reserve Bulletin* provided information on those new state banks that took out membership in the Federal Reserve. An extensive search of the bank examiners' reports revealed that 677 nonmember banks, 32 state member banks, and 253 national banks were chartered in this period.[61]

The selected determinants of membership were minimum capital requirements, branching restrictions, portfolio restrictions, par clearance, state deposit insurance, and total and vault cash reserve requirements on demand and time deposits. The minimum capital and reserve requirement variables were measured as the difference between the Federal Reserve and state regulations for 1924 for each bank. In the state of New York, for example, the vault cash reserve requirement on demand deposits for country banks was 6 percent compared to the Federal Reserve's requirement of 7 percent. The difference, 1 percent, was the independent variable used. It was hypothesized that the greater the difference in favor of the state, the greater the probability that a bank would become a state nonmember. If the regulation did constrain bank behavior and influence its membership decision, the estimated coefficient should be positive and significant.

As explained in Chapter 1, state banks in rural areas tended to hold a much larger portion of their assets in mortgages and real estate–based loans than urban state or national banks. State banks were able to offer more loans and discounts on real estate owing to the weaker state restrictions on their portfolios. Thus, state banks had more profitable loans open to them in agricultural areas than national banks had, but at the same time they had a portfolio containing paper that was not generally acceptable at the discount window. It was hypoth-

[61] For a more detailed discussion of the data, see Appendix A.

esized that banks in rural areas would thus be less likely to join the Federal Reserve. In order to capture the advantages and disadvantages that state institutions enjoyed because of their ability to lend on real estate in rural areas, a variable representing the opportunity to offer loans was necessary. For this purpose, a proxy, the ratio of rural to total state population, was chosen, with rural population defined to be those people living in communities of 2,500 or less. As data are not available for the middle of the decade, the figures for 1920 and 1930 were averaged. It was hypothesized that the higher this ratio was, that is, the more rural the state, the more likely it would be for a bank to be a nonmember. A positive sign on the coefficient was expected.

If a state permitted state-wide or limited branch banking, a dummy variable was set equal to one to capture the possible effects. It is not possible to determine a priori whether branching would increase the probability of a bank joining the Federal Reserve, as state member banks could enter the system and retain this privilege. Furthermore, the interpretation of this variable is complicated by the fact that new banks chartered by the state authorities might decrease in number relative to those chartered by the Comptroller, as expansion of the state system took place through an increase in bank offices rather than new banks. The sign of the coefficient on the branching dummy variable could be either positive or negative accordingly. National banks were at a disadvantage as they could open only limited agencies for deposit in branching states, but in states that allowed only limited agencies they were apparently competing on an equal basis. A dummy variable was set equal to one in states that permitted only limited agencies. As the advantages were equal for all banks—national, state member, and nonmember—the coefficient on this variable should not be significant.

There were two types of state deposit guarantee systems, compulsory and voluntary. A dummy variable was used to account for each type. The cost of deposit insurance rose in the 1920s, as increased bank failures forced up insurance premiums. When the premiums or assessments became too high, banks sought to avoid deposit insurance. A bank could easily drop voluntary insurance, and the coefficient was not expected to be significant for this variable. To evade the higher cost of compulsory insurance, a bank would have to abandon its state for a national charter. A negative and significant coefficient was expected for this variable, indicating that it drove banks into the Federal Reserve System.

State banks were reluctant to give up the practice of nonpar clearance, claiming that it was an important source of income. There is no easy method for determining how nonpar clearance increased the profitability of some banks. In an attempt to get at the supposed advantages of nonpar clearance, a proxy, the ratio of nonpar banks to all banks in each Federal Reserve district, was used. This variable was selected because preference for exchange charges was clearly regional in character.

The practice had almost entirely died out by itself in New England and the Mid-Atlantic. If nonpar clearance represented additional profitable opportunities, then it might reasonably be expected to be reflected in the percentage of banks practicing it in each Federal Reserve district. Each district could be loosely considered as a trade area for the banks within it, which would use the same correspondents. A bank's ability to charge exchange would also be enhanced if other banks in the area did so as well. If nonpar clearance induced banks to stay out of the Federal Reserve, then the coefficient on this variable should be positive and significant.

The use of the discount window and other free services conferred benefits on member banks, but no separate variable was included to measure these advantages. A dummy variable would have corresponded exactly to the dichotomous division of membership and was therefore not used. Instead these advantages should be captured in the intercept term. A negative and significant coefficient would provide partial evidence that the Federal Reserve's provision of these services made joining the system more attractive.

The membership decision model used here is:

$$Y_i = b_0 + b_1x_{1i} + b_2x_{2i} + b_3x_{3i} + b_4x_{4i} + b_5x_{5i} + b_6x_{6i} + b_7x_{7i}$$
$$+ b_8x_{8i} + b_9x_{9i} + b_{10}x_{10i} + b_{11}x_{11i} \qquad (1)$$

where $Y_i = 0$ when the ith bank joined the Federal Reserve and $Y_i = 1$ when the ith bank joined a state banking system. For the ith bank, the independent variables are x_{1i}, the difference between the state and national minimum capital requirements; x_{2i}, a dummy variable for branch banking; x_{3i}, a dummy variable for limited agencies; x_{4i}, the ratio of the rural to total population in a given state; x_{5i}, the ratio of nonpar banks to all banks in a Federal Reserve district; x_{6i}, a dummy variable for voluntary deposit insurance; x_{7i}, a dummy variable for compulsory deposit insurance; x_{8i}, the difference between state and national vault cash reserve requirements on demand deposits; x_{9i}, the difference between state and national vault cash reserve requirements on time deposits; x_{10i}, the difference between state and national total reserve requirements on demand deposits; and x_{11i}, the difference between state and national total reserve requirements on time deposits. The probit procedure transforms equation (1) with a cumulative normal density function to:

$$P(E_i) = F(b_0 + b_1x_{1i} + b_2x_{2i} + b_3x_{3i} + b_4x_{4i} + b_5x_{5i} + b_6x_{6i}$$
$$+ b_7x_{7i} + b_8x_{8i} + b_9x_{9i} + b_{10}x_{10i} + b_{11}x_{11i}) \qquad (2)$$

or

$$P(E_i) = F(I_i) \qquad (3)$$

where $P(E_i)$ is both the probability of a single bank being a state nonmember and the percentage of banks in a given state choosing to remain outside the Federal Reserve. I_i is the critical value that yields that probability from the normal distribution.

The estimated coefficients and approximate t-statistics of the probit model using three different specifications are presented in Table 3.7. The large sample containing 962 observations should provide a clear indication of a variable's significance. One measure of goodness of fit, the log likelihood ratio test, showed that all equations explaining the membership decision were significant.[62] Another measure of goodness of fit, the pseudo-R^2, is low; however, as explained in Chapter 2, this could have occurred if some of the regulations were not binding.

In general the model supported the hypotheses put forward. In all estimations the coefficients on the minimum capital requirement variable were positive and significant as hypothesized. The branch banking dummy variable had a negative and significant coefficient in all three models. The sign on this variable probably indicates that in states that permitted branching the state banking systems expanded by opening new branches rather than new banks, whereas in the national system expansion took the form of opening new individual banks. It is interesting that the coefficient on the dummy variables for states that allowed the establishment of limited agencies was not significant. This points to the fact that where all commercial banks had equal opportunities to open additional offices, the membership decision was not affected.

The proxy for the advantages state-chartered banks had to make loans on real estate, the ratio of rural to total population, was positive and significant as expected. This coefficient and the coefficient for the minimum capital requirements are remarkably similar to the estimates for 1908–1910, reflecting the continuity of the factors determining membership in the federal system.

[62] At the 5 percent level the critical value of the test with nine degrees of freedom is 16.9; with eleven degrees of freedom it is 19.7.

Table 3.7
Federal Reserve Membership Probit Estimates, 1923–1925

	Model I	Model II	Model III
Independent Variables			
Intercept	0.079	0.174	0.019
	(0.417)	(1.474)	(0.117)
Minimum capital	0.009	0.008	0.008
requirement	(4.500*)	(4.000*)	(4.000*)
Branch banking	−0.272	−0.301	−0.309
	(−2.229*)	(−2.529*)	(−2.575*)
Limited agencies	−0.021	−0.056	−0.035
	(−0.153)	(−0.412)	(−0.257*)
Ratio of rural	1.109	1.065	0.978
to total state	(4.004*)	(3.917*)	(3.649*)
population			
Par clearance	0.569	0.375	0.408
	(1.448)	(1.014)	(1.074)
Total reserve	0.016		0.004
requirements on	(0.889)		(0.250)
demand deposits			
Vault cash reserve	−0.058	−0.017	
requirements on	(−2.000*)	(−0.680)	
demand deposits			
Total reserve	−0.040		−0.032
requirements on	(−3.333*)		(−4.000*)
time deposits			
Vault cash reserve	0.051	−0.042	
requirements on	(1.417)	(1.555)	
time deposits			
Voluntary deposit	−0.130	−0.402	−0.309
insurance	(−0.506)	(−1.648*)	(−1.298)
Compulsory deposit	−0.610	−0.615	−0.672
insurance	(−3.788*)	(−3.819*)	(−4.450*)
Goodness of Fit			
Log likelihood	86.5*	71.9*	82.4*
ratio test statistic			
Pseudo-R^2	0.199	0.148	0.153

NOTE: The numbers in parentheses are approximate *t*-statistics obtained by dividing the estimated coefficients by their estimated standard errors.
* Significant at the 0.05 level.

As hypothesized, the variable for the attractions offered by nonpar clearance to nonmember banks was positive, but it was not significant. Banks that preferred to remain off the Federal Reserve's par list were primarily located in rural states, and this variable was positively correlated with the ratio of rural to total population.[63] Multicollinearity, the intercorrelation here between these two variables, may have drawn off some of its significance. When the population variable was dropped, the par clearance variable became significant. It may thus have been a factor influencing the membership decision, although it is difficult to unscramble the contribution of each variable.

The signs of the coefficients of the deposit insurance variables switched from positive for the period 1908–1910 to negative for the period 1923–1925. This reflects the observed flight of banks from the failing systems of deposit insurance. The sign on the dummy variable for voluntary insurance was not significant for Models I or III, providing some evidence that banks could easily drop out of these guarantee systems. On the other hand, the coefficient on the compulsory insurance dummy was significant, indicating that banks seeking to avoid the rising costs of insurance assessments were driven to take out national charters.

As was the case for the period 1908–1910, some of the reserve requirement variables were closely correlated.[64] The existence of multicollinearity makes the analysis of the effects of the differences in reserve requirements on the membership decision difficult. Taken alone in Model II, the vault cash reserve requirements are both not significant at the 5 percent level; but in Model I, when the other reserve requirements are present, the sign on time deposits flips from negative to positive and the sign on demand deposits becomes significant. The signs on the total reserve requirement coefficients are

[63] The coefficient of correlation was 0.538.
[64] The strongest simple correlations ranged from 0.305 to 0.728.

more stable—the sign on demand deposits is positive and not significant, and the sign on time deposits is negative and significant in both Models I and III. The large reductions in reserve requirements by the Federal Reserve caused the vault cash reserve requirements to fall to levels equal to or lower than state requirements. It appears that, correlation between the variables aside, vault cash reserve requirements did not strongly influence membership as the requirements may have fallen considerably below the amount of vault cash banks ordinarily kept. The total reserve requirement on demand deposits was also consistently not significant, probably for the same reasons. The only variable difficult to account for is the total reserve requirements on time deposits, which is strongly significant. This may speak to the effect that the federal authorities had in undermining the states' advantage when they lowered the total requirement on time deposits to 3 percent. Nonmember banks who held a larger portion of their liabilities in time deposits were generally allowed to keep a portion of their reserves on deposit with reserve agents. The latter were invariably larger city banks, and hence more likely to be members of the Federal Reserve. The attractiveness of membership may have been enhanced by the states permitting banks under their supervision to hold part of their reserves in the form of bankers' balances.[65]

The last interesting feature of the empirical results is the positive sign on the intercept term. This should not occur if the Federal Reserve's discount window and its free services to members were powerful attractions. Apparently, these did not outweigh the other unspecified factors, such as weaker

[65] The total effect of reserve requirements on the membership decision, as measured by a log likelihood ratio test on all four coefficients, was significant at the 5 percent level, as were the reserve requirements in other paired groupings. However, the different positive and negative inducements to join the Federal Reserve System tended to cancel out, and the overall effect of reserve requirements on the membership decision was small for most states.

supervision, that would have kept banks from joining the Federal Reserve. This evidence is corroborated by Frodin's finding that the benefits from the discount window and other services per dollar of member deposits were very low in the 1920s.[66]

Government Policy and Membership in the Federal Reserve System

Alternative policies to maintain and increase the Federal Reserve's membership can be evaluated using the method elaborated in Chapter 1. The estimated coefficients, which represent weighted contributions to the critical value, are multiplied by their independent variables to generate a critical value for each class of banks in each state. This value when plugged into a normal distribution will yield a prediction of the percentage of banks in each state choosing a state system. These percentages may then be multiplied by the total number of new banks in the state to predict how many will take out membership in the state systems.[67] The estimates from Model I were used since the model had the highest log likelihood ratio statistic, indicating it explained more variation than the other two specifications. The predicted numbers of Federal Reserve members and nonmembers compared very favorably to the actual numbers. In the period October 31, 1923, to October 30, 1925, 285 (29.6%) newly chartered banks joined the Federal Reserve, and 677 (70.4%) joined the state banking systems. The model predicted these to be 276 (28.7%) and 686 (71.3%) respectively.

The effects of changes in Federal Reserve regulations on membership may be examined by substituting the values for the alternative regulations for the actual, multiplying these

[66] Frodin, "The Tax/Subsidy Relation," Table 1 and Figure 2.
[67] This technique is explained in Appendix B.

by the estimated coefficients to obtain the critical value that will yield the counterfactual percentages of members and non-members. One possible change in regulations to attract members would have been to abolish the Federal Reserve's minimum capital requirement and only require member banks to conform to state laws. If this course of action had been followed, the Federal Reserve would have gained 375, or 39.0 percent, of the 962 new banks formed in the period 1923–1925, instead of the 276, or 29.6 percent it actually acquired. This indicates that there would have been a reasonable gain in membership. It would also be interesting to know how the distribution of deposits between the banking systems would have been affected. As this policy change would have tended to draw in smaller country banks, this question can be given an approximate answer by calculating how much these banks would have brought in if each was of average deposit size for nonmembers. This should also be compared with the actual growth of the Federal Reserve System. Between 1920 and 1928, the number of Federal Reserve member banks fell from 9,398, or 32.3 percent of all commercial banks, possessing 70.3 percent of all deposits, to 8,774, or 34.6 percent of all banks, possessing 72.7 percent of all deposits held in commercial banks. The federal system was, thus, fairly stable. The falling number but rising proportion of banks reflects the higher mortality of nonmembers in a period of failure in rural areas and some consolidation through branching, as indicated in Table 3.2. Over the years 1920–1928, the average deposits of nonmember banks rose from $544,000 to $795,000.

The effects of a policy of lowering capital requirements on the distribution of deposits may be analyzed if it is assumed that all banks in the long run would have made their membership decisions on the same basis as newly chartered banks. Furthermore, it is assumed that all banks entering the federal system were the average size of nonmembers in 1925; that is, they had deposits of $790,000. This is not unreasonable and probably overstates the size of the new banks and hence the impact of the policy. The elimination of federal capital requirements would have increased membership to 39.0 percent of all banks and the Federal Reserve's share of commercial-bank deposits to 75.0 percent under these assumptions. The population would have increased noticeably, but the Federal Reserve's portion of deposits would have changed little, owing to the small size of the nonmember banks that would have joined.

Another possible regulatory change that might have enhanced membership would have been to drop entirely the restrictions placed on national banks offering loans on real estate. In the 1923–1925 sample, this alteration would have led 466, or 48.5 percent, of the new banks to join the Federal Reserve and 496, or 51.5 percent, to enter the state banking systems. If this policy change would have affected all banks in the same manner, then the federal system would have found itself with 78.9 percent of all commercial-bank deposits in 1925.

It is interesting to consider what would have happened to membership if the Federal Reserve had been successful in forcing all banks to clear at par. According to the probit estimates, universal par clearance might have denied some profitable operations to banks located in the West and the South. Assuming that banks continued to make rational decisions and were not piqued by being coerced to clear at par, it is possible to determine how many more would have joined the Federal Reserve if this practice had been prohibited. Forcing all banks to clear at par would have increased the number of member banks in the sample from 285 to 326, or 33.9 percent of the total. As this variable was not significant in Model I of the probit estimation, its effect here was very small.

All of the three regulatory changes above would have affected banks in rural areas. If the Federal Reserve had wanted to make an all-out effort to draw small rural banks into its system, it could have eliminated capital requirements and portfolio restrictions and enforced par clearance. If this policy had been pursued, then, according to the estimation, 518, or 53.8 percent of the banks in the sample, would have taken out membership in the Federal Reserve. If the whole bank population were similarly affected, another 4,854 banks would have joined the Federal Reserve, bringing the system's share of commercial-bank deposits to 81.1 percent in 1928. Although 11,702 banks would still have remained outside the system, the Federal Reserve's share of deposits would have risen by 7.8 percent, reflecting a moderate degree of success for this type of policy.

Requiring all banks to meet federal reserve requirements was another measure that might have been employed to strengthen the system.[68] The nonsignificant signs on some of the reserve requirement coefficients for this period seem to indicate that the Federal Reserve had already lowered requirements to the point where the difference in the cost of holding reserves was not an important factor in the membership decision. If the Federal Reserve had imposed uniform reserve requirements on all banks, members and nonmembers alike, 294 of the 962 new banks, or 30.6 percent, would have joined. This represents virtually no change from the 285 who actually did join, and it would not have noticeably added to the number of members in 1928 or their deposits. This result appears to be quite reasonable in light of the low reserves and relatively easy credit conditions that allowed banks to avoid using the discount window. The real failure to attract members was, thus, not caused by too high reserve requirements, but by restrictions that fostered small rural unit banks that were, on the whole, averse to joining the Federal Reserve System.

---

[68] The power to require nonmember banks to adhere to federal requirements has been recently granted to the Federal Reserve by the Depository Institutions Deregulation and Monetary Control Act of 1980.

This counterfactual analysis cannot be applied to what may have been a very important factor in determining Federal Reserve membership, branching. The negative and significant coefficients indicate that branch banking decreased the number of new banks. In branching states, the number of offices was expanded by branches rather than by new banks. More liberal branching laws, on the order of state-wide branching, would have substantially modified the nation's banking structure in such a way that the type of marginal analysis applied above is not useful to examine the effects of increased branching on membership. Analysis of this change must be carried out in a less rigorous fashion.

One of the distinguishing characteristics of banks joining the Federal Reserve System was that they were among the largest banks in the country. This can be seen in the changes in the average size of banks in the years 1916–1918, when the Federal Reserve made its greatest gains in membership. From 1916 to 1918, the number of national banks rose by 128; and the average deposit size of national banks grew from $1,436,000 to $1,820,000. For the most part, this reflected the expansion of the business of established banks rather than the addition of new large banks. In 1916, the 34 state members, averaging $7,676,000 in deposits, were much larger than the national banks. They dwarfed the nonmembers, whose average deposits were $588,000.

The amendments to the Federal Reserve Act encouraged many state banks to join. In 1917, there were 53 state members, averaging $11,867,000 in deposits. The admission of these very large banks was followed by the entry of slightly smaller banks, so that in 1918 there were 513 state members whose average deposits were $9,627,000. The admission of a few banks increased the Federal Reserve's percentage of all commercial banks from 29.0 in 1916 to 29.9 in 1918 and raised its share of deposits from 50.4 to 67.7 percent. This was the system's greatest gain; thereafter its membership and deposits drifted slowly upward, not so much by attracting banks as by the failures of nonmembers. The impact of this tremendous spurt on state nonmember banks is interesting. After rising in size from an average of $588,000 in deposits in 1916 to $651,000 in 1917, they fell to $469,000 in 1918. This represents the loss of the largest banks to the Federal Reserve.

Branching was one of the most important factors affecting a bank's size and its propensity to join the Federal Reserve. This has been recognized in the modern literature on the Federal Reserve's membership problem. Gambs and Rasche have argued that the advantages of membership seem to be a function of size and that banks grow most rapidly in branching states.[69] Providing evidence on why big banks join the Federal Reserve, R. Alton Gilbert has found that larger banks use its free services more intensively. He computed the implicit rate of return on reserve balances and found it to be much higher for large banks than for small ones.[70]

To assess the contribution of branching to bank size, an ordinary least squares regression of the average deposit size of each type of bank by state in 1924 on regulatory and population density variables was performed. The results are presented in Table 3.8. All the equations explaining the variations in the dependent variable are significant, as their F-statistics were significant at the 5 percent level. As capital and reserve requirements did not vary across states for national and state member banks, these terms were omitted from their regressions. For both these types of member banks, the dummy for any type of branch banking and the population density variable, the averaged population density for 1920 and 1930, are significant at the 5 percent level. The dummy variable for the

[69] Carl Gambs and Robert Rasche, "The Costs of Reserves and the Relative Size of Member and Nonmember Bank Demand Deposits," pp. 715–717.
[70] R. Alton Gilbert, "Utilization of Federal Reserve Bank Services by Member Banks: Implications for the Costs and Benefits of Membership," p. 9.

Table 3.8
Ordinary Least Squares Estimates of the Determinants of Bank Size, 1924

	National Banks	State Member Banks	Nonmember Banks
Independent Variables			
Intercept	1.156	−0.662	0.148
	(5.048*)	(−0.393)	(1.185*)
Minimum capital			0.014
requirement			(3.285*)
Branch banking	0.711	7.873	0.225
	(1.758*)	(2.753*)	(1.383)
Limited Agencies	0.533	0.462	0.058
	(0.843)	(0.459)	(0.232)
Population	0.006	0.051	0.003
density	(4.103*)	(5.363*)	(5.549*)
Vault cash reserve			0.038
requirements on			(0.983)
demand deposits			
Vault cash reserve			−0.035
requirements on			(−0.909)
time deposits			
Goodness of Fit			
R^2	0.344	0.519	0.722
F-statistic	9.23*	16.83*	17.70*

NOTE: The dependent variable is average bank deposits in millions of dollars by state in 1924. The numbers in parentheses are *t*-statistics.
* Significant at the 0.05 level.

establishment of limited agencies is not significant. For non-member banks, population density and the state minimum capital and reserve requirements were the only significant variables. Although branching is not significant, it may still be important, as a dummy variable is a poor way to capture the effects of widely differing branching laws.

The most interesting feature of Table 3.8 is the relative consistency in magnitude between the coefficients on the branching and those on the population density variable. The coefficients indicate that banks needed a population density

of over 100 persons per square mile to attain the same average
size as they could with some form of branching.[71] This also
suggests that there was considerable potential for growth in
the size of banks, had at least some limited types of branching
been allowed. Only ten states—Connecticut (307.2), Delaware
(117.0), Illinois (126.0), Maryland (155.4), Massachusetts (508.3),
New Jersey (478.6), New York (240.2), Ohio (151.5), Pennsylvania (204.2), and Rhode Island (608.1)—had population
densities higher than 100. Many states could easily have increased bank size through liberalization of branching laws.

In an attempt to determine the effects of bank size on the
portion of commercial-bank deposits in the Federal Reserve
System, an ordinary least squares regression was performed
on state data for 1924:

$$\text{MEM} = 0.582 + 0.035 \text{ SIZE}$$
$$(25.379) \quad (3.798)$$
$$R^2 = 0.238 \quad F_{1,\,47} = 14.42$$

The dependent variable, MEM, was the percentage of all commercial-bank deposits in the Federal Reserve System, and the
sole independent variable, SIZE, was the average deposit size
of all commercial banks in millions of dollars. The numbers
in parentheses are t-statistics. The independent variable was
significant at the 5 percent level. The coefficient does appear
to be quite reasonable in light of additional evidence presented below. The model indicates that if the average size of
commercial banks in a state was $8 million, then 85.5 percent
of the state's total deposits would be held by members of the
Federal Reserve.

Another simple way to assess the importance of branching
is to examine those states in which branching was not only

[71] This can be seen by multiplying the coefficient on population density by
100. The resulting number will be approximately equal to the coefficient on
branching.

permitted but supported by the state banking authorities. The *Federal Reserve Bulletin* singled out six states—California, Louisiana, Massachusetts, Michigan, New York, and Ohio—where branching was highly developed.[72] It was in these states that the Federal Reserve System was strongest. In 1914, the commercial banks in these states held 35.5 percent of all of the nation's deposits. National banks held 46.8 percent of all deposits in the six states, not very different from the national banks in the rest of the country, which possessed 51.1 percent of all deposits in the remaining states.[73] By 1919, this situation was altered dramatically as state banks permitted to branch joined the Federal Reserve. The six states in that year accounted for 43.3 percent of the nation's commercial-bank deposits. Federal Reserve members in these states held 79.4 percent of all the deposits in these states, which amounted to 34.4 percent of all U.S. commercial-bank deposits. All the rest of the banks in the Federal Reserve System had deposits accounting for 35.3 percent of all the nation's deposits. By 1924, Federal Reserve member banks had expanded their position in these six states to hold 86.3 percent of all commercial-bank deposits in them. This was equal to 37.0 percent of all United States deposits. The rest of the member banks in the country held 35.7 percent. Also, the percentage of deposits in the Federal Reserve System in the rest of the states was considerably less, 62.5. This again points to the importance of branching, although it should be noted that several of these states had high population densities which would also contribute to the large size of banks. This evidence suggests that if the rest of the country had eased its branching restrictions to a degree comparable to that found in these six states, the

[72] Board of Governors of the Federal Reserve System, *Federal Reserve Bulletin*, 13 (May 1927), pp. 317 ff.

[73] These figures are calculated from Board of Governors of the Federal Reserve System, *Banking and Monetary Statistics*, pp. 24–33.

Federal Reserve might have had somewhere around 86.3 percent of all bank deposits—substantially higher than its actual
72.7 percent.

What is impossible to determine is how free state-wide or
nationwide branching would have affected membership. Yet
all the evidence, historical and contemporary, does indicate
that branching on such a scale would have promoted the growth
of very large banks which would most likely have become
members of the Federal Reserve.

The Limits on Membership in the Federal Reserve System

From its inception, the Federal Reserve System's membership problems stemmed from its inability to draw in the smaller
unit state banks which were located more in rural than urban
areas. These institutions often could not meet the minimum
capital requirements of the Federal Reserve and possessed
little eligible paper for rediscounting. They found the higher
reserve requirements, stricter supervision, and par clearance
onerous. The Federal Reserve tried to coax them into the
system but to no avail. The empirical evidence in this chapter
indicates that more radical changes lowering reserve and capital requirements would still not have brought in most of the
nonmember banks. The alternative means for expanding
membership in the Federal Reserve System was to liberalize
branching. The absorption of smaller banks into branching
banks would have overcome the dependence on persuading
individual banks to join. Branching, however, was also fiercely
resisted by the unit banking lobbies in Washington and the
state capitals. Unless Congress was willing to dilute completely
the Federal Reserve's regulations or ease the restrictions on
branching, there was no means, short of coercion, to extend
the system's coverage. The dual banking system continued to
be a headache for federal regulators who feared that their

ability to control the expansion of credit was hindered by the large number of banks that remained beyond their regulatory reach. They were convinced that the Federal Reserve could not carry out its mission unless the banking system was unified under their control.

4

State Banking Reforms:
Deposit Insurance as a Solution
to the Problems of the
Banking System

The States and Banking Reform

CONGRESS and the state legislatures responded to the panic of 1907 with legislation aimed at strengthening the nation's banking system. Most studies of banking reform focus solely on the events at the federal level that led to the creation of the Federal Reserve System, conveying the impression that there was little activity at the state level.[1] The state legislatures did not, however, stand by idly, waiting for the federal government to act. The response of several states to the panic was to propose the establishment of state-sponsored deposit guarantee funds. This began a spirited debate that defined sharply the points of conflict between the different schools of banking reform and widened the rifts between them. Where it was adopted deposit insurance strongly influenced the development of banking and caused some serious problems. The

[1] Robert Craig West, *Banking Reform and the Federal Reserve, 1863–1923.* Robert H. Wiebe, *Businessmen and Reform: A Study of the Progressive Movement.* These very useful studies focus almost exclusively on reform at the federal level.

debate over the establishment of federal deposit insurance followed the earlier arguments over the state guarantee funds. Although the creation of the Federal Deposit Insurance Corporation was a victory for those opposed to a more radical reform of banking, the new federal system benefited from the mistakes of its predecessors.

Although federal and state banking reforms took different directions after the panic of 1907, there was a certain similarity in their overall purpose. Neither tried to reverse the effects of past legislation, which had promoted the growth of thousands of unit banks. Instead, their legislation attempted to correct the banking system's malfunctioning while preserving the structure of the banking industry. The Federal Reserve Act sought to accomplish this by providing discounting facilities sufficient to prevent another liquidity crisis. As the control of the monetary base was a prerogative of the federal government, states could not follow suit. One alternative for them was deposit insurance. States could remove the motive behind panics by guaranteeing depositors recovery of their assets. The public, alert to the potential benefits of deposit insurance, switched its deposits from uninsured national banks to insured state banks. This led to a spectacular increase in the deposits and number of state banks relative to national banks. Insurance of deposits thus increased the attractiveness of a state charter. Even though this was not the primary motive behind this legislation it did help to counter the attempt by Congress to broaden federal control of banking by lowering reserve requirements for national banks and those state banks that joined the Federal Reserve System.

Previous Attempts to Insure Bank Liabilities

State insurance of banking liabilities was not a novel idea. Prior to the National Banking Act of 1864 and its amendments, which demolished the antebellum state banking systems, several states had insurance schemes designed primarily to protect bank-note issue. Preeminent among these was the New York Safety Fund created in 1829. Assessing banks on their capital, New York provided a fund that gave 100 percent protection to subscribing banks' liabilities. Financial crises placed a heavy strain on it, but the Safety Fund and the systems of Indiana, Iowa, Michigan, and Ohio were able to withstand all the antebellum crises. Only the Vermont system failed to give insured claimants payment in full.[2] When the national banks were allowed to monopolize the issue of bank notes, they were required to back them with U.S. bonds, and the total volume of notes was strictly limited. With bank notes secured in this fashion, insurance was superfluous.

The resurgence in the 1880s of state-chartered banks was based on the development of deposit banking, which circumvented the national-bank monopoly of bank notes. The idea of insuring deposits was first widely considered after the panic of 1893. In that panic, unlike that of 1907, banks did not preemptively suspend payments, and 491 commercial banks failed compared to a total of 243 for 1907–1908.[3] To alleviate the plight of the failed banks' depositors, William Jennings Bryan presented a bill to Congress in 1893 to establish a deposit insurance fund. Several state legislatures in the West also debated the issue, but no action was taken, even though banks continued to fail at an alarmingly high rate after the panic was over.[4] This was primarily the result of an agricultural depression, and bank failures were significantly higher in the South and the West.[5] There was little that deposit in-

[2] Carter H. Golembe, "The Deposit Insurance Legislation of 1933: An Examination of Its Antecedents and Purposes," pp. 183–187.

[3] A. Piatt Andrew, "Substitutes for Cash in the Panic of 1907," pp. 513–514. Board of Governors of the Federal Reserve System, *Banking and Monetary Statistics, 1914–1941*, p. 283.

[4] W. E. Kuhn, *History of Nebraska Banking: A Centennial Retrospect*, p. 13.

[5] Hugh Rockoff, "Regional Interest Rates and Bank Failures, 1870–1914," p. 92.

surance could do to prevent these failures, and interest in deposit insurance waned in the late 1890s when agricultural prices began to recover.

The Debate over Deposit Insurance

The panic of 1907 reawakened interest in deposit insurance, and nowhere did the idea enjoy greater currency than in the populist West. At the height of the crisis in December 1907, the Oklahoma legislature passed the first law since the Civil War to guarantee bank liabilities. Its example was followed shortly by the legislatures of Kansas, Nebraska, South Dakota, and Texas. The remaining state deposit insurance systems of Mississippi, North Dakota, and Washington were established after the founding of the Federal Reserve System. While deposit insurance legislation was passed by these states under a variety of circumstances, their banking systems all had similar characteristics.

The states in which deposit insurance was adopted had, by previous legislation, all firmly established unit banking within their boundaries and were all in relatively undiversified regions where business prosperity in general depended on one or two commodities. Support for deposit insurance came primarily from small-town country bankers. The opposition to the guarantee of deposits came largely from city bankers, and in states in which they were the dominant element in the industry, deposit insurance was not seriously considered.

The divisions within the banking industry over the question of deposit insurance and reform in general arose principally from differences in the size and scope of banks' operations. These were, in turn, the product of differences in regional conditions and state regulations. The size of banks was determined by population density, minimum capital requirements, and branching restrictions. Widespread prohibition of branching meant the vast majority of banks were restricted to a single office. Population density limited to a large degree the potential number of depositors and borrowers of single-office banks. Minimum capital requirements imposed a lower bound on bank size. Rural states with low population densities had, typically, low capital requirements to ensure that small communities would not be deprived of bank offices. This created banking systems in the southern and western states dominated by hundreds of small unit banks. Greater population density coupled with higher capital requirements and some branching established larger, more diversified banks in the East.

In states in which regulation and low population density had created many small unit banks, the banking industry was particularly vulnerable to economic fluctuations, owing to each bank's small number of depositors and undiversified loan portfolios. Country bankers often looked favorably on deposit insurance, viewing it as a means of protecting themselves and their depositors from the danger of a panic. The alternative was to allow increased branching. This would have permitted banks to insure themselves by gaining more depositors, lessening the probability of large unexpected withdrawals, and by offering loans to more types of business, decreasing the danger of investing too heavily in one type of activity.

Although most country bankers were unwilling to consider branch banking as an alternative, many contemporary observers recognized the superior safety offered by branch banking. In an article in the *Quarterly Journal of Economics* in 1903, Oliver M. W. Sprague of Harvard argued that branch banking provided banks with a form of insurance:

> The larger the number of individual borrowers, the smaller is the likelihood, in general, of serious loss from their failure to meet obligations. The danger of heavy losses at any one time is further reduced if the bank is engaged in business over a wide geographical area, with loans based upon more kinds of business than is possible to local banks, except in large centers

of population. . . . The larger the number of depositors and the more varied their business, the less likely are their demands to come at any one time. Such demands vary with the season of the year, both in different trades and different sections of the country. . . . The bank with many branches can concentrate its reserves whenever the demand arises.[6]

This potential for diversification enabled branching banks to reduce their exposure to risk, lessening their desire for government-provided insurance which might force them to join a system with smaller less well diversified banks.

In spite of its recognized benefits, branch banking was severely limited at the turn of the century by the ban on national banks' and most state banks' branching. Thus, branching banks held only a fraction of total bank assets or offices. Most of the nation's banks were small unit banks spread out over the country. This dispersion also reduced the possibility of interbank cooperation which might have substituted for the intrabank coordination that strengthened branching banks. Deposit insurance appeared to offer an alternative to branching and interbank cooperation, and it was thus promoted as protecting the small country bank from panics. Deposit holders in these banks wanted to protect their assets, and the guarantee of deposits offered a solution that was acceptable to their bankers, holding at bay the populist menace of the large bankers' "money trust."

None of the states in which large banks were dominant ever seriously considered deposit insurance. In a few states, relatively higher capital requirements and some provision for branching ensured the growth of larger banks that could manage financial crises more easily. Conservative bankers in the Northeast and the mid-Atlantic states were adamantly opposed to deposit insurance. James B. Forgan, one of the leading Chicago bankers, wrote a pamphlet attacking the idea of deposit insurance. He expressed the fears of many of his

[6] Oliver M. W. Sprague, "Branch Banking in the United States," p. 243.

associates: "Is there anything in the relations existing between banks and their customers to justify the proposition that in the banking business the good should be taxed to pay for the bad; ability taxed to pay for incompetency; honesty taxed to pay for dishonesty; experience and training taxed to pay for the errors of inexperience and lack of training; and knowledge taxed to pay for the mistakes of ignorance?"[7] This fear of bankers in the major financial centers that they would have to pay for the weakness and recklessness of other bankers was widespread. It was reflected in an editorial published by the *Philadelphia Enquirer* in 1909 when several states were considering deposit insurance legislation. The author anathematized deposit insurance: "The idea of furnishing a guarantee for bank deposits is one of those crude, half-baked, ill-digested notions in which the populist West is so prolific. A bad deposit is a debt like any other and there is no more reason why it should be guaranteed by law than there is in the case of any other kind of indebtedness."[8] Many of these bankers thought that the only way to strengthen the banking system was to increase branching.

The argument that the adoption of deposit insurance by a state was determined by the interests of its banking community is supported by the "economic" theory of regulation. As laid out by Stigler and Posner, the economic theory of regulation posits that regulation is a good like any other which will be supplied to those who value it the most.[9] In place of price signals in the marketplace, political pressure is applied in the legislature. The more highly a particular type of regulation is valued by an industry or interest group, the greater the lobbying effort it will make. In contrast to the theory of

[7] James B. Forgan, *Guaranty of National Bank Deposits*, p. 3, quoted in Thomas B. Robb, *The Guaranty of Bank Deposits*, p. 193.

[8] Kuhn, *History of Nebraska Banking*, p. 18.

[9] George Stigler, "The Theory of Economic Regulation." Richard Posner, "Theories of Economic Regulation."

cartels, which posits that an industry will be more successful at setting a joint price and securing its subsequent enforcement if the number of firms is small, the economic theory of regulation argues that an industry will be more likely to obtain favorable regulation (and hence, prices and profits) when it is made up of many firms. The costs of forming and maintaining a cartel are too high when there is a large number of firms; however, the existence of many firms may enhance an industry's ability to lobby. In the banking industry there were thousands of firms well distributed throughout the country, and banks were able to exert considerable pressure on Congress and the state legislatures. Another factor likely to increase political activity is an asymmetry of interests within an industry.[10] If there are divisions in the industry, each group will be drawn into politics. The banking industry, in which the interests of the larger banks conflicted with those of the smaller banks, is an example of such asymmetry, which created an incentive for banks to try to influence the legislatures.

The struggle by each section of the banking industry to protect its position is revealed in the legislative struggles over deposit insurance. The smaller, usually rural, banks eager to have the state legislatures establish deposit insurance encountered strong opposition from the larger, more conservative banks. The Texas legislature made membership in the state guarantee fund compulsory but sought to accommodate both parties by giving its state banks a choice between joining the Depositors Guaranty Fund where they paid in annually 1 percent of their average daily deposits, or the Bond Security System where they posted a bond of indemnity equal to their capital with a surety company.[11] In Nebraska and Mississippi, the state bankers' associations organized by the larger state banks vigorously lobbied their state legislatures to block de-

---

[10] Posner, "Theories of Economic Regulation," pp. 10–14.

[11] Joseph M. Grant and Lawrence L. Crum, *The Development of State-Chartered Banking in Texas*, pp. 82–83.

posit insurance laws but to no avail. The Nebraska Bankers' Association challenged the constitutionality of its state's statute, but the law was upheld by the Supreme Court in 1911.[12] The larger state banks in Nebraska and other states responded by taking out national bank charters to avoid compulsory insurance. Kansas, South Dakota, and Washington avoided these battles by offering voluntary deposit insurance. Not only did eight states pass deposit insurance legislation and several others seriously consider it, but 150 bills for guaranteeing deposits were also submitted to Congress between 1907 and 1933. Most of these came from the representatives of the southern and western states where unit banking was firmly established. One-third of the bills were sponsored by representatives from the states of Kansas, Nebraska, Oklahoma, and Texas.[13]

Branch banking and deposit insurance were incompatible. No state that permitted branch banking seriously entertained the idea of deposit insurance. In contrast to other western states, California responded to the panic of 1907 by passing the most liberal contemporary branch banking law; a deposit guarantee fund was not considered. In the unit banking state of Minnesota there was strong agitation for deposit insurance, but the country bankers failed to overcome the resistance of the Twin Cities bankers. However, when the latter began to open branch offices in the early 1920s, the country bankers, allied with certain city bankers, obtained a law prohibiting branching.[14] In southern and western states, the state bankers associations were dominated by unit banks, and they mounted successful campaigns to limit or prohibit branching in their states. They tried to enlist the support of their customers, playing on fears that funds would be siphoned off to the big city and local credit would dry up. One indication of their

[12] Robb, *The Guaranty of Bank Deposits*, pp. 162–170.
[13] Golembe, "The Deposit Insurance Legislation of 1933."
[14] Charles S. Popple, *Development of Two Bank Groups in the Central Northwest*, p. 113.

success was the defeat in a 1924 Illinois referendum of a law to permit branching by a two-to-one margin.[15] In the state of Washington, they were able to overturn a long-established law permitting branching and secure the passage of a law creating a deposit guarantee fund.[16]

Banking reformers were thus divided into two hostile camps, one bent on preserving, the other on eliminating unit banking. These positions were maintained and sharpened in succeeding years, and the debate over the creation of the Federal Deposit Insurance Corporation reflected this division. The Comptroller of the Currency, John Pole, commented on the Banking Act of 1933. He stated: "I am in agreement with the ultimate purpose of this bill, namely, greater safety to the depositor. The method proposed by the bill and the principles which I advocate stand at opposite poles. A general guaranty of bank deposits is the very antithesis of branch banking."[17] An opponent of Pole and a key supporter of the bill, Representative Henry Steagall, chairman of the House Committee on Banking and Currency, agreed that the bill would defend unit banking. He argued that: "This bill will preserve independent dual banking in the United States . . . that is what this bill is intended to do."[18]

The Structure of the Banking Industry and the Demand for Deposit Insurance

If the characterization of the division on the question of banking reform presented above is correct, then the disposition of each state's legislature toward deposit insurance should have been influenced by the existing banking legislation and the banking structure it created. States in which the small unit

---

[15] Shirley D. Southworth, *Branch Banking in the United States*, pp. 17–71.
[16] State Bank Examiner of the State of Washington, *Annual Report*.
[17] Golembe, "The Deposit Insurance Legislation of 1933," p. 197.
[18] Ibid., p. 198.

bank was uncontested should have been inclined to consider seriously or adopt deposit insurance, while states in which larger banks predominated and some branching was allowed should have opposed the guarantee of deposits.

To test the hypothesis that a state's existing banking structure conditioned its response to deposit insurance proposals, a probit analysis was employed. Qualitative-response analysis is appropriate here since the dependent variable, the establishment of deposit insurance, is dichotomous. There are two approaches to examining the choice of deposit insurance. The first examines the individual factors that affected the banks' ability to diversify their activities to insure themselves and hence affected their desire for state-provided deposit insurance. It includes as independent variables the three major regulations determining the structure of the banking industry; the minimum capital requirements for non-reserve-city banks, a dummy variable for branch banking, and the reserve requirement for non-reserve-city banks.[19] It was hypothesized that higher capital requirements and provision for some branching, which would tend to eliminate smaller unit banks, would make deposit insurance less likely, while higher reserve requirements would make it more probable as these reduced the profitability of banking. The fourth variable was the ratio of rural to total state population, taken from the 1910 census.[20] The hypothesis here was that the lower the population density, the smaller the average size of banks and the more vulnerable they would be to irregularities in withdrawals of deposits, increasing the need for deposit insurance. The last

[19] These data were obtained from Samuel A. Welldon, *Digest of State Banking Statutes*, supplemented by the Board of Governors of the Federal Reserve System, *Federal Reserve Bulletin*, 4 (October 1917), pp. 768–795, 10 (March 1924), pp. 154–181, and U.S. Comptroller of the Currency, *Annual Report*, various years.

[20] U.S. Department of Commerce, *Historical Statistics of the United States*, pp. 24–37. Rural population is defined as those people living in towns of 2,500 or less.

variable was the ratio of assets in the failed state banks to the total assets of state banks for the period 1903–1909. It was expected that the higher the failure rate the more likely a state would be to adopt deposit insurance.[21] The second formulation of the model has as its argument that the distribution of the size of banks influenced the adoption of deposit insurance. Its independent variables are the average size of state and national banks by state in 1908.[22] The hypothesis here was that the smaller the average bank size, the greater the pressure applied by banks on the legislature to secure deposit insurance to protect them.

The probit estimates of the coefficients and standard errors are presented in Table 4.1, with the approximate t-statistics. The log likelihood ratio test indicated that both equations were significant at the 5 percent level, and the pseudo-R^2 was found to be equal to 0.305 and 0.361 for Model I and Model II respectively.[23]

The results in Table 4.1 support the hypothesis that a state's banking regulation or structure determined its response to deposit insurance. For Model I all the estimated coefficients had the expected sign, except for the ratio of rural to total population. Branch banking, minimum capital, and reserve requirements were all significant at the 10 percent level, while the ratio of rural to total population and the failure rate were not. Alternative measures of the last two variables were employed to determine if the estimates were sensitive to any

[21] U.S. Comptroller of the Currency, *Annual Report*, 1903–1909. For states adopting deposit insurance later, the failure rate was adjusted.

[22] This uses data from U.S. Comptroller of the Currency, *Annual Report*, 1908. It would have been desirable to include other moments of the distribution of bank size (variance and skewness) to judge the relative strength of the different groups. Unfortunately these were too costly to calculate given the over 19,000 banks in existence in this year.

[23] The statistic for Model I was 13.18 and for Model II, 11.27. The pseudo-R^2 was calculated for each equation and found to be 0.305 and 0.261 for Models I and II respectively. See Appendix B for a discussion of these measures of goodness of fit.

Table 4.1
State Selection of Deposit Insurance, Probit Estimates

	Model I	Model II
Independent Variables		
Intercept	−0.706	0.438
	(−0.428)	(0.752)
Minimum capital requirement	−0.074	
	(−1.559*)	
Branch banking	−5.493	
	(−1.454*)	
Total reserve requirements	0.065	
on demand deposits	(1.415*)	
Ratio of rural to total state	−0.075	
population	(−0.045)	
State bank failure rate	30.429	
	(1.291)	
Average size of national banks		−0.290
		(−0.401)
Average size of state banks		−4.569
		(−1.593*)
Goodness of Fit		
Log likelihood ratio test statistic	13.18*	11.27*
Pseudo-R^2	0.305	0.261

NOTE: The numbers in parentheses are approximate *t*-statistics obtained by dividing the estimated coefficients by their estimated standard errors.
   * Significant at the 0.10 level.

particular measure. Population density measured as inhabitants per square mile in 1910 and national-, non-national-, and commercial-bank failure rates in terms of assets or the number of banks were substituted for the nonsignificant variables; but they did not substantially alter the results.

One possible explanation for the lack of significance of the bank failure rate may be that to the extent that differences in failure rates were a consequence of differences in the structure of the banking industry in each state, the regulation variables would pick this up directly. Only other sources of failure would be indicated by this coefficient, and these may be slight. Agricultural prosperity after the turn of the century helped to diminish regional differences in failure rates. The marked convergence of failure rates in all regions may thus ensure this variable's weakness.[24]

In Model II the average size of state banks is significant, although the average size of national banks does have the correct sign. It seems plausible to find that national banks did not exert an influence on the choice of deposit insurance for they were prohibited by the U.S. Attorney General from joining the state deposit guarantee systems in 1908.

It is not surprising that both models perform equally well. The average size of state banks can, to a large degree, be explained by the regulations imposed by each state on its industry. In an ordinary least squares regression of the average size of state banks on the minimum capital requirements, the branching dummy, and the ratio of rural to total population, all significantly contributed to explaining average bank size at the 5 percent level. The coefficient on reserve requirements was not significant. The equation explained 58 percent of the variance in the average size of banks.[25]

The explanatory power of the models may be gauged by their ability to predict which states actually adopted deposit insurance. Prediction is based on the estimated probit coefficients.[26] The probabilities of any state passing a law guaranteeing deposits given the estimated value of its probit index are presented in Table 4.2 for Model I and Table 4.3 for Model II.

It is striking that in Table 4.2 no state with branch banking had greater than a 5 percent probability of adopting deposit insurance and that in Table 4.3 there are only three excep-

[24] Rockoff, "Regional Interest Rates and Bank Failures, 1870–1914," p. 92.

[25] The dependent variable was the total assets of state banks in thousands of dollars divided by the number of banks, or "size." The regression equation was: size = 0.53 + 0.025 minimum capital requirement + 0.33 branching dummy − 0.005 total reserve requirement + 0.009 vault cash reserve requirement − 0.84 population density. All the estimates were significant at the 5 percent level except for reserve requirements. The F-statistic was equal to 13.6, being significant at 5 percent and the R^2 was equal to 0.58.

[26] For a more detailed description of the procedure see Appendix B.

Table 4.2

Model I: Probability that a State Selects Deposit Insurance Given the Estimated Value of Its Probit Index
(in percent)

0–5	6–10	11–20	21–30	31–40	41–50	51 and over
Arizona	Illinois	Michigan	Arkansas	Wisconsin	Minnesota	North Carolina
California[a]	Iowa	Pennsylvania	South Carolina	North Dakota[b]	South Dakota[b]	Montana
Delaware[a]	New Mexico	Kentucky	Idaho	Kansas[b]	Wyoming	Texas[b]
Florida[a]	Mississippi[b]	Alabama	Nebraska[b]		Washington[b]	
Georgia[a]	Ohio		Nevada			
Louisiana[a]	Virginia		Oklahoma[b]			
Maine[a]	Colorado		Utah			
Massachusetts[a]	Indiana		Maryland			
Missouri[a]						
New Jersey						
New York[a]						
Oregon						
Rhode Island[a]						
Tennessee[a]						
Vermont						
New Hampshire						
Connecticut						
West Virginia						

SOURCE: The probabilities are calculated from the estimates of Model I in Table 4.1 using the method described in Appendix B.

NOTE: In each category the states are listed in ascending order of probability.

[a] Permitted some form of branch banking.

[b] Adopted deposit insurance.

Table 4.3
Model II: Probability that a State Selects Deposit Insurance Given the Estimated Value of Its Probit Index
(in percent)

0–5	6–10	11–20	21–30	31–40	41–50	51 and over
California[a]	Maryland	Wisconsin	Florida[a]	Colorado	Wyoming	North Dakota[b]
Connecticut	West Virginia	Virginia	South Carolina	Idaho	Texas[b]	Oklahoma[b]
Delaware[a]	Arizona	Iowa	Georgia[a]	Minnesota	South Dakota[b]	
Illinois	Montana	Alabama	Mississippi[b]	North Carolina		
Maine[a]		Kentucky		Arkansas		
Massachusetts[a]		Indiana		New Mexico		
Michigan		Tennessee[a]		Kansas[b]		
New Jersey		New Hampshire		Nebraska[b]		
New York[a]		Vermont				
Ohio						
Pennsylvania						
Rhode Island[a]						
Utah						
Louisiana[a]						
Missouri[a]						
Nevada						
Washington[b]						
Oregon						

SOURCE: The probabilities are calculated from the estimates of Model II in Table 4.1 using the method described in Appendix B.

NOTE: In each category the states are listed in ascending order of probability.
[a] Permitted some form of branch banking.
[b] Adopted deposit insurance.

tions. Those states that set their minimum capital requirement greater than or equal to the National Banking System's $25,000 minimum never had greater than a 10 percent chance of guaranteeing deposits. The appearance of Mississippi and Washington as outliers may be explained by the fact that in both cases deposit insurance was hastily imposed by the state legislature in response to crises other than panics. Although there had been some support in the state of Washington for deposit insurance after the panic of 1907, bills before the legislature were routinely defeated. But in 1917, while the bill was being debated, four banks in the city of Seattle failed; and the opposition to the act was overwhelmed.[27] Up to the time Washington passed its act to guarantee deposits, a limited form of branching had permitted the growth of relatively large commercial banks compared to other states in the West. The high average size of state banks in Washington accounts for its low probability of adopting deposit insurance in Table 4.3. Mississippi adopted deposit insurance not in response to a panic but to the disastrous cotton crop of 1913, which caused many banks to fail. The states that had high probabilities of guaranteeing deposits but failed to do so may also be accounted for. Although information on agitation for deposit insurance in each state is scant, it does appear that many of those states that had high probabilities had strong movements pressing for such legislation. There was considerable sentiment in Montana and Minnesota for the establishment of deposit guarantee funds. The Wisconsin legislature seriously considered deposit insurance but voted down the bill when, in the midst of hearings on a projected fund, the Oklahoma system of insurance broke down.[28] Thus it may be concluded that states that favored unit banking through their legislation were inclined to adopt deposit insurance to provide banks with additional protection.

[27] Robb, *The Guaranty of Bank Deposits*, pp. 170–172.
[28] Ibid., pp. 161–162 and Popple, *Development of Two Bank Groups*, p. 101.

A Comparison between the American and the Canadian Banking Systems

It is instructive to compare how Canada, a country similar to the United States in many ways, resolved the problem of guaranteeing the convertibility of deposits. In the early twentieth century, there was no interest in insuring deposits in Canada. This may be attributed to the fact that Canada's banking system permitted free nationwide branching. The minimum capital requirement of $500,000 was greater than that for any class of state or national bank in the United States. This promoted a system of large branching banks whose offices were spread across the country.[29] Branching was well established and spreading rapidly. In 1890 there were 38 chartered banks with 426 branches, while in 1910 there were 28 banks with a total of 2,367 branches.[30] Compared to the American system, Canadian banking was virtually unregulated. There were no reserve requirements or state supervision. The most important regulation was that chartered banks could not issue bank notes in excess of the par value of their capital. Banks recognized their interdependence, and the small number made cooperation relatively easy. As the economic theory of regulation predicts, a cartellike association rather than government provision of insurance was the means by which Canadian banks guaranteed their deposits and notes. In 1892, the chartered banks formed the Canadian Bankers' Association. This organization coordinated the reform efforts of bankers; and, in 1900, this voluntary association was given the status of a public corporation with the primary purpose of superintending the issue of notes. Banks agreed to open

[29] Joseph French Johnson, *The Canadian Banking System*, pp. 18–19.
[30] Benjamin Haggot Beckhart, "The Banking System in Canada," in Henry Parker Willis and Benjamin Haggot Beckhart, *Foreign Banking Systems*, pp. 327, 362.

enough provincial redemption centers to ensure that their notes would not be discounted, but circulate at par.[31]

The same factors that caused money markets to tighten in the United States in 1907 and precipitated the panic were present in Canada. But, while credit became very tight and there were some bank failures, no panic occurred. The Canadian banks were well aware of their mutual interdependence and of how the failure of one bank to meet its obligations in a time of financial stringency could prejudice the interests of the others and a run on the banks begin. When the Bank of Ontario failed in October 1906, bankers were afraid that this bank's failure to sustain convertibility might endanger them all. To prevent this, the Bank of Montreal agreed to take over the Bank of Ontario's assets and pay all liabilities, provided the other banks would agree to accept a share of its losses. This was all done behind closed doors on the day of the bank's demise. The next day the bank and all its branches opened as part of the Bank of Montreal. Similarly, when the Sovereign Bank was close to suspending its operations in 1908, its business was taken over by twelve other institutions.[32] Most of Canada's mergers in this period were begun when small banks approaching insolvency solicited offers from larger banks.[33] This private action by industry contrasts with what happened in the United States in 1907 when Knickerbocker Trust Company failed to obtain a loan from another city bank, precipitating a run on the bank and igniting the panic.[34]

This comparison of the American and Canadian banking systems supports the propositions of the economic theory of

---

[31] Roeliff Morton Breckenridge, *History of Banking in Canada*, pp. 131–134.

[32] Johnson, *The Canadian Banking System*, pp. 124–127.

[33] Beckhart, "The Banking System in Canada," in Willis and Beckhart, *Foreign Banking Systems*, p. 340.

[34] Milton Friedman and Anna J. Schwartz, *A Monetary History of the United States, 1867–1960*, pp. 159–163. Interbank cooperation was not unknown in the United States. The actions of the Chicago Clearinghouse in 1905 probably prevented a panic. See Chapter 2 for a description of these events.

regulation and suggests that the number of firms may determine how a banking industry will seek to insure its liabilities. The fact that there were so few Canadian banks enabled them to cooperate in a mutual guarantee of their note issue and deposits. In the United States it was virtually impossible for the large number of banks to cooperate when a panic threatened. The larger banks sought to increase branching to strengthen the industry but met the opposition of the smaller banks. Anxious to protect themselves from absorption by larger banks, the small, country banks promoted state-sponsored deposit insurance as a means of guaranteeing bank liabilities.

The Design of the State Guarantee Funds and Their Demise

The American experiment with deposit insurance had two phases. In the first, the state banking authorities learned from bitter experience what modern economists have established on a theoretical basis. Provision of deposit insurance where the premium or assessment is fixed and free of the risk characteristics of a bank's portfolio, and where the bank's asset choice is left free and unsupervised, will create an incentive to hold very risky portfolios.[35] The "moral hazard" created by fixed-premium insurance encouraged banks to substitute state-supplied insurance for self-insurance in the form of greater capital and surplus.[36] The insurer—the state—thus found itself faced with a rising number of bank failures and imposed

[35] John H. Karekan and Neil Wallace, "Deposit Insurance and Bank Regulation: A Partial Equilibrium Exposition."

[36] The theory is laid out in Isaac Ehrlich and Gary Becker, "Market Insurance, Self-Protection, and Self-Insurance." Sam Peltzman found that in spite of capital-to-asset restrictions, federal deposit insurance has led banks to substitute deposit insurance for capital. Sam Peltzman, "Capital Investment in Commercial Banking and Its Relationship to Portfolio Regulation." Although later studies have offered some contradictory evidence, the hypothesis that banks substitute FDIC insurance for capital cannot be ruled out. See Gerald P. Dwyer, Jr., "The Effects of the Banking Acts of 1933 and 1935 on Capital Investment in Commercial Banking."

additional regulations on capital as well as other controls to limit the risk to which banks exposed themselves. In the second phase, the state legislatures were forced to terminate deposit insurance when the rising number of bank failures brought about by a regional depression bankrupted the guarantee funds. What the states did not foresee was that while deposit insurance, if properly designed, could prevent bank failures by reducing the motive behind a panic, it could not stem a wave of failures brought about by a general economic downturn. The principal characteristics of each state's deposit insurance law are presented in Table 4.4.

OKLAHOMA

Oklahoma had rushed to establish a deposit guarantee system in 1907, and little attention was given to its design. An assessment on bank capital was levied to create an insurance fund, all deposits were insured, immediate payment upon closure was promised, and advertisement of insurance was allowed. The Oklahoma legislature had intended the fund to provide protection for all commercial banking institutions, but the United States Attorney General ruled in 1908 that national banks could not join, and thus deposit insurance was limited to state banks and trust companies.[37] With virtually no supervision or further regulation, deposit insurance decreased banks' risks considerably and led to a rapid expansion of state banks. Between March 1908, when the legislation went into effect, and November 1909, state banks increased from 470 to 662, with their deposits rising from $18 million to $50 million. National banks, on the other hand, declined from 312 to 220 as banks took out state charters. Their deposits rose slightly, from $38 million to $42 million.[38] These developments offer a striking contrast to the slower growth, nationwide, of banks after the panic of 1907. State banks had increased at an annual rate of 15.9 percent, and national banks

[37] Thornton Cooke, "The Insurance of Bank Deposits in the West," p. 90.
[38] Robb, *The Guaranty of Bank Deposits*, pp. 82–87.

at 7.8 percent in the period 1897–1907, but this slowed to 4.9 and 2.4 percent, respectively, for 1907–1914.[39] Meanwhile, membership in Oklahoma's banking system jumped 40.8 percent in a little over a year.

This frenzy of activity resulted in severe problems for the deposit guarantee fund. The crisis began with the collapse of the largest bank in the state, the Columbia Bank and Trust Company. This bank had greatly overextended itself, increasing its loans with inadequate collateral without increasing its capital. Its deposits climbed from $365,000 in September 1908 to $2,806,000 in September 1909. The bank's demise in 1909 immediately threatened the insurance fund, which contained only $400,000, and a special levy on all other member banks was required to pay off the depositors.[40]

This was only the first in a rising number of failures which undermined the system of deposit insurance. The Oklahoma legislature responded to this crisis by overhauling the deposit guarantee law in 1909. The new law tried to ensure that the fund would not be exhausted. It provided for fixed annual assessments of 0.25 percent of average daily deposits to raise the fund gradually from its original 1 percent to 5 percent of average daily deposits, and special assessments of up to 2 percent a year were allowed to maintain the fund.[41] The legislature also imposed additional restraints on banks to reduce the possibility of failure. Banks, henceforth, were to receive deposits up to at most ten times their capital and surplus. Supervision of banks was also improved. Previously the composition of the state banking board was purely political, consisting of the governor, the lieutenant governor, the president of the Board of Agriculture, the state treasurer, and the state auditor. The conservative bankers of the state bankers asso-

---

[39] Calculated from U.S. Department of Commerce, *Historical Statistics*, pp. 1025–1030.

[40] Cooke, "The Insurance of Bank Deposits in the West," pp. 328–332 and Robb, *The Guaranty of Bank Deposits*, pp. 43–57.

[41] Cooke, "The Insurance of Bank Deposits in the West," pp. 336–338.

Table 4.4
Characteristics of State Deposit Insurance Systems

State	Date of Legislation	Participation	First Assessment	Annual Assessment
Oklahoma	1907	Compulsory	1% of deposits	To maintain fund
	1909	Compulsory	1% of deposits	0.25% of deposits
Texas	1909			
Deposit guarantee		Choice of one compulsory	1% of deposits	0.25% of deposits
Bond security			Bond equal to capital	
Kansas	1909	Voluntary	$500 cash or bonds for each $100,000 deposits	0.05% of deposits
Washington	1917	Voluntary	$1,000 cash or bonds for each $100,000 deposits	0.5% of deposits
Nebraska	1909	Compulsory	1% of deposits	0.1% of deposits
South Dakota	1909	Voluntary	0.1% of deposits	0.1% of deposits
North Dakota	1915	Compulsory	0.25% of deposits	0.25% of deposits
	1917	Compulsory	0.05% of deposits	0.05% of deposits
Mississippi	1914	Compulsory	$500 cash or bonds for each $100,000 deposits	0.05% of deposits

SOURCES: Thornton Cooke, "The Insurance of Bank Deposits in the West." Joseph M. Grant and Lawrence L. Crum, *The Development of State-Chartered Banking in Texas*, pp. 74–87. Thomas B. Robb, *The Guaranty of Bank Deposits*.

Deposits Insured	Payment	Capital Ratio	Limit on Interest Rates	Advertising
All	Immediately	None	3%	Permitted
All	Immediately	Deposits limited to 10 times capital and surplus	3%	Permitted but penalty for advertising state protection
Non-interest bearing	Immediately	Deposits limited by size of capital	None	Permitted but penalty for advertising state protection
All	6% bonds provided until bank liquidated	Deposits limited to 10 times capital and surplus	3%	Permitted but penalty for advertising state protection
All	Upon liquidation of bank's assets	Deposits limited to 20 times capital	Set by Guaranty Board	Permitted but penalty for advertising state protection
All	When receiver determines deficiency	Investments limited to 8 times capital and surplus	None	Permitted
All	When receiver determines deficiency	Deposits limited to 15 times capital and surplus	5%	No provision
All	Unchanged	Unchanged	5%	Limited
All	When receiver determines deficiency	Set by Guaranty Board	Set by Guaranty Board	Permitted
All	When receiver determines deficiency	Deposits limited to 10 times capital and surplus	4%	No Provision

ciation put pressure on the legislature, and the law was amended to form a board composed of the state bank commissioner, his assistant, and three bankers selected by the governor from a list of nominees presented to him by the state bankers association.[42] A stiff fine was imposed on banks that advertised that deposits were guaranteed by the state rather than the deposit guarantee fund. The state bank commissioner was also given considerable discretion to determine which new banks merited a charter. This reorganization of state institutions and new controls slowly brought the situation under control. In 1914 the guarantee fund still owed depositors of failed banks over $800,000. Through regular assessments and increased authority over banking this deficit was eliminated in 1920.[43] Efforts to restore the system to solvency by increased assessments undermined it by producing what is known in the insurance literature as "adverse selection." This behavior was associated with the larger, usually more conservatively managed banks.[44] These banks had a lower probability of failure, and they took out national charters to avoid paying the special assessments brought about by the failure of the smaller banks. By 1914 only two state banks remained that had capital greater than the minimum required of national banks.[45] This flight from the banking system automatically increased the burden on those remaining in the system and threatened the fund's operation.

TEXAS

The lessons of the Oklahoma experience were not easily learned. Texas compounded Oklahoma's errors by creating its dual system of deposit insurance. The legislature, noting Oklahoma's problems, tried to limit risk taking, fixing capital-

[42] Robb, *The Guaranty of Bank Deposits*, pp. 28–29.
[43] Ibid., pp. 105–106.
[44] For a theoretical treatment of this subject, see Mark Pauly, "Overinsurance and Public Provision of Insurance: The Roles of Moral Hazard and Adverse Selection."
[45] Robb, *The Guaranty of Bank Deposits*, p. 87.

to-deposit ratios for state banks. Banks with a capital of $10,000 had to restrict their deposits to five times their capital and surplus, those with a capital of $10,000–$20,000 to six times, those with $20,000–$40,000 to seven times, those with $40,000–$75,000 to eight times, those with $75,000–$100,000 to nine times, and those with a capital of over $100,000 to ten times.[46]

Most banks opted for the less costly Depositors Guaranty Fund; 541 joined it and 43 joined the bond scheme in the first year. Bank supervision was, however, notoriously lax. Bank charters were easy to obtain, and state banks' investments were not scrutinized. Just as in Oklahoma, the number of state banks increased dramatically as a consequence of offering deposit insurance. Between 1909 and 1914, the number of state banks rose from 502 to 849, an annual rate of 17.3 percent, while national banks dropped from 535 to 519. Most of the new banks were very small and located in rural areas. When agricultural prices began to fall in the 1920s, many of these rural banks began to fail, placing a heavy burden on the fund. Additional levies on the remaining members of the fund became necessary. Eventually pressure from the banks forced the legislature to alter the 1909 statute and allow banks to switch from one system to another. Banks abandoned the Depositors Guaranty Fund en masse. By 1926, a year after the law was changed, there were only 75 banks left in the fund, and they were subjected to a 8.5 percent levy on their capital to replenish the fund. The odium of this heavy tax and widespread hostility to the bond scheme forced the legislature to abolish both types of deposit insurance in 1927.[47]

KANSAS

The Kansas deposit guarantee law of 1909, in contrast to the laws of Texas and Oklahoma, provided for voluntary deposit insurance and offered interest-bearing certificates to de-

[46] Grant and Crum, *The Development of State-Chartered Banking in Texas*, pp. 82–83.

[47] Ibid., pp. 123–184.

positors of failed banks to be redeemed upon the banks' liquidation. Each bank had to submit to a close inspection of its
books and officials. A capital-to-deposit ratio of 10 percent
was established, and advertisement of insurance was strictly
limited to giving notice that deposits were protected by the
guarantee fund not the state. Despite these tight restrictions,
designed to control the perverse incentives created by fixed
premium insurance, over half the Kansas state banks joined
the system. Owing to these regulations, the rise in the number
of state banks was not exceptional. Between 1905 and 1909
state banks had increased in number from 558 to 777, or 9.8
percent a year, and their deposits from $51 million to $93
million. In 1914 the number of banks had grown to 927, an
increase of 5.4 percent a year, with deposits of $108 million.
After growing from 171 banks with deposits of $50 million
in 1905 to 209 banks with $68 million, the National Banking
System in Kansas stagnated; and by 1914 it contained 213
banks with deposits of $69 million.[48] Kansas's close regulation
of banks taking out deposit insurance limited the growth of
state banking and tended to exclude the smaller banks with
more risky portfolios. The larger banks dominated the system
so that while only one-half of the banks subscribed to the
guarantee fund, its members held over 80 percent of the
deposits of state banks. These conservative policies contributed to the absence of failures among the member banks.[49]

The only known system of private deposit insurance appeared in Kansas. The Bankers' Deposit Guaranty and Surety
Company was founded by the national banks excluded by the
ruling of the U.S. Attorney General from joining the state
deposit guarantee fund. They feared that without deposit
insurance they would lose deposits to state banks. The company's premium was set at $0.50 per $1,000 of deposits up
to the amount of a bank's capital and surplus. The remaining

[48] Robb, *The Guaranty of Bank Deposits*, pp. 120–125.
[49] Ibid., p. 123.

deposits were insured at a rate of $1 per $1,000 of deposits. Banks were subject to close inspection, and an increase in their own capital appears to have been an attractive substitute for insurance. There were no failures in the company's first ten years, but interest died out when the competition for deposits from the closely regulated state-insured banks did not materialize. The banks that had taken out private insurance were sound, and many let their policies lapse. By 1921 the company had shifted almost entirely to other types of insurance.[50]

The absence of other private deposit insurance companies is not surprising. Insurance of deposits is very much unlike other types of insurance. Fires, for example, occur randomly, and the probability that all buildings will burn down at the same time is small. On the other hand, the probability of large numbers of banks all failing at the same time is much greater. A downturn in the economy may induce widespread failures of banks and other firms. More important for banks, a panic may force all of them to close their doors temporarily, if not permanently. Private companies probably cannot insure against these economy-wide risks. The appearance of the Bankers' Deposit Guaranty and Surety Company was predominantly a defensive reaction of the national banks to the state's provision of insurance to the state banks. The company had a small clientele and quickly moved into other kinds of business.

WASHINGTON, NEBRASKA, THE DAKOTAS, AND MISSISSIPPI

The state of Washington's system of deposit insurance was very similar to Kansas's guarantee fund. Like the Kansas system, the Washington insurance plan never obtained anything like complete coverage, and less than one-half of the banks joined it.[51]

In the heartland of populism, Nebraska gained a deposit guarantee law in 1909 with the support and approbation of

[50] Ibid., p. 116.
[51] Ibid., pp. 170–172.

William Jennings Bryan and Governor Ashton C. Shallenberger. Nebraska benefited from the errors of other states. The law provided for the fund to be sustained at a level of 1 percent of average daily deposits, and it was managed by a board of bankers appointed by the governor. Banking expansion was constrained by limiting investments to eight times a bank's capital and surplus. However even in Bryan's home state, deposit insurance had its enemies. The large state banks, which had bitterly opposed this compulsory insurance, responded by taking out national charters. Nevertheless, once the legal questions were resolved, the number of state banks swelled from 661 with $76 million in 1911 to 910 banks with $232 million in 1914, a rise of 12.6 percent a year, well above the national average of 4.9 percent. In comparison, national banks decreased in number in this period from 246 to 191. More national banks took out state charters than state banks moved into the federal system.[52]

South Dakota's deposit insurance law also took the Kansas law as its model, but the refusal of many banks to join led the legislature to amend the law in 1915 and compel banks to join. This act was based on the Nebraska statute and adhered to most of its details. North Dakota passed its deposit insurance law in 1917, adapting the South Dakota and Nebraska codes. Like the Washington state law, it was passed well into the wartime boom, which makes it difficult to evaluate its impact on the banks within the state's boundaries.[53]

In Mississippi, the boll weevil did its part to promote deposit insurance. The destruction of a large part of the cotton crop in 1912 and 1913 brought down twenty-nine banks in the state. The Mississippi legislature ignored the protests of the state bankers association and passed a deposit guarantee law in 1914. This law established a state banking department and created a unique system of compulsory deposit insurance.

[52] Ibid., pp. 139–141.
[53] Ibid., pp. 162–165, 172–174.

Although it drew on the Kansas law for some features, the deposit guarantee fund was supervised by three examiners, one elected from each of the three state supreme court districts. In spite of the direct election of examiners and other peculiar features, bank examination appears to have been conducted in good faith.[54]

THE COLLAPSE OF THE STATE SYSTEMS

While the other deposit insurance statutes had been passed largely in response to the need to curtail panics, the passage of the Mississippi Act at the outset of a depression indicated a serious misunderstanding of the purpose behind the guarantee of deposits. Deposit insurance could only allay a loss of depositor confidence and successfully operate by itself when the economy was in good health. If a depression gripped the local or national economy, some other instrument, open market operations or massive discounting, would be necessary to prevent banks from going under. The decline in agricultural prices in the 1920s spelled trouble for the banks in the West and the South. In 1923 the first wave of bank failures that crippled the deposit insurance funds hit these regions. The governing boards were forced either to default on payments or to levy increasingly high assessments on the remaining banks in the system. The voluntary systems began to melt away. For the state of Washington, 1922 was the last year when receipts from assessments exceeded the disbursements to depositors from failed banks. A year later membership had fallen off, and the guarantee fund was exhausted, paying out only a fraction of the value of insured deposits.[55]

The compulsory systems struggled on a little longer. In Nebraska the bank commission tried to cope with the situation by refusing to levy a special assessment to replenish the fund.

---

[54] Ibid., pp. 165–170.
[55] State Bank Examiner of the State of Washington, *Annual Report*, 1922 and 1923.

Instead, it took over the operation of technically insolvent banks, if creditors would agree, in the expectation that liabilities could be reduced without resorting to the deposit guarantee fund. However by 1928 even these extraordinary measures failed, and a special assessment had to be levied. This was resisted tooth and nail by the state banks, which obtained a court injunction to halt the assessment. The legislature, acknowledging defeat, repealed the deposit insurance law in 1930.[56] The agricultural depression wrecked the rest of the systems as liabilities of the guarantee funds greatly exceeded their assets. By 1929, South Dakota's fund, for example, had $1 million of resources and $37.8 million worth of claims against it. The state legislature dissolved the fund, and after administrative expenses were met the fund paid out less than 1 percent on its outstanding debts.[57]

The Relationship between Branching and Bank Failures

Branching was a viable policy alternative to deposit insurance, and it appears that banks might have been strengthened and the number of failures decreased if there had been more branching in the 1920s. This assertion is supported by evidence from several sources. An inverse relationship was found to exist between branching and bank failures. The correlation coefficients between two measures of branching, the ratio of branching banks to all commercial banks and branch bank offices to all commercial banks in each state for 1925 were -0.196 and -0.214 respectively. When the bank suspension variable was replaced by the ratio of deposits of suspended banks to the deposits of all commercial banks in a state, the coefficients were -0.211 and -0.203.[58] Although these cor-

---

[56] Kuhn, *History of Nebraska Banking*, pp. 15–20.

[57] Superintendent of Banks, *Biennial Report*, 1930, p. 306; 1932, p. 345.

[58] The data for this analysis came from Board of Governors of the Federal Reserve System, *Banking and Monetary Statistics*, pp. 296–300 and Board of

relations do not evince a particularly strong inverse relationship, they do suggest that branching did impart additional
strength to the banking systems of those states that permitted
it. Detection of a relation between branching and failures is
difficult because branching was still quite limited in the 1920s.
In 1925, for example, only 2.5 percent of all banks were
branching banks, and 10.5 percent of all offices were branch
bank offices.

Another means of assessing the relationship between failures and branching is to examine the six states—California,
Louisiana, Massachusetts, Michigan, New York, and Ohio—
that the *Federal Reserve Bulletin* singled out as having firmly
established branch banking. In these states in 1925, branching
banks accounted for 9.1 percent of all commercial banks and
branch bank offices for 30.7 percent of all bank offices. The
six states' banks, possessing $20,346 million of deposits, had
13 banks, holding deposits of $6.1 million, fail. The rest of
the country's total deposits were $27,223 million. These states
had 618 bank failures, affecting deposits of $167.5 million in
1925. The eight states with deposit insurance systems suffered
from an expansion of banking and a decline in demand for
their agricultural products. The result was that they bore a
disproportionate share of the bank failures. Their total deposits amounted to only $3,379 million, but in 1925 they had
204 banks, holding deposits of $46.9 million, fail.[59]

The Canadian experience also suggests that branch banking
reduced the incidence of bank failure. Between 1920 and
1926 only one bank in Canada, with liabilities of $18.5 million,
closed its doors, compared to 3,063 banks with liabilities of
$1,085 million that failed in the United States in the same

Governors of the Federal Reserve System, *All Bank Statistics, United States,
1896–1955*. The statistics were all significant at the 10 percent level.

[59] Board of Governors of the Federal Reserve System, *Banking and Monetary
Statistics*, pp. 284–285 and Board of Governors of the Federal Reserve System,
All Bank Statistics.

period. The average annual ratio of liabilities of failed banks
to total banking liabilities in this period was 0.27 percent for
the United States and 0.09 percent for Canada.[60] In this period the Canadian system offered greater safety than the
American system. The depositors of the only failed institution,
the Hamilton Bank lost nothing, as the bank was absorbed by
the Canadian Bank of Commerce.[61] Furthermore, in contrast
to the United States banking system, which was plagued by
bank failures in the 1930s, the Canadian system was relatively
unscathed by the Great Depression.[62]

State-Sponsored Deposit Insurance in Retrospect

The failure of these deposit guarantee systems to stem the
bank failures of the twenties and the weakness of the banking
industry during the crises of the 1930s induced many states
to move away from efforts to shore up unit banking and
toward branching as a means of strengthening the industry
and increasing the number of offices.

State deposit insurance schemes all ended in dismal failure.
They had contributed to the rapid growth of many small
vulnerable unit banks in the least economically diversified
areas of the country. With no means to counter the agricultural depression of the 1920s, states were powerless to prevent
the rising tide of bank failures from crippling their deposit
guarantee funds. Unable to protect their unit banking systems
from this and the more severe crises of the 1930s, states began
to ease restrictions on branch banking. By 1939, Washington
and South Dakota allowed state-wide and Mississippi and North

[60] Calculated from data in Beckhart, "The Banking System in Canada," in
Willis and Beckhart, *Foreign Banking Systems*, p. 483; Board of Governors of
the Federal Reserve System, *All Bank Statistics*; and M. C. Urquhart and
K.A.H. Buckley, *Historical Statistics of Canada*, pp. 240–241.

[61] Beckhart, "The Banking System in Canada," in Willis and Beckhart,
Foreign Banking Systems, p. 338.

[62] George Morrison, *Liquidity Preferences of Commercial Banks*, pp. 63–77.

Dakota permitted limited branch banking.[63] This turn of events marked the beginnings of a national shift away from unit and toward branch banking. The major beneficiary of state experimentation with deposit insurance was the Federal Deposit Insurance Corporation, whose design avoided the errors embodied in previous legislation.[64]

The establishment of state and later of federal deposit insurance was a consequence of nineteenth-century antibranching statutes, which created a banking system dominated by unit banks. Self-insurance and interbank cooperation to prevent panics via the growth of a nationwide system of branch banking along Canadian lines were unacceptable to the smaller banks, and they sought government insurance instead. The problem plagued banking structure and engendered a weak solution in the form of state deposit insurance. The inherent weakness of the state guarantee funds, in turn, contributed to the problems of the banking industry.[65] It was appropriate that the federal government should finally assume the job of insuring banks. With a well-designed system, an individual state could insure banks only as long as a deflation or other general financial disturbance did not bring about widespread bank failures. The Federal Deposit Insurance Corporation's successful operation was not threatened by this problem, as the risk to which the entire banking system was exposed could be controlled by the Federal Reserve System's open market operations or discounting. This was, however, not the only

[63] Frederick A. Bradford, *The Legal Status of Branch Banking in the United States*, pp. 22–23.

[64] Golembe, "The Deposit Insurance Legislation of 1933," pp. 195–200. The FDIC has not entirely escaped the problems that plagued its predecessors. The corporation is continually worried about "capital adequacy," fearing that banks have not increased their capital to match their growth of assets. However, the power of the FDIC to arrange mergers for troubled or failing banks has prevented bank failures from depleting its insurance fund.

[65] The limitations on branching probably kept many banks from attaining an optimal scale of operations.

policy alternative, as witnessed by the state legislatures' easing of the constraints on branching. The irony is that the federal insurance of deposits, which had long been promoted by its supporters to protect unit banking, was installed by the Congress even as state legislatures began to ease the constraints on branching. Federal deposit insurance was an expedient solution; but as the states had belatedly realized, it was inferior to the establishment of a system of branch banking which, in conjunction with the proper use of other monetary instruments, could have more easily allayed the danger of a panic.

Conclusion

THE FEDERAL and state legislation adopted in the second half of the nineteenth century to regulate banking led to the development of an industry composed of thousands of independent banks. The federal ban on branching by national banks and the almost complete prohibition of branching by the states ensured the preeminence of the single-office bank. In the first years of the twentieth century, the increasing population density in urban areas allowed some banks to grow to a substantial size, but the distinguishing feature of the banking system was the large and growing number of very small unit banks. These small banks were not isolated; they were integrated with the rest of the financial system. The need to clear interbank claims and the drive to find the most profitable investments for their funds led them to establish correspondent relations with the larger city banks. The city banks assisted their correspondents with interbank clearing and acted as their agents in the city money markets. These relationships were strengthened by the imposition of reserve requirements, permitting banks to place a portion of their reserves on deposit with reserve-city or central-reserve-city banks where they might earn interest.

The larger cities and, in particular, New York became the foci of the money markets, linking together the thousands of unit banks. Whereas in a system of branching banks, such as Canada developed, clearing and financial flows between regions were largely internalized by banks, the seasonal and cyclical movements of funds in the United States had to be channeled through the correspondent network by the major city banks. In the absence of a central bank capable of temporarily increasing bank liquidity, such a system was vulnerable to financial crises. At the center of the correspondent system, the largest banks attempted to thwart crises by organizing mutual assistance through the offices of the clearinghouses. Although this did not correct the weaknesses of the banking system, it did help to stave off some financial crises.

For most contemporary analysts, the reform of the banking system required the establishment of new institutions to strengthen its areas of weakness. Both the Federal Reserve System and the state deposit guarantee funds were creations of this approach. Rarely were attempts made to get at the root cause of many of the system's difficulties—the restrictive regulation that had produced the industry's structure and most of its problems. Although it was sometimes suggested that branch banking could improve the banking system by increasing the number of offices, equalizing interest rates, decreasing failures, and increasing membership in the National Banking System, it remained a remedy untried by Congress and almost all state legislatures. The political opposition to branch banking was far too strong. At the time statutes restricting branching were adopted there appeared to be little interest in the issue, but the tremendous expansion of the economy and the banking system in the late nineteenth century developed an industry that had a stake in maintaining the regulations under which it had grown up. The banking legislation had created its own lobby, and the preservation of independent unit banking from the city bankers and the dual banking system from the federal bureaucrats became this lobby's key objectives.

The reform legislation that was passed complied in form,

if not always in substance, with the interests of the unit and state bankers' lobbies. The banking structure was not altered, and membership in the federal banking system remained voluntary. The result was that the Federal Reserve System and the state deposit guarantee funds failed in many ways to accomplish the objectives of the banking reformers. The same factors that kept banks from joining the National Banking System limited the Federal Reserve's membership. The smaller and more rural banks preferred to remain in the state banking systems, attracted by lower capital and reserve requirements, fewer portfolio restrictions, and weaker supervision. When the Federal Reserve eased its regulations, the states easily undermined its increased attractiveness by weakening their requirements. There were no compelling reasons for small banks to join the Federal Reserve System to clear interbank payments or gain access to the discount window. The correspondent banks and the clearinghouses continued to offer their clients clearing services, and the increased liquidity provided by discounting operations was also available to nonmembers through their correspondent banks' intermediation. Furthermore, the Federal Reserve Act did not sever the connection between the stock market and the major New York City banks as its authors believed it would. Their optimism blinded them to the fact that markets could not be restructured simply by offering some alternative government institutions. The Federal Reserve did, however, increase its effectiveness when it moved away from the real bills concept of monetary policy and began to discover how to coordinate open market and discount operations to achieve policy goals.

The attempts of the state legislatures to strengthen their banking systems by providing deposit insurance were a more dismal failure. Lacking the federal power to increase banking liquidity, there was nothing the states could do to prevent the bankruptcy of the guarantee funds. These were drained by a rising number of failures brought about by an agricultural depression that the states could not control.

The key factor that could have increased Federal Reserve membership, diminished the role of the correspondent banks, and improved the resistance of banks to failure and panic alike was branch banking. The struggle to permit more branching in the 1920s concluded with the passage of the McFadden Act which only extended branching so far as to equalize privileges between national and state member banks of the Federal Reserve. Congress then abandoned the idea of interstate branching, and the focus of branching reform shifted to the state legislatures. Branch banking grew in the 1920s, but it was still seriously constrained by state legislation. These barriers began to weaken only when the profound crises of the 1930s emphasized again the weakness of small unit banks and temporarily undermined the political influence of the unit banking lobby in many states.

The atomistic nature of the banking industry made the American banking system particularly susceptible to periodic crises. The most severe crises, in which many banks failed and there was a general suspension of convertibility, occurred when banks tried to improve their liquidity positions vis-à-vis other banks by converting their bankers' balances into currency. This contrasted with the situation north of the border where cooperative arrangements between Canadian banks prevented financial crises of the same magnitude. City bankers in the United States also cooperated in times of trouble; however their efforts only had a limited success as the very large number of country banks prevented any cooperation on a national level. Free branch banking would have reduced the number of banks and facilitated banks' mutual assistance in times of crisis.

Increased branching would have strengthened the individual bank as well. Free branch banking would have created banks with more geographically diversified portfolios, decreasing their vulnerability to economic conditions in one area. More diversified portfolios would have reduced the number of banks lacking assets eligible for discounting with the Federal Reserve banks. The emergency credit provided by the Federal Reserve would thereby have been more readily available. Increased branching would have substantially strengthened the banking system and probably have prevented the wave of bank failures in the 1930s, even if the Federal Reserve had pursued the same monetary policy. The contrast between the American and Canadian experience during the Great Depression is striking. Although Canada suffered a general economic contraction like the United States, there was no collapse of the banking system. Free branch banking would not have prevented the depression in the United States, but it might have been less severe.

Since the 1930s intrastate branch banking has spread to all but thirteen states, but interstate branching is still forbidden. Free intrastate and interstate branching would create much larger banks and, no doubt, raise the specter of a new "money trust"; but free branching could very well solve the Federal Reserve's membership problem. The key to strengthening the banking system is to be found in deregulation of the banking industry rather than in the creation of new government agencies or regulations.

Appendix A: Data for
Probit Analysis

THE DETERMINANTS of membership in the National Banking System and the Federal Reserve System are examined in this study by the application of the probit qualitative-response model to two cross-section samples of newly chartered banks. As the published sources of information on banking were inadequate for testing the model, these samples were collected to provide an appropriate data base.

Necessary to the successful application of the probit model, described in Appendix B, were samples of banks that had just incorporated under federal or state laws and opened for business. Data on national banks chartered by the Comptroller of the Currency were easily obtained from the Comptroller's *Annual Reports*, but information on banks chartered by the states was not found in one source. The reports of all the state bank examiners had to be consulted.

Both samples are for two-year periods, October 31, 1908, to October 30, 1910, and October 31, 1923, to October 30, 1925, which represented two reporting periods for the Comptroller of the Currency. This time framework was chosen because several states issued biennial reports that did not indicate the date of each bank's opening.

The first sample period was chosen because of the information made available about state banking regulations in Samuel Welldon's volume for the National Monetary Commission, *Digest of State Banking Statutes.* A list of state bank examiners' reports used in this study is found at the end of this appendix. Each state bank examiner's report was examined to find either those banks chartered within this specific period or those chartered during a comparable period. Kansas, for example, did not publish the date of each bank's charter, providing only the number and names of banks chartered between June 1, 1908, and June 1, 1910. Thirty-five states published annual or biennial reports for the period 1908–1910. Collection of banks for the sample from these states was straightforward.

Reports for twelve other states—Alabama, Arkansas, Georgia, Indiana, Iowa, Kentucky, Louisiana, Maryland, Nevada, New Mexico, Utah, and Wisconsin—were not available for this period. Most of these states did not begin publication of reports on their state banks until later. To find the banks chartered in this period for these states, the earliest available bank examiners' reports were consulted. These reports published the year of incorporation with each bank's balance sheet. The entire list of each state's banks was then examined to find those banks chartered in this period. Some banks may have been omitted by this procedure if they failed between the time of incorporation and the first available bank examiner's report, but the error was presumed to be small as relatively few of the total number of banks in the United States failed in the intervening years.

The only state that did not provide any bank reports was Wyoming. In the absence of such information, the number of newly chartered state banks was deduced from the change in the total number of state banks reported in George Barnett's *State Banks and Trust Companies since the Passage of the National-Bank Act.* This figure was adjusted for the number of bank failures but did not include any voluntary liquidations.

This search yielded a total of 2,242 new state banks and trust companies and 620 national banks for the years 1908–

State	1908–1910		1923–1925	
	National Banks	State Banks and Trust Companies	Federal Reserve Members	Non-members
Alabama	5	33	1	16
Arizona	1	5	0	1
Arkansas	7	55	2	8
California	52	39	23	14
Colorado	12	68	2	6
Connecticut	1	0	2	8
Delaware	1	1	0	1
Florida	4	13	4	35
Georgia	16	47	1	11
Idaho	8	35	1	6
Illinois	34	94	8	20
Indiana	23	59	3	27
Iowa	17	21	5	26
Kansas	10	131	3	16
Kentucky	14	41	2	13
Louisiana	2	21	2	10
Maine	2	0	0	0
Maryland	9	2	1	6
Massachusetts	3	7	3	2
Michigan	11	53	4	24
Minnesota	14	88	6	18
Mississippi	4	15	5	5
Missouri	11	61	13	54
Montana	17	37	4	5
Nebraska	26	55	4	10
Nevada	3	1	0	1
New Hampshire	1	0	0	2
New Jersey	20	3	40	34
New Mexico	3	2	6	2
New York	32	13	35	10
North Carolina	6	43	3	5
North Dakota	20	97	3	19
Ohio	20	30	1	24
Oklahoma	17	213	8	3
Oregon	12	42	2	6
Pennsylvania	23	57	21	42
Rhode Island	0	0	0	0
South Carolina	11	43	1	22

Table A.1 (*cont.*)

| | 1908–1910 | | 1923–1925 | |
State	National Banks	State Banks and Trust Companies	Federal Reserve Members	Non-members
South Dakota	12	157	8	12
Tennessee	18	21	2	0
Texas	19	365	26	112
Utah	2	13	0	2
Vermont	1	0	0	0
Virginia	18	26	3	4
Washington	19	48	3	9
West Virginia	11	12	5	7
Wisconsin	6	66	7	7
Wyoming	2	9	2	12

NOTE: The chartering period runs from October 31 to October 30.

1910. Table A.1 lists the number of banks chartered by the federal and state authorities for the two sample periods by state.

The second time period, 1923–1925, was chosen because the Federal Reserve's basic regulations and policy had been hammered out, and no basic changes were made. This allowed the use of contemporary regulations for independent variables because unchanging regulations ensured that banks were incorporating on the basis of the current, established regulations rather than on the basis of any expected new regulations. New national banks were obtained from the Comptroller of the Currency's *Annual Reports* for 1924 and 1925. The *Federal Reserve Bulletin* provided information on the state banks that took out Federal Reserve membership. This list of state member banks was then compared to the state bank examiners' reports to weed out those banks that were already established and were simply changing their affiliation. This check ensured that the sample contained only banks chartered within this period.

By the 1920s all states with the exception of Wyoming were publishing either annual or biennial reports on their state banks. The search for newly chartered banks was, therefore, considerably easier than it was for the earlier period. For Wyoming, the same method was employed to determine the number of new state banks. The federal and state documents revealed that 253 national banks, 32 state member banks, and 677 nonmember banks were chartered in the period 1923–1925.

State Bank Examiners' Reports

Alabama, Banking Department. *Summary of the Condition of the State Banks of Alabama.*

Arizona, Bank Comptroller. *Condensed Statement of Reports of the Territorial and National Banks of Arizona.*

Arizona, Superintendent of Banks. *Condensed Statement of Reports of the State and National Banks of Arizona.*

Arkansas, Bank Commissioner. *Annual Report.*

California, Banking Department. *Annual Report.*

Colorado, Division of Banking. *Statement of Condition of State Banks and Industrial Banks in the State of Colorado.*

Connecticut, Office of the Bank Commissioner. *Report.*

Delaware; Office of the State Bank Commissioner. *Annual Report.*

Florida, Division of Banking. *Report.*

Georgia, Department of Banking and Finance. *Annual Report.*

Idaho, Department of Finance, Bank Commissioner. *Report.*

Illinois, Auditor's Office. *Statement Showing the Condition of the Illinois State Banks.*

Indiana, Bank Department. *Annual Report.*

Iowa, Department of Banking. *Annual Report of the Superintendent of Banking.*

Kansas, Banking Department. *Biennial Report of the Bank Commissioner.*

Kentucky, Department of Banking and Securities. *Annual Report.*

Louisiana, Banking Department. *Report.*

Maine, Department of Banks and Banking. *Report of the Bank Commissioner.*

Maryland, Banks Commissioner. *Annual Report Showing the Condition of the State Banks, Trust Companies and Savings Institutions.*

Massachusetts, Department of Banking and Insurance, Division of Banks and Loan Agencies. *Annual Report of the Commissioner of Banks.*

Michigan, Banking Department. *Report of the Commissioner of Banking.*

Minnesota, Banking Division. *Biennial Report.*

Mississippi, Banking Department. *Statements Showing the Condition of the State and National Banks.*

Missouri, Department of Business and Administration, Division of Finance. *Report of the Commissioner of Finance.*

Montana, State Examiner. *Annual Report of the State Examiner.*

Nebraska, State Banking Board. *Report of the Secretary of the State Banking Board.*

Nevada, Office of the Superintendent of Banks and Small Loan Companies. *Biennial Report of the Superintendent.*

New Hampshire, Bank Commissioner's Office. *Annual Report of the Bank Commissioner.*

New Jersey, Division of Banking. *Annual Report.*

New Mexico, Department of Banking. *Report.*

New York, Banking Department. *Annual Report.*

North Carolina, Banking Department. *Report of the Commissioner of Banks.*

North Dakota, Department of Banking and Financial Institutions. *Biennial Report.*

Ohio, Division of Banks. *Annual Report.*

Oklahoma, State Bank Commissioner. *Report.*

Oregon, Banking Division. *Annual Report of the Superintendent of Banks.*

Pennsylvania, Banking Department. *Annual Report.*

Rhode Island, Banking Division. *Annual Report.*

South Carolina, State Bank Examiner. *Annual Report.*

South Dakota, Department of Banking and Finance. *Biennial Report.*

Tennessee, Department of Insurance. *Annual Report.*

Texas, Department of Insurance and Banking. *Annual Report of the Commissioner of Insurance and Banking.*

Utah, Department of Financial Institutions. *Biennial Report of the Commissioner of Financial Institutions.*

Vermont, Department of Banking and Insurance, Banking Division. *Annual Report of the Bank Commissioner.*

Virginia, Bureau of Banking. *Annual Report.*

Washington, Division of Banking. *Report of the Supervisor of Banking.*

West Virginia, Auditor's Office. *Biennial Report.*

Wisconsin, Office of the Commissioner of Banking. *Abstract of the Reports of State and Mutual Savings Banks and Trust Companies of Wisconsin.*

Appendix B: Probit Analysis

CHAPTERS 1 and 3 analyze the determinants of membership in the National Banking System and the Federal Reserve System. A microeconomic approach was taken in which the individual bank was the unit of observation. Any prospective financial institution intending to go into the business of commercial banking had a choice of incorporating under state or federal law. Both the federal and the state banking systems were heavily regulated, and every new bank was faced with the decision of selecting the regulatory regime under which it would earn the highest profits. The appropriate statistical model for analysis of this simple dichotomous choice is a qualitative-response model, where the variable reflecting a firm's decision can take on either of two values, zero or one, representing respectively membership in the federal or state system. The model then uses the proportion of banks entering the state system as the dependent variable. In Chapter 4, the creation of deposit guarantee funds by the states is examined using a very similar model. The statistical methods described below were also applied to the analysis of why certain states chose to establish systems of deposit insurance.

Two types of independent variables were used in the analysis of bank membership. Some variables were measured as the difference between state and federal regulations. For example, if the federal minimum capital requirement was $25,000 and one state's requirement was $15,000, then the explanatory variable was $10,000 for a bank incorporating in that state. It was hypothesized that the larger this number, the more likely a bank would be to incorporate under state regulations, if the capital constraint was binding. The effects of other regulations were captured by variables measuring the investment opportunities open to state banks relative to national banks or by dummy variables representing the option of branching or deposit insurance open to state banks. The advantages of membership in the state banking system relative to the federal banking system for each class of banks, country or reserve-city, in each state were measured by the vector x_i. The greater the advantages or disadvantages of the state system, the more or less likely a bank would be to join it.

Probit analysis was the qualitative-response method employed. This assumes that there is some index, I_i, equal to $x_i'B$, that is the data matrix times the true response coefficients, for each class of banks in each state. If it is assumed that the larger I_i is, the greater the probability a bank will choose state membership, then there is a monotonic relation between the value of I_i and the probability of it entering a state system. For the membership model, this simply means that the more profitable membership in the state banking system became, the greater the probability of an individual bank or the larger the percentage of banks in a given class joining the state system. The "true" probability function will then have the characteristics of a cumulative density function (CDF). Probit analysis assumes the CDF is normal. The choice of the probit procedure is justified by assuming that the membership decision is made by comparing I_i to some critical value I^*, where if $I_i \geq I^*$, a bank takes out membership in the state system. Given the large sample size, the central limit theorem may be invoked to justify the assumption that I^* is a normally distributed random variable. The conditional probability of an institution joining a state system, E, given I_i, is:

$$\text{prob}(E/I_i) = \text{prob}(I^* \leq I_i) = F(x_i'B)$$

where $F(\cdot)$ is the normal CDF evaluated at the value of $x_i'B$ $= I_i$.[1]

If the true proportion, P_i, of banks in each class in each state selecting the state system is related to the index $I_i = x_i'B$ by way of the standard normal CDF, then

$$P_i = \frac{1}{\sqrt{2\pi}} \int_{-\infty}^{I_i} e^{-\frac{1}{2}t^2}\, dt = F(I_i).$$

The true proportions were, of course, not available; and the sample proportions, $P_i = P_i + e_i$, were used. It then follows from this relation that $F^{-1}(p_i) = F^{-1}(P_i + e_i)$ where F^{-1} is the inverse of the normal CDF. From this expression, the following relation may be derived:

$$F^{-1}(p_i) = F^{-1}(P_i) + e_i/Z(P_i) = x_i'B + e_i/Z(P_i)$$

where $F^{-1}(p_i)$ and $F^{-1}(P_i)$ are the observed and true probits.[2] $F^{-1}(P_i) = I_i$, and $Z(P_i)$ is the value of the standard normal density function evaluated at P_i. As,

$$\text{var}[e_i/Z(P_i)] = P_i(1-P_i)/n_i[Z(P_i)]^2,$$

the generalized least squares estimator for B is

$$\hat{B} = (x'\hat{\phi}^{-1}x)^{-1}x'\hat{\phi}^{-1}v$$

where v is the vector of the observed probits $F^{-1}(p_i)$ and $\hat{\phi}$ is a matrix whose elements are consistent estimates of $\text{var}[e_i/Z(P_i)]$.[3]

The SOUPAC program at the University of Illinois at Champaign-Urbana contained a probit program which used

[1] George G. Judge, William E. Griffiths, R. Carter Hill, and Tsoung-Chao Lee, *The Theory and Practice of Econometrics*, p. 591.

[2] Ibid., p. 592.

[3] Ibid.

a maximum likelihood estimation technique ensuring that the estimated coefficients and standard errors were asymptotically consistent. The significance of the coefficients was examined by approximate t-statistics obtained by dividing the coefficient by the standard error. The goodness of fit of the model was evaluated in three ways. The log of the likelihood function of the unconstrained model, $L(\hat{B})$, and the log of the likelihood function where only the intercept term is included, $L(B_0)$, were used in two tests. The significance of the entire equation was tested using the log likelihood ratio test statistic. This is asymptotically distributed as chi-square. The statistic is equal to minus two times the unconstrained less the constrained log of the likelihood functions. This is analogous to an F-test for an ordinary least squares regression. The analogue to the R^2 is the likelihood ratio index or pseudo-R^2:

$$\rho^z = 1 - L(\hat{B})/L(B_0).^4$$

The last measure of goodness of fit used was a comparison of the actual with the predicted number of banks choosing the state system for each class of bank in each state. The predicted number was obtained from an estimate of the index $\hat{I}_i = x_i'B$. This was then used to obtain:

$$\hat{p}_i = F(x_i'\hat{B}).$$

This $\hat{p}_i$ was multiplied by the total number of banks in the ith class to get the predicted number of banks choosing state membership in that class. The number of predicted banks in all classes was summed, yielding the predicted number of banks nationwide to join the state banking systems. For state deposit insurance, $\hat{p}_i$ was itself examined to determine the predicted probability of each state deciding to create a deposit guarantee fund.

The potential effects of changes in state and federal regulations on membership in the National Banking System and

[4] Ibid., p. 601.

the Federal Reserve System were also examined using the probit estimates. For each regulatory change a new data matrix, y_i, was substituted for x_i. This was used to obtain a new predicted proportion:

$$\hat{p}_i = F(y_i'\hat{B}).$$

This $\hat{p}_i$ was then multiplied by the total number of banks in the ith class to get an estimate of how many more or how many fewer banks would have joined the state banking systems. The sum of all classes gave the estimate of the total change nationwide that would have been caused by an alteration in the regulations.

Bibliography

Aldrich, Nelson W. *A Suggested Plan for Monetary Reform*. Washington, D.C.: U.S. Government Printing Office, 1911.

Andrew, A. Piatt. "Hoarding in the Panic of 1907." *Quarterly Journal of Economics*, 22 (February 1908), pp. 290–299.

———. "Substitutes for Cash in the Panic of 1907." *Quarterly Journal of Economics*, 22 (August 1908), pp. 497–516.

———. "The Treasury and the Banks Under Secretary Shaw." *Quarterly Journal of Economics*, 21 (August 1907), pp. 519–568.

Baltensperger, Ernst. "Alternative Approaches to the Theory of the Banking Firm." *Journal of Monetary Economics*, 6 (1980), pp. 1–37.

Barnett, George. *State Banks and Trust Companies since the Passage of the National-Bank Act*. Washington, D.C.: U.S. Government Printing Office, 1910.

Bell, John Fred. " The Growth and Development of Banking Activities of Trust Companies." Ph.D. dissertation, University of Illinois, Urbana, 1928.

Benston, George J. "Economies of Scale in Financial Institutions." *Journal of Money, Credit and Banking*, 4 (May 1972), pp. 312–341.

———. *Federal Reserve Membership: Consequences, Costs, Benefits and Alternatives*. Chicago: Association of Reserve City Bankers, 1978.

Board of Governors of the Federal Reserve System. *All Bank Statistics, United States, 1896–1955*. Washington, D.C.: Board of Governors of the Federal Reserve System, 1959.

———. *Annual Report*. Washington, D.C.: Board of Governors of the Federal Reserve System, 1914–1929.

———. *Banking and Monetary Statistics, 1914–1941*. Washington, D.C.: Board of Governors of the Federal Reserve System, 1943.

———. *Federal Reserve Bulletin*. Washington, D.C.: Board of Governors of the Federal Reserve System, 1914–1938.

Bradford, Frederick A. *The Legal Status of Branch Banking in the United*

States. New York: Economic Policy Commission, American Bankers Association, 1940.

Breckenridge, Roeliff Morton. *History of Banking in Canada*. Washington, D.C.: U.S. Government Printing Office, 1910.

Cagan, Phillip. *Determinants and Effects of Changes in the Money Stock, 1875–1960*. New York: National Bureau of Economic Research, 1965.

————. "The First Fifty Years of the National Banking System." In Deane Carson, *Banking and Monetary Studies*. Homewood, Ill.: R. D. Irwin, 1963.

Cannon, James Graham. *Clearing Houses*. Washington, D.C.: U.S. Government Printing Office, 1910.

"The Central Bank Question." *Banking Law Journal*, 20 (October 1909), pp. 941–979.

Chandler, Lester V. *Benjamin Strong, Central Banker*. Washington, D.C.: The Brookings Institution, 1958.

Cooke, Thornton. "The Insurance of Bank Deposits in the West." *Quarterly Journal of Economics*, pt. 1, 24 (November 1909), pp. 85–108; pt. 2, 24 (February 1910), pp. 327–391.

Cowing, Cedric B. *Populists, Plungers, and Progressives: A Social History of Stock and Commodity Speculation, 1890–1936*. Princeton: Princeton University Press, 1965.

Dwyer, Gerald P., Jr. "The Effects of the Banking Acts of 1933 and 1935 on Capital Investment in Commercial Banking." *Journal of Money, Credit and Banking*, 13 (May 1981), pp. 192–204.

Ehrlich, Isaac and Becker, Gary. "Market Insurance, Self-Protection, and Self-Insurance." *Journal of Political Economy*, 80 (July/August 1972), pp. 623–648.

Fisher, Gerald C. *American Banking Structure*. New York: Columbia University Press, 1968.

Frame, Andrew Jay. *Address on Panic Panaceas before the Convention of the American Bankers Association*. Waukesha, Wisc., 1904.

Friedman, Milton and Schwartz, Anna J. *A Monetary History of the United States, 1867–1960*. Princeton: Princeton University Press, 1963.

Frodin, Joanna Haywood. "The Tax/Subsidy Relation between Member Banks and the Federal Reserve System." *Journal of Monetary Economics*, 6 (1980), pp. 105–120.

Gambs, Carl and Rasche, Robert. "The Costs of Reserves and the Relative Size of Member and Nonmember Bank Demand Deposits." *Journal of Monetary Economics*, 4 (1978), pp. 715–733.

Gilbert, R. Alton. "Utilization of Federal Reserve Bank Services by Member Banks: Implications for the Costs and Benefits of Membership." *Federal Reserve Bank of St. Louis Review*, 59 (August 1977), pp. 2–15.

Golembe, Carter H. "The Deposit Insurance Legislation of 1933: An Examination of Its Antecedents and Purposes." *Political Science Quarterly*, 75 (June 1960), pp. 181–200.

Goodhart, Charles E. A. *The New York Money Market and the Finance of Trade 1900–1914*. Cambridge, Mass.: Harvard University Press, 1969.

———. "Profit on National Bank Notes, 1900–1913." *Journal of Political Economy*, 73 (October 1965), pp. 516–522.

Grant, Joseph M. and Crum, Lawrence L. *The Development of State-Chartered Banking in Texas*. Austin: Bureau of Business Research, University of Texas, 1978.

Hammond, Bray. *Banks and Politics in America*. Princeton: Princeton University Press, 1957.

James, John A. "The Conundrum of the Low Issue of National Bank Notes." *Journal of Political Economy*, 84 (April 1976), pp. 362–367.

———. "Cost Functions of Postbellum National Banks." *Explorations in Economic History*, 15 (April 1978), pp. 184–195.

———. *Money and Capital Markets in Postbellum America*. Princeton: Princeton University Press, 1978.

Johnson, Joseph French. *The Canadian Banking System*. Washington, D.C.: U.S. Government Printing Office, 1910.

Johnston, J. *Econometric Methods*. New York: McGraw-Hill Book Co., 1972.

Judge, George G.; Griffiths, William E.; Hill, R. Carter; and Lee, Tsoung-Chao. *The Theory and Practice of Econometrics*. New York: J. Wiley Co., 1980.

Karekan, John H. and Wallace, Neil. "Deposit Insurance and Bank Regulation: A Partial Equilibrium Exposition." *Journal of Business*, 51 (1978), pp. 413–438.

Knight, Robert E. "Comparative Burdens of Federal Reserve Member and Nonmember Banks." *Monthly Review of the Federal Reserve Bank of Kansas City* (March 1977), pp. 13–28.

Kuhn, W. E. *History of Nebraska Banking: A Centennial Retrospect*. Lincoln: University of Nebraska Bureau of Business Research, Bulletin no. 72, 1968.

Lockhart, Oliver C. "The Development of Interbank Borrowing in the National Banking System, 1869–1914." *Journal of Political Econ-*

omy, pt. 1, 29 (February 1921), pp. 138–160; pt. 2, 29 (March 1921), pp. 222–240.

Maddala, G. S. *Econometrics.* New York: McGraw-Hill Book Co., 1977.

"More on Correspondent Banking." *Monthly Bulletin of the Federal Reserve Bank of Kansas City* (July/August 1965), pp. 14–63.

Morrison, George. *Liquidity Preferences of Commercial Banks.* Chicago: University of Chicago Press, 1966.

Neal, Larry. "Trust Companies and Financial Innovation." *Business History Review,* 45 (Spring 1971), pp. 35–51.

Pauly, Mark. "Overinsurance and Public Provision of Insurance: The Roles of Moral Hazard and Adverse Selection." *Quarterly Journal of Economics,* 89 (February 1974), pp. 44–62.

Peltzman, Sam. "Capital Investment in Commercial Banking and Its Relationship to Portfolio Regulation." *Journal of Political Economy,* 78 (January/February 1970), pp. 1–26.

Popple, Charles S. *Development of Two Bank Groups in the Central Northwest.* Cambridge, Mass.: Harvard University Press, 1944.

Posner, Richard. "Theories of Economic Regulation." *Bell Journal of Economics and Management Science,* 5 (Autumn 1974), pp. 335–358.

Preston, Howard H. *History of Banking in Iowa.* Iowa City: State Historical Society of Iowa, 1922.

———. "Recent Developments in Branch Banking." *American Economic Review,* 14 (September 1924), pp. 443–462.

Prestopino, C. J. "Do Higher Reserve Requirements Discourage Federal Reserve Membership?" *Journal of Finance,* 31 (December 1976), pp. 1471–1480.

Redlich, Fritz. *The Molding of American Banking: Men and Ideas.* 2 vols. New York: Johnson Reprint Co., 1968.

Robb, Thomas B. *The Guaranty of Bank Deposits.* Boston: Houghton Mifflin Co., 1921.

Robertson, Ross. *The Comptroller and Bank Supervision, An Historical Appraisal.* Washington, D.C.: Office of the Comptroller of the Currency, 1968.

Rockoff, Hugh. "Regional Interest Rates and Bank Failures, 1870–1914." *Explorations in Economic History,* 14 (January 1977), pp. 90–95.

Southworth, Shirley D. *Branch Banking in the United States.* New York: McGraw-Hill Book Co., 1928.

Spahr, Walter Earl. *The Clearing and Collection of Checks.* New York: The Bankers Publishing Co., 1926.

Sprague, Oliver M. W. "Branch Banking in the United States." *Quarterly Journal of Economics*, 17 (February 1903), pp. 242–260.

––––––. *Crises of the National Banking System*. Washington, D.C.: U.S. Government Printing Office, 1909.

State Bank Examiner of the State of Washington. *Annual Report*. Olympia, Wash.: State Bank Examiner, 1919, 1922, 1923.

Stigler, George. "The Theory of Economic Regulation." *Bell Journal of Economics and Management Science*, 2 (Spring 1971), pp. 3–21.

Superintendent of Banks. *Biennial Report*. Pierre, S. Dak.: State Bank Examiner, 1930, 1932.

Sylla, Richard E. *The American Capital Market, 1846–1914: A Study of the Effects of Public Policy on Economic Development*. New York: Arno Press, 1975.

Timberlake, Richard H., Jr. *Origins of Central Banking in the United States*. Cambridge, Mass.: Harvard University Press, 1978.

Tippetts, Charles S. *State Banks and the Federal Reserve System*. New York: Columbia University Press, 1929.

Urquhart, M. C. and Buckley, K.A.H. *Historical Statistics of Canada*. Toronto: Cambridge University Press, 1965.

U.S. Comptroller of the Currency. *Annual Report*. Washington, D.C.: U.S. Government Printing Office, 1870–1934.

U.S. Congress, House of Representatives. *The Money Trust Investigation before the Subcommittee on Banking and Currency*, 63rd Cong., 1st sess., 1913.

U.S. Department of Commerce. *Historical Statistics of the United States*. 2 vols. Washington, D.C.: U.S. Government Printing Office, 1975.

U.S. Department of the Treasury. *Annual Report*. Washington, D.C.: U.S. Government Printing Office, 1870–1929.

Watkins, Leonard L. *Bankers' Balances*. Chicago: A. W. Shaw Co., 1929.

Welldon, Samuel A. *Digest of State Banking Statutes*. Washington, D.C.: U.S. Government Printing Office, 1909.

West, Robert Craig. *Banking Reform and the Federal Reserve, 1863–1923*. Ithaca: Cornell University Press, 1977.

Westerfield, Ray B. *Historical Survey of Branch Banking in the United States*. New York: American Bankers Association, Economic Policy Commission, 1939.

Wicker, Elmus R. *Federal Reserve Monetary Policy 1917–1933*. New York: Random House, 1966.

Wiebe, Robert H. *Businessmen and Reform: A Study of the Progressive Movement*. Cambridge, Mass.: Harvard University Press, 1962.

Willis, Henry Parker. *The Federal Reserve.* Garden City, N.Y.: Doubleday, Page & Co., 1915.

————. *The Federal Reserve System.* New York: Ronald Press Co., 1923.

Willis, Henry Parker and Beckhart, B. H. *Foreign Banking Systems.* New York: Henry Holt and Co., 1929.

Index

Library of Congress Cataloging in Publication Data
White, Eugene Nelson, 1952-
The regulation and reform of the American banking system, 1900-1929.
Bibliography: p.
Includes index.
1. Banks and banking—United States—History—20th century.
2. Banking law—United States—History—20th century. I. Title.
HG2481.W47   1983   332.1′0973   82-61395
ISBN 0-691-04232-2